Macroeconomics

Macroeconomics

Oskar Zorrilla

The MIT Press
Cambridge, Massachusetts
London, England

The MIT Press
Massachusetts Institute of Technology
77 Massachusetts Avenue, Cambridge, MA 02139
mitpress.mit.edu

The MIT Press would like to thank the anonymous peer reviewers who provided comments on drafts of this book. The generous work of academic experts is essential for establishing the authority and quality of our publications. We acknowledge with gratitude the contributions of these otherwise uncredited readers.

This book was set in Times New Roman by Westchester Publishing Services. Printed and bound in the United States of America.

Library of Congress Cataloging-in-Publication Data

Names: Zorrilla, Oskar, author.
Title: Macroeconomics : an active learning approach / Oskar Zorrilla.
Description: Cambridge, Massachusetts : The MIT Press, [2025] | Includes
   bibliographical references and index.
Identifiers: LCCN 2024040440 (print) | LCCN 2024040441 (ebook) | ISBN
   9780262552332 (paperback) | ISBN 9780262383134 (pdf) | ISBN
   9780262383141 (epub)
Subjects: LCSH: Macroeconomics.
Classification: LCC HB172.5 .Z67 2025 (print) | LCC HB172.5 (ebook) | DDC
   339–dc23/eng/20241223
LC record available at https://lccn.loc.gov/2024040440
LC ebook record available at https://lccn.loc.gov/2024040441

10 9 8 7 6 5 4 3 2 1

EU Authorised Representative: Easy Access System Europe, Mustamäe tee 50, 10621 Tallinn, Estonia | Email:
gpsr.requests@easproject.com

To my teachers—in the math department at Exeter and the econ department at Columbia.

Contents

List of Figures

List of Tables

Introduction

The purpose of this book is to develop your ability to think like a macroeconomist. Unlike a traditional textbook, it is not a detailed transcript of lectures. There is no chapter 3, section 4 that talks about inflation. Rather than *tell* you what macroeconomics has to say, the book invites you to *do* macroeconomics. It helps you pose and answer the questions that macro-economists ask. To accomplish this, the book is centered on problems, not topics. Because knowledge is cumulative, the problems are interrelated. But since knowledge does not stack up neatly on itself, this relationship is less like a line and more like a network. Techniques, themes, and results will emerge as you work through the problems.

You should approach each problem as an exploration, with curiosity about what you might discover. The problems in this book are structured as signposts along the way, but you are responsible for the journey. You should not expect that each problem will deliver a set of facts for you to memorize. Nor should you expect the problem to reveal itself to you. Solving problems is much more challenging than reading and note-taking. It requires both creativity and persistence. Creativity will allow you to make leaps, to "try something new"; persistence will allow you to keep trying when your first try doesn't get you all the way there. It requires you to be aware of both the details and the big picture. Without the details, you will lose your grasp of the problem; without the big picture you will not be able to integrate previous knowledge into your solution strategy.

Although the tools you use will vary from problem to problem, there are a few general principles of successful problem-solving. Here are some of them:

Write down what you are given: All problems start with raw materials: these can be assumptions, equations, parameters, functions, or datasets. Make sure you account for all of them *in writing*. Overlooking one of them is oftentimes the reason problems become intractable. The chances that you overlook something are much higher when you keep a mental list; it is much better to keep a physical list written out on paper.

Be clear about what the problem is asking you to do: If the information given at the beginning of the problem is your start point, what the problem is asking you to do is your destination. You need both before you set off. If you begin "trying things" without knowing what you are being asked to do, you will almost certainly make very little progress. If you are unsure about what the question is asking, reread the problem more carefully, or go back to previous problems. Sometimes knowing what the end is will immediately suggest a solution method. For example, if you are being asked to calculate a macroeconomic statistic, then the definition of that statistic will tell you what you need to do in order to calculate it.

Distinguish between the exogenous and endogenous variables: Exogenous variables, also called parameters, are taken at face value and are external to the model. Endogenous variables, also called outcome variables, are the variables that the model aims to explain. Distinguishing between the two types of variables is perhaps the easiest way to put into practice the previous two principles since solving a model is really an exercise in writing the endogenous variables as functions of the exogenous variables. There is a useful, if imperfect, rule of thumb to tell them apart. Exogenous variables are often, though not always, denoted by Greek letters; endogenous variables are often, though not always, denoted by Latin letters.

Draw accurate diagrams: An equation and its graph contain the same information. Yet the graph conveys that information more transparently and compellingly than its corresponding equation. This is why textbooks are replete with graphs. Since this is a problem book, the responsibility of creating those graphs falls on you. Be careful to assign each variable its proper axis. Label your axes clearly and consistently. Make sure you understand what type of function you are being asked to graph: is it linear, quadratic, logarithmic? Is it increasing or decreasing? If a diagram is not an accurate representation of its equation, the economic conclusions you draw from the diagram will be incorrect.

Keep track of the units: Variables and their units both follow mathematical rules. Units multiply and divide, and you cannot add or subtract variables of different units. This makes units a simple diagnostic that you can use to your advantage. If you find yourself adding two variables with different units, something's wrong. Once you finish deriving an equation, check that the units on one side are the same as the units on the other; an apple can't equal an orange. Because units tell you what the variables in your equations and diagrams represent they can also help you make economic sense of your mathematical results.

Write down all of your steps: It is tempting to write only the setup and the solution, especially when the answer comes to you easily. Recall, however, that you are building a body of knowledge for *your future self.* What may be obvious in the moment might be less so when you need it to solve a subsequent problem many days later. Or when you need it to study for an exam. Or if you realize, whether in class the next day or ten minutes later in the following section, that you have made a mistake. Without your work written out in front of you, retracing your steps will be very difficult. Even if your work is incorrect, it is still very valuable—it helps you keep track of all the paths that you have tried and that have not been fruitful. Keeping a clear written record of all your work is the single most important problem-solving strategy.

Make use of what you already know: Results build on each other. The insights from one problem will almost certainly be useful elsewhere, either as a way to help you solve another problem, or when integrated with another insight to reach an even deeper understanding. Keep that in mind as you work through a problem. If you focus on the problem too narrowly, you will miss its connections to other problems. In some cases, those connections will make solving a particular problem much simpler. And if you have a written record of your work, you don't even need to commit any of these prior results to memory. All you have to do is look them up in your notes.

If the strategies outlined above seem like they are taken out of a math course, it is because economics, like most other sciences, has adopted math as its primary tool. But this is not a math course: math is only the means. Every economics question can be posed as a mathematical problem. By the same token, every mathematical result has an economic interpretation. At this stage in your economics education, this book takes care of the first part. It translates the economic questions into mathematical models. The second part is up to you. Solving a problem goes beyond deriving an equation—it requires that you translate the mathematical result into a meaningful economic statement.

Before we begin, a brief introduction into the subject is in order. Macroeconomics is concerned with the joint allocation of three *aggregates*—capital, labor, and output—in a specific place and across time. We call them aggregates because they define an entire class rather than a unique type, and it is in this sense that macroeconomics is *macro*. For example, an airplane is obviously different from a building, but we classify them both as capital. As macroeconomists we are interested in the allocation of capital as a whole, not in the allocations of airplanes or buildings. Furthermore, we are not interested merely in the allocation of capital in isolation, but in the simultaneous allocations of capital, labor and output, and their evolution through time. While we can define the scope of our inquiry parsimoniously, the inquiry itself is vast. Understanding these allocations naturally raises a variety of challenging questions, sheds light on many facts—both about the behavior of individual agents as well as the behavior of aggregate outcomes—and helps guide public policy.

1 The Med

Imagine the economy of a small Mediterranean island where people eat grapes and drink wine. A farmer who owns all of the vineyards on the island hires workers to pick the grapes. There is only one winery on the island; the winemaker buys grapes from the farmer and hires workers to turn those grapes into wine. The island also maintains marines for the purpose of national defense. Everyone on the island consumes three things: grapes to eat, wine to drink and national defense for tranquility.

There are three related questions that, as macroeconomists, we would like to answer. First, how valuable is the island's production? This requires that we calculate its *output*. Second, is this island rich or poor? This requires that we calculate its *income*. Third, what are the expenditures on the island? This requires that we calculate *aggregate demand*.

Farmer: Grapes sell for $2.00 per bunch. At this price the farmer harvests twelve million bunches of grapes a year. Since some of her vines die each year, she keeps three million bunches to plant more vines and sells the remaining nine million. She hires labor to tend the vines and pick the grapes, and the total wage bill comes to $13 million. Finally, she pays the government $1 million in taxes.

Winemaker: Wine sells in two markets; it is purchased domestically by the households on the island and it is exported abroad. It sells for $12.00 per bottle in the domestic market and $13.00 per bottle in the foreign market. The winemaker sells two million bottles in the domestic market and one million bottles abroad. He needs two bunches of grapes per bottle. Since there is no glass industry on the island, he must buy three million glass bottles from abroad for $1.00 each. He also hires labor and his total wage bill is $12 million. The government taxes the winery twice. First, it charges an export tax of $2.00 per bottle. Second, it collects $2 million in taxes from the winemaker.

Government: The government collects taxes and uses all the proceeds to pay the marines their wages. It collects corporate taxes from the farm and the winery totaling $3 million, export taxes totaling $2 million, and $3 million in income taxes from workers for a total of $8 million.

Households: Residents of the island make up the households. Households are sometimes also referred to as consumers. Households consume grapes, wine, and national defense, the last of which is provided by the government. The three types of household are the workers, the farmer, and the winemaker.

1.1   Output

1. If the farmer did not hire any workers, how many grapes could be harvested from the vineyard?

2. Without a vineyard, how many grapes would the workers be able to harvest?

3. The farmer hires workers to work on her vineyard. What is the market value that this relationship generates?

4. The winemaker hires workers to work at his winery. How much value does this relationship *add* to the grapes and glass bottles that are used as raw materials in the production of wine?

5. We define as *final* those goods or services that are not used as inputs to produce other goods or services. What are the three final goods and services produced in this economy?

6. We define *intermediate* goods as those that are used as inputs in the production chain. Are there any intermediate goods?

7. List the inputs needed to produce wine. If any of those are intermediate goods, what are their own inputs?

8. How much value do the inhabitants of the island dedicate to national defense?

9. Compute the quantity and total value of all goods and services produced.

10. Compute the quantity and total value of the intermediate goods, if there are any.

11. Subtract the value of the intermediate goods (computed in question 10) from the value of all goods and services produced (computed in question 9). Explain why this difference reflects the value of all *final* goods and services produced.

12. How much value does the farmer add to the economy? How much value does the winemaker add? How much value do the marines add? Sum the value added by all three. How does it compare to the value of all final goods and services produced?

1.2   Income

1. What are the two inputs required to make grapes?

2. What is the income left to the farmer she pays the workers?

3. If wages compensate the workers' labor, what does the farmers' income compensate?

4. What is the share of the value of the grapes that compensates the workers? What is the share of the value of the grapes that compensates the farmer as the owner of the vineyard?

5. What is the income left to the winemaker after he pays for intermediate goods and labor?

6. From your answers above we can conclude that the value of the wine becomes pre-tax income—directly and indirectly—for four different parties. List them.

7. How are these parties different from each other? How are they similar? Group them into two pairs. What criteria did you use? Why?
[Hint: Who else do the farmer and winemaker have to pay?]

8. Laborers can work for the government, for the farmer or for the winemaker. What is the total after-tax income that goes to labor in this economy?

9. What is the total after-tax income that goes to capital in this economy?
[Hint: Who owns the capital in this economy?]

10. Who else receives income in this economy? How much income do they receive?

11. Add up the net income of all of the agents on the island. How does it compare to the value of all final goods and services produced on the island?

1.3 Aggregate Demand

1. On what two goods do consumers spend their after-tax income?

2. We define *consumption expenditures* (denoted by C) as the component of aggregate demand that comes from households. Calculate the total expenditure of households. How does this compare to household income?

3. What is the value of the grapes that the farmer keeps to replace her vines?

4. Do the grapes that are kept for replanting satisfy the definition of *consumption expenditures*? Discuss.

5. We define *investment* (denoted by I) as the component of aggregate demand that goes toward accumulating or replacing capital. Do any agents on the island incur investment? If so, what is the value of investment expenditures?

6. What are government purchases (denoted by G)?

7. The total value of exports minus the total value of imports has two names. We refer to this difference as either the *trade balance*—and denote it TB—or as *net exports*—and denote it NX. The two have the same meaning. What are the net exports of the island?

8. Aggregate demand is the sum of $C + I + G + NX$. What is the total aggregate demand on the island? How does it compare to the income of the island?

Reference

Langfeld, J., E. Seskin, & B. Fraumeni (2008). Taking the pulse of the economy: Measuring GDP. *Journal of Economic Perspectives, 22*(2), 193–216.

2 Twins

Though deceptively simple, the equilibrium relationship between output, income, and aggregate demand imposes some restrictions on the equilibrium relationships of other macroeconomic variables. Here we will consider the relationship among three such variables: savings, investment, and the balance of trade.

We consider an economy with households and a government. The government receives income, T, from taxes and makes purchases, G, of total output. The government can borrow from households by issuing bonds and pays households interest, R, on its outstanding debt.

1. Write down an expression for total government expenditures.

2. The *fiscal deficit*, D, is the difference between government expenditures and tax revenue. This is the additional amount the government must borrow to pay for its expenditures. Write down the deficit as a function of G, R, and T.

3. Show that the government's budget constraint can be written as:

$$T + D = G + R \tag{2.1}$$

4. Label the expenditure side of the above budget constraint.

5. When the deficit is negative we say the government is running a *surplus*. If the government runs a surplus, which one is larger: tax revenues or government expenditures?

Households earn income, Y, from economic activity; additionally, they receive interest payments, R, from the government. They pay the government a total tax bill, T, and consume C.

6. Write down an expression for total household expenditures.

7. We define *savings*, S, as the difference between total earnings and total expenditures. Write down household savings as a function of Y, R, T, and C.

8. Show that the households' budget constraint can be written as:

$$Y + R = C + T + S \tag{2.2}$$

9. Label the earnings side of the above budget constraint.

Having derived the the two budget constraints, we exploit the fact that they must both hold in equilibrium.

10. Combine the two budget constraints to show that, in equilibrium, the following holds:

$$Y = C + G + S - D \tag{2.3}$$

11. S is also called *private savings*, while $-D$ is also called *public savings*. What does the expression $S - D$ measure?
[Hint: $S - D = S + (-D)$]

We now consider a second equilibrium relationship: Income, Y, equals aggregate demand, $C + I + G + NX$.

12. Name the four components of aggregate demand.

13. Suppose this is a closed economy, so that there are neither imports nor exports. Show that in equilibrium:

$$I = S - D \tag{2.4}$$

14. Explain the above equation in words.

15. Now, suppose that this is an open economy with imports and exports. Show that in equilibrium:

$$NX + I = S - D \tag{2.5}$$

16. Explain the above equation in words.

17. Suppose that investment, I, increases but total savings, $S - D$, stay constant. What must happen to net exports, NX?

18. Suppose that the fiscal deficit increases, but investment and private savings stay constant. What must happen to net exports?

19. We say a country is running a *trade deficit* if net exports are negative. Given your answer to the previous question, offer a brief explanation as to why the fiscal deficit and the trade deficit are often called the *twin deficits*.

3 Rates and Logs

Most macroeconomic data are reported as a rate; inflation, GDP growth, and unemployment are all examples. When economic data are plotted against time, they are usually plotted on a natural log scale rather than a linear scale. As it turns out, there is a close relationship between rates and the natural log; it is an indispensable tool in both empirical and theoretical economics. We want to understand why it arises and how to use it.

3.1 Income per Capita

Perhaps the defining fact of the past two centuries is that—unlike the thousands of years before—income per capita has grown consistently almost everywhere. Figure 3.1 shows the trajectory of real income per capita over the past 140 years in two developed and two developing countries in different continents. We say *real* because it is measured using a consistent unit across countries and years: the 2011 US dollar. Both panels in figure 3.1 contain the same information. Panel (a) plots income per capita while panel (b) plots the natural log of income per capita.

1. Just by "eyeballing" figure 3.1(a), which of the four countries grew at the highest rate between 1880 and 2018?

Table 3.1 has the initial and final values of income per capita plotted in figure 3.1(a). Pick any one of the four countries to answer the following questions. Let Y denote income per capita.

2. How many times larger is Y in 2018 than in 1880?

3. Calculate the *yearly* percentage rate, in decimals, that income per capita grew between 1880 and 2018 if it had done so at a constant rate.
[Hint: You need to solve an exponential equation.]

4. Graph Y as a function of time.

5. If you superimposed your graph onto figure 3.1(a) what would it look like?

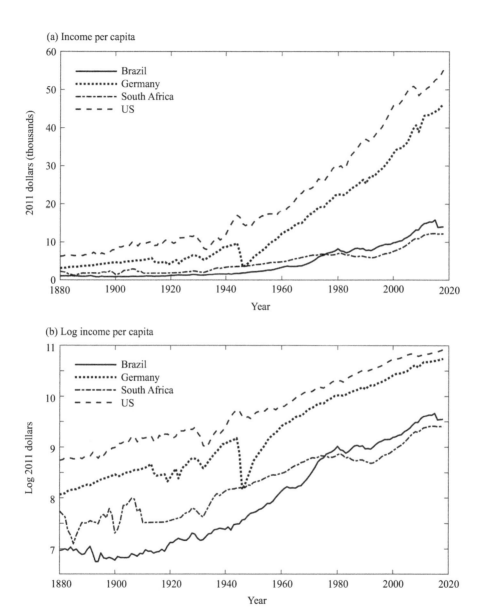

Figure 3.1
Real income per capita (2011 US dollars) between 1880 and 2018. *Source*: Maddison Project Database.

Table 3.1
Real income per capita in 1880 and 2018. Entries correspond to initial and final values
plotted in figure 3.1(a).

	Brazil	Germany	S. Africa	US
1880	1,058	3,174	2,294	6,256
2018	14,034	46,178	12,166	55,335

Source: Maddison Project Database.

6. Define $y \equiv \log(Y)$. Show that y can be written as the following linear function of time:

$$y = \log(1 + r)t + y_0 \tag{3.1}$$

where y_0 denotes the log of the initial value of income per capita.

7. What is the slope of the resulting line?

8. Take the natural log of the initial and final values in table 3.1.

9. Use your answers above to write down the equation of the line that goes through the initial and final points of the graph in figure 3.1(b).

10. If you superimposed the line onto figure 3.1(b) what would it look like?

11. How does the slope of the line that you fit compare to the rate of growth you calculated in question 3?

12. Given your answer above, just by "eyeballing" figure 3.1(b), which of the four countries grew at the highest rate between 1880 and 2018?

13. In which of the two panels in figure 3.1 is it easier to see the growth rate of income per capita?

3.2   What Is So Natural about the Natural Log?

Unlike mathematicians, economists do not use the term $\ln(\cdot)$ to refer to the natural log. We simply write $\log(\cdot)$. Unless otherwise noted, every time you see the log function in an economics context, including this book, you should interpret it as the natural log.

1. Graph the function $\log(x)$. Make sure to label some critical points ($x = 0$, $x = 1$, $x \to \infty$) properly.

We will now consider the properties of this function around a very special point: $x = 1$.

2. What is the value of the function $\log(x)$ when $x = 1$?

3. Take the derivative of the log function. What is the value of this derivative when $x = 1$?

4. What is the equation of the line tangent to the function $\log(x)$ at $x = 1$?
[Hint: Recall that if you know the slope and one point of a line you can write its equation using point-slope form.]

5. Consider a small decimal r and evaluate $\log(1 + r)$ using a calculator. Now evaluate the tangent line that you derived above at $x = (1 + r)$. Calculate the difference between the two values.

6. What does the size of the difference suggest about evaluating the function $\log(1 + r)$ when r is small?

7. Use your answer above to show that the slope of the line (3.1) can be written more simply as the growth rate, r.

3.3   Growth

Consider data of a variable over time, $\{Y_t, Y_{t+1}, Y_{t+2}, \ldots, Y_{t+n}\}$. The variable of interest could be US output each quarter, the number of new daily coronavirus infections, or even your GPA each semester. Often we are interested in the rate at which these variables change over time. There are two ways to express this rate. The first is the percentage change (in decimals), which we call the *net growth rate*. If the net growth rate is r then the *gross growth rate* is $(1 + r)$.

1. Suppose you are at time $t + 1$. Write down the formula you would use to calculate the *net* growth rate between time t and $t + 1$. We will denote the *net* growth rate, r.

2. Rewrite your equation above to show that the *gross* growth rate is equal to the following ratio:

$$\frac{Y_{t+1}}{Y_t} = 1 + r \tag{3.2}$$

3. Define $y_t \equiv \log Y_t$. Show that

$$y_{t+1} - y_t = \log(1 + r) \tag{3.3}$$

4. Can the right-hand side of equation (3.3) be simplified further? If so, explain under what conditions this simplification is possible.

5. Use your answer above to suggest an alternative way of computing *net* growth rates.

Reference

Bolt, J., & J. Luiten van Zanden (2020). Maddison style estimates of the evolution of the world economy. A new 2020 update. *Maddison Project Database*. Accessed online at https://www.rug.nl/ggdc/historicaldevelopment /maddison/releases/maddison-project-database-2020

4 Grade Inflation

Academic grades have risen significantly over the past sixty years. According to Arthur Levine and Diane Dean, only 7 percent of undergraduates in 1969 earned grades above a B+, while 25 percent earned grades below a B−. By 2013 those shares were 41 percent and 5 percent, respectively. Is this the result of grade inflation or are students learning more? How can we tell and why do we care?

To explore these questions we are going to build a simple example. Consider a small economics department that teaches the same three classes every semester: macro, micro and metrics. Because macro and micro are easier than metrics they have higher average grades and also higher enrollment. Using the 4.0 scale, the average grade in macro and micro is 2.5, and they each enroll $\frac{2}{5}$ of the student body. The average grade in metrics is 2.0 and it enrolls the remaining $\frac{1}{5}$ of students.

1. What is the average GPA in the department?

2. Given Levine and Dean's estimates, at what yearly rate did the percentage of grades above a B+ grow between 1969 and 2013?

3. Given Levine and Dean's estimates, at what semesterly rate did the percentage of grades below a B− shrink between 1969 and 2013?

Now suppose the professors decide to relax their standards. They do this using a very simple procedure: while they continue to grade in the same way as before, they now add 0.1 to all final grades. This implies the average grade in macro and micro is now 2.6, while the average grade in metrics is now 2.1. As a shorthand we will call the original grading standard s_0 and the new, relaxed standard s_1.

4. What is the new average GPA in the department?

5. How many times larger is the new GPA relative to the original one?

6. At what rate did the GPA increase?

7. Does this higher GPA reflect a *real* increase in performance, or is it merely a *nominal* increase due to grade inflation?

8. Suppose that professors' salaries are tied to student performance as measured by the average GPA in the department. Now suppose you are the administrator who makes the decision on salaries. You observe the higher GPA, but of course professors do not tell you that they decided to be more lenient. Would you want to make a decision on salaries based only on the new GPA?

9. How could you solve this problem before you make a decision on salary increases?

Now suppose that not only did professors relax their standards—moving from s_0 to s_1—but also students got better on average. The average GPA in macro jumps from 2.5 to 2.8, the average GPA in micro jumps from 2.5 to 2.6, and the average grade in metrics jumps from 2.0 to 2.2.

10. What is the new average GPA in the department?

11. How many times larger is the new GPA relative to the original one? (original student ability, original grading policy).

12. At what rate did the GPA increase?

13. Is it possible to work out how much of the average GPA increase is due to student improvement and how much of it is due to grade inflation? If so, calculate the GPA increase due solely to student improvement. If not, explain why not.

14. Divide the *nominal* GPA of the department by the *real* GPA that measures only student improvement. By how much does the nominal figure overstate the real one? We will call this ratio the GPA *deflator.*

15. At what rate did the real GPA increase?

16. Compare the rate at which the real GPA increased to the rate at which the nominal GPA increased. What does the difference in the two rates measure?

After a few years of grading according to s_1, professors once again decide to change their standards. This time, however, they disagree about how much to do so. The metrics professor decides to add an additional 0.4 points to final grades. The micro professor decides to stay at s_1 and continue adding 0.1 points to final grades. The macro professor—who has reached the salary cap—decides to revert to the original grading system s_0 and add no additional points. Professors continue to grade according to s_0, but now the metrics professor adds a total of 0.5 points after grading, the micro professor adds 0.1 points after grading, and the macro professor adds no extra points. We will call this grading system s_2.

This has an effect on student enrollment. Since micro is now the easiest course, enrollment balloons from $\frac{2}{5}$ to $\frac{1}{2}$ of the student population. Macro and metrics are now equally difficult, so $\frac{1}{4}$ of students enroll in macro, down from $\frac{2}{5}$, while the other $\frac{1}{4}$ enroll in metrics, up from $\frac{1}{5}$. Under this new grading system, the average GPA in metrics jumps from 2.2 to 2.8, the average GPA in macro remains at 2.8, and the average GPA in micro jumps from 2.6 to 3.0.

17. What is the new average GPA in the department?

18. How many times larger is the new average GPA under s_2 than the GPA under s_1?

19. At what rate did the GPA increase? How does it compare to the growth rate you computed in question 12?

20. Is it possible to work out how much of the average GPA increase is due to student improvement and how much of it is due to grade inflation? If so, calculate the GPA increase due solely to student improvement. If not, explain why not.

21. Divide the *nominal* GPA of the department by the *real* GPA that measures only student improvement. By how much does the nominal figure overstate the real one?

22. How does the deflator for s_1 (computed in question 14) compare to the deflator for s_2 (computed above)?

23. At what rate did the real GPA increase? How does it compare to real GPA increase from s_0 to s_1 (computed in question 15)?

Reference

Levin, A., & D. Dean (2012). *Generation on a tightrope: A portrait of today's college student.* San Francisco: Wiley.

5 Standardized Tests

Comparing students from different schools according to their transcripts is always challenging. College admissions offices deal with this problem every year, as do companies deciding on job applications from soon-to-be college graduates, MBAs, and JDs. Most colleges and many companies solve this problem by requiring applicants to take a *standardized* test. In recent years, however, standardized tests have come under heavy criticism. Are there feasible alternatives to standardized tests? To answer this question we will analyze a sequence of increasingly difficult comparisons between two applicants.

Let's start with the simplest case. Alex and Blake go to the same school and take the same classes. The school has a uniform grading system, so even if the classes are offered in different semesters, or by different professors, the standard is exactly the same.

1. If the admissions committee is interested only in academic performance, does it face a problem in comparing Alex and Blake using their respective GPAs? If yes, explain why. Otherwise, explain who the committee will choose.

Now suppose, not unreasonably, that Alex and Blake have different interests. Even though they go to the same school they have taken different classes. Table 5.1 displays their respective transcripts. Courses are identified by subject and number, with higher numbers indicating more advanced courses. Grades are out of 4.0.

2. Compute their respective GPAs.

3. What makes comparing Alex and Blake according to their GPAs in this case different from the case where they took the same classes?

4. Are there specific elements of their transcripts that make the GPA comparison problematic? If so, list them.

5. Are there specific elements of their transcripts that make a comparison possible? If so, list them.

6. Build and compute a one-number measure that can serve as an alternative to compare Alex and Blake. We will call this measure PGPA, where P stands for *parity*. According to the PGPA, who would the admissions committee choose?
[Hint: Think about your answers to the two previous questions.]

Table 5.1
Transcripts for Alex and Blake.

Alex		Blake	
Course	Grade	Course	Grade
Chemistry 401	3.0	Chemistry 401	3.0
Literature 301	3.5	Physics 204	4.0
Biology 300	3.5	Philosophy 324	4.0
Economics 312	2.0	Economics 312	3.0
History 333	4.0	History 333	2.0

Finally, suppose that the transcripts above do not come from the same school. To keep it simple, we will assume that the schools use the same textbooks and use the same numbering system; for example, Chemistry 401 in Alex's school covers the same material from the same textbook as Chemistry 401 in Blake's school.

7. Explain whether the PGPAs you computed in the the previous question still offer an effective comparison statistic to differentiate between Alex and Blake.

8. Some high schools and colleges now include the school average GPA as part of their transcripts for individual students. Why might this information be useful to the admissions committee comparing Alex and Blake?

9. Suppose that the average GPA in Alex's school is 3.5, while the average GPA in Blake's school is 3.0. Both schools include this information in their transcripts. By what factor, on average, are grades higher at Alex's school?

10. Explain how this factor can be used to adjust the PGPAs you computed in question 6 to make them comparable once again. After the adjustment is made, who would the admissions committee choose?

11. What are the two problems that admissions committees face when comparing different students from different schools?

12. Explain how a standardized test solves both of these problems. Explain how the adjusted PGPA solves both of these problems.

6 The Big Mac Index

Brits and Americans have at least three things in common: Big Macs, Coca Cola, and aircraft carriers. According to *The Economist*, in 2012 the price of a Big Mac was $4.42 in the United States and $3.82 in the United Kingdom. Suppose that Coke was the same price in both countries: $1. While Big Macs and Coke are the same in the two countries, the same is not true for carriers. The *Queen Elizabeth* class and the *Ford* class are very different beasts. Unsurprisingly, while the cost of the *Queen Elizabeth* was $5 billion, the *Gerald Ford* cost $13 billion.

Suppose that output in the two countries consists only of Big Macs, Coke, and carriers. Table 6.1 contains prices and quantities for the three goods in the years 2012 and 2013. All prices are quoted in US dollars so there is no need to know the exchange rate. The easiest way to complete this chapter is in a spreadsheet such as Microsoft Excel or Google Sheets.

6.1 Levels

1. *Nominal GDP* measures the market value of all final goods and services produced in a year using that same year's prices. Compute the nominal GDP in both countries for both years.

2. *Real GDP* measures the market value of all final goods and services produced in a year using the prices of an arbitrary year. We call that year the *base* year. Compute the real GDP in both countries for both years using 2012 as the base year.

3. Compute real GDP in both countries for both years using 2013 as the base year.

4. How do the nominal GDP figures compare to the real GDP figures in each country across time? Briefly explain why this is the case.

The GDP *deflator*, $\lambda_t(T)$, is the ratio of nominal GDP, $NGDP_t$, to real GDP, $RGDP_t$, in year t, where real GDP is computed using prices from base year T.

$$\lambda_t(T) \equiv \frac{NGDP_t}{RGDP_t(T)} \tag{6.1}$$

Table 6.1
Prices and quantities in the US and UK for 2013–2014.

US

	2012		2013	
	Price	Quantity	Price	Quantity
Big Mac	4.42	300 million	4.78	310 million
Coke	1	300 million	1.05	315 million
Carrier	13 billion	1	13 billion	1

UK

	2012		2013	
	Price	Quantity	Price	Quantity
Big Mac	3.82	80 million	4	82 million
Coke	1	70 million	1.05	71.75 million
Carrier	5 billion	1	5.1 billion	1

Source: The Economist.

Note that t and T need not be different.

1. Calculate the log of the GDP deflator for both years for both countries and using both 2012 and 2013 as base years.
[Hint: You will end up with eight different calculations, two deflators per year per country. Another hint: Half of the deflators will be trivial to calculate.]

6.2   Log Differences

1. Solve for nominal GDP in equation (6.1).

2. Use your answer above to show that:

$$\log(NGDP_t) = \log(RGDP_t(T)) + \log(\lambda_t(T))$$

3. What is the relationship between the net growth rates of the nominal GDP, real GDP and the GDP deflator?
[Hint: Recall that the net growth rate of a variable X_t is equal to $\log(X_t) - \log(X_{t-1})$.]

4. Calculate the growth rate of nominal GDP in each country.

5. Calculate the growth rate of real GDP using 2012 and 2013 as the base year in both countries.

6. Calculate the growth rate of the GDP deflator using 2012 and 2013 as the base year in both countries.

7. Briefly explain why the growth rate of the GDP deflator measures the rate of change of prices. This rate of change is called the rate of *inflation*.

8. Discuss the differences between the inflation rate using 2012 versus 2013 as the base year.

6.3 Personal Consumption Expenditures

The GDP deflator tells us about the price level for the overall economy. But we may instead be interested in the price level of what consumers purchase. After all, the cost of a carrier has little effect on the cost of living of either Americans or Brits.

1. Calculate the *nominal expenditures* in the US for *only* Big Macs and Coke for both 2012 and 2013.

2. What component of *nominal* aggregate demand did you calculate in the previous question?

3. Calculate the *real* expenditures in the US for *only* Big Macs and Coke for both 2012 and 2013, using 2012 as the base year.

4. Calculate the *real* expenditures in the US for *only* Big Macs and Coke for both 2012 and 2013, using 2013 as the base year.

5. In the questions above you have calculated both nominal and real *personal consumption expenditures*. Calculate the corresponding deflators for both 2012 and 2013, using both 2012 and 2013 as base years.
[Hint: You should end up with four deflators, two of which are trivial.]

6. What is the inflation rate according to this deflator? How does it compare to the inflation rate of the GDP deflator?

7. This deflator is called the *personal consumption expenditures price index*, or PCEPI; the growth rate of this index is the preferred measure of inflation that the Federal Reserve targets. How does the inflation rate compare when you use 2012 versus 2013 as the base year?

6.4 Purchasing Power Parity

Consider real GDP in the US and real GDP in the UK in 2013 using 2012 as the base year.

1. Real GDP allows us to control for differences in prices *across time*. Compute the ratio of UK-to-US real GDP. Why might we worry that comparing real US GDP and real UK GDP might be misleading?

2. Now calculate GDP in the UK for 2013 using *2012 US prices*. What is the ratio of this alternate real UK GDP to real US GDP?

3. Discuss the difference between the two ratios.

4. Repeat the previous steps for real consumption expenditures.
[Hint: Consumption expenditures include Big Macs and Coke only.]

5. How do the ratios change when you use US prices to calculate consumption expenditures in the UK?

6. Consider the following consumption basket: 1 Big Mac and 1 Coke. What is the cost of purchasing this consumption basket in the US in 2013 dollars? What is the cost of purchasing this consumption basket in the UK in 2013 dollars?

7. Divide the cost of the consumption basket in the US by the cost of the consumption basket in the UK. Is it above or below one? And what does that suggest about comparing real US GDP in 2013 with real UK GDP in 2013?

8. Now multiply this ratio by the real value of UK consumption expenditures in 2013 (Consumption expenditures in the UK in 2013 valued at 2012 UK prices). You have calculated UK consumption expenditures at *purchasing power parity*. How does this value compare to the value you got when you evaluated UK consumption expenditures using US prices in question 4 of this subsection?

Reference

Economist, The (2013). *The Big Mac index*. Accessed online at https://economist.com/big-mac-index

7 Exchange Rates, Purchasing Power, and the Terms of Trade

Consider a two-country, two-good world. Each country produces one good but consumes both. This opens up the countries to trade. They have different currencies, however, so trade requires a foreign exchange market and, more specifically, an exchange rate. We will denote the countries with the superscript d for domestic and f for foreign. For concreteness, we will say that the domestic country uses dollars and the foreign country uses francs.

1. Let X denote the franc to dollar exchange rate. It tell us how many dollars can be purchased with one franc. If X is two, how many francs do you need to buy one dollar?

2. What are the units of X?

3. Suppose that the domestic country produces good a. Let P_a^f denote the price of good a in the francs. Write down the price in *domestic* currency, dollars, of selling good a abroad.

4. Let P_a^d denote the domestic price of good a. If $XP_a^f > P_a^d$, to which market would the firm sell to, the domestic or the foreign a?

5. If $XP_a^f < P_a^d$, to which market would the firm sell to, the domestic or the foreign one?

6. Given your answers above, if both countries are buying good a, what must be true about the domestic and foreign price (in dollars) of the good? Use your answer to show that the following relationship must hold in equilibrium:

$$X = \frac{P_a^d}{P_a^f} \tag{7.1}$$

7. Now consider the foreign country producing good b. Use the same reasoning as above to show that, in equilibrium:

$$\frac{1}{X}P_b^d = P_b^f \tag{7.2}$$

8. Equations (7.1) and (7.2) are examples of the *law of one price*. What do economists mean by this?

[Hint: Think about how you derived these relationships.]

9. Combine your results above to show that this implies:

$$\frac{P_a^f}{P_b^f} = \frac{P_a^d}{P_b^d} \tag{7.3}$$

This result is called the *purchasing power parity hypothesis.*

10. Suppose that *a* stands for apples and *b* for bananas. What are the units of P_a/P_b? Why doesn't the superscript matter?

11. Use you answer above to write down the economic interpretation of equation (7.3).

12. Recall that the domestic country exports apples to the rest of the world and imports bananas. The price ratio between its exports and imports, P_a/P_b, is called its *terms of trade.* Write down an expression for the terms of trade of the foreign country.

13. Suppose that the terms of trade improve for the domestic country. If the quantity of exports and the quantity of imports stays the same, what happens to the value of its trade balance? What happens to the value of the trade balance of the foreign country?

Now suppose that *a* stands for alcohol and *b* stands for bartending. The domestic country continues to be the only producer of alcohol, but now both countries produce bartending.

14. Explain why the two countries can continue to trade alcohol, but not bartending.

15. If bartending is more expensive in the domestic country, will it be possible for the foreign country to sell bartending services only to the domestic country?

16. Given your answer above, will equation (7.2) necessarily continue to hold?

17. For what kinds of goods and services do you expect the purchasing power parity hypothesis to hold?

Reference

Obstfeld, M., & K. Rogoff (1995). Exchange rate dynamics redux. *Journal of Political Economy, 103*(3), 624–660.

8 Bumble

Bumble is a location-based dating app. Users upload a profile of themselves and browse through the profiles of other users, swiping right for the profiles that interest them and left for those profiles that do not seem like a good fit. In heterosexual matches, only female users can make the first contact with matched male users. To put it dispassionately, females review potential male candidates who have expressed interest and reach out only to those who make the cut. What outcomes do we expect from this design? In particular, how many women, how many men, and how many matches do we expect Bumble to generate? To answer these questions we will develop a simple model of the heterosexual dating market on Bumble.

Let K denote the total number of females and N denote the total number of males on Bumble. To make our analysis clearer we will make a few simplifying assumptions. First, we will assume that when a woman sends a message to a man, she invites him to dinner that night and the man always says yes; we will call this outcome a match. We also assume that when the couple goes out to dinner they each get an equal amount of enjoyment that can be equated to a dollar amount, y. Because we are in the twenty-first century, we expect that both will chip in to pay for the bill. We will denote the total cost of the dinner by c, and the amount paid by the woman by w.

8.1 Matches

How do matches happen? Let M denote the total number of matches on the app. We can think of the app as a technology that takes men and women as inputs and *produces* matches; in other words, we can think of it mathematically as a *matching function*, $F(\cdot)$:

$$M = AF(N, K) \tag{8.1}$$

1. What economic interpretation can we give A?

2. Imagine that suddenly all of the women quit the app; what should happen to the number of matches? Substitute the values of M and K that correspond to this scenario in equation (8.1).

3. Imagine that suddenly all of the men quit the app; what should happen to the number of matches? Substitute the values of M and N that correspond to this scenario in equation (8.1).

4. Given your answers above, explain why we call both men and women *essential inputs* for matching.

5. Consider a fixed number of men, N. What do we expect to happen to the number of matches if one additional woman joins the app?

6. Your answer to the question above implies an inequality when the inputs are (N, K) versus when the inputs are $(N, K + 1)$. Write down the inequality.

7. Consider a fixed number of women, K. What do we expect to happen to the number of matches if one additional man joins the app?

8. Your answer to the question above implies an inequality when the inputs are (N, K) versus when the inputs are $(N + 1, K)$. Write down the inequality.

9. When the inequalities above hold, we say that the matching function exhibits *positive marginal returns* with respect to its inputs. Explain what we mean by *marginal returns* and what we mean by *positive*.

Suppose that the app is launched in a single college campus and then becomes available in a second—identical—campus where the exact same number of men and women join. By introducing the app into this second campus we say we have *scaled* the inputs by a factor of two.

10. What should happen to the number of overall matches when there are suddenly twice the number of men and women as there were before?

11. In the example above we scaled the number of men and women by a factor of two. If we instead scaled both men and women by an arbitrary factor, λ, by what factor do we expect the number of matches to scale?

12. Substitute λK and λN and your answer to the question above in equation (8.1).

13. Explain why we say that the matching function displays *constant returns to scale*.

8.2   What Men Want (A Movie from the Year 2019)

Given the properties of the matching function (i.e., the app), let's consider the prospects of the men who sign up and how those prospects determine how many men sign up.

1. If there are M matches and N men on the app, what is the fraction of men who find a match? Explain why this fraction is also the probability that a man who joins gets a match.

2. Let p denote the probability of a man getting matched. Write down p as a function of A, K, and N.

3. Let $k \equiv K/N$ denote the female-to-male ratio. Apply the fact that the matching function, $F(N, K)$, exhibits constant returns to scale to show that the probability of getting a match can be written only as a function of k:

$$p = AF(1, k) \tag{8.2}$$

[Hint: Dividing by N is the same thing as multiplying by $1/N$.]

4. We say a variable is *exogenous* when its value is external to the model. We say a variable is *endogenous* when its value is determined by the model. Is k an endogenous or an exogenous variable?
[Hint: What outcomes does our model aim to explain?]

If a man on Bumble gets a date he'll get an enjoyment of y and end up paying $c - w$ for dinner. Of course, if he doesn't get a date, he still has to eat dinner. We denote by b the dollar equivalent of the net benefit he gets from having dinner alone.

5. What is the man's net payoff from getting a date?

6. What is the man's net payoff from not getting a date?

7. What is the *average* payoff for the men who look for dates on Bumble?
[Hint: The average payoff is the weighted sum of the possible payoffs; and the weights are the probabilities of each payoff. You have already calculated the two possible payoffs and the probabilities of each.]

8. Assume that $y = c$. What is the romantic meaning of this assumption?

9. Let x denote the average payoff. Substitute the assumption above into your expression for x and write the average payoff as a function of p, b, and w.

$$x = p(w - b) + b \tag{8.3}$$

10. We call $w - b$ the *surplus* the man gets from getting a date. Is the surplus the *gross* value of going on the date or the *net* value of going on the date?

11. Is N an increasing or decreasing function of x?

We have that the total number of men who join depends on the average payoff of joining, but the average payoff of joining depends on the female-to-male ratio, which itself depends on the number of men who join. How is this ratio determined? This brings us to what women want.

8.3 What Women Want (A Movie from the Year 2000)

Recall that women also get a benefit equal to a monetary value y of getting a date. We assume that women on Bumble have to pay a fixed cost θ when reviewing potential matches. Importantly, they have to pay this cost whether they decide to reach out to a guy or not. We normalize the value to women of not finding a date to 0.

1. If there are M matches and K women on the app, what is the fraction of women who find a match? Explain why this fraction is also the probability that a woman gets a match.

2. Let q be the probability of a woman getting matched. Write down q as a function of A, K, and N.

3. Recall that k is the female-to-male ratio on Bumble. Apply the fact that the matching function, $F(N, K)$, exhibits constant returns to scale to show that the probability of getting a match can be written only as a function of k:

$$q = AF\left(\frac{1}{k}, 1\right) \tag{8.4}$$

4. If more women relative to men join the app, do you expect their probability of matching, q, to increase or decrease? Is equation (8.4) consistent with this intuition?

5. What is payoff for a woman who gets a date?
[Hint: Remember she will pay w to cover the tab.]

6. What is the payoff for a woman who does not get a date?
[Hint: Remember she pays θ regardless of whether she finds a date or not.]

7. What is the average payoff of women who are on the app?

8. What will happen to the number of women on the app if the average payoff is positive? How about if the average payoff is negative? At what point will the number of women joining neither increase nor decrease?

9. Given your answers above, show that the following equation will hold *in equilibrium:*

$$q = \frac{\theta}{y - w}$$

We call this equilibrium condition the *free entry condition.*

10. What is the *surplus* of going on the date for the woman?
[Hint: Recall that the surplus is the net rather than the gross value of going on a date.]

11. Show that the female-to-male ratio, k, is a function of the exogenous variables θ, y, w, and A:

$$F\left(\frac{1}{k}, 1\right) = \frac{\theta}{A(y - w)} \tag{8.5}$$

What is the economic interpretation of each of these variables?

References

Diamond, P. (1982). Wage determination and efficiency in search equilibrium. *Review of Economics Studies, 49*(2), 217–227.

Pissarides, C. (1985). Short-run equilibrium dynamics of unemployment, vacancies and real wages. *American Economic Review, 75*(4), 676–690.

Pissarides, C. (1990). *Equilibrium unemployment theory.* Oxford: Blackwell.

9 The Search for Dates and Jobs

Modeling the dating market might seem like an odd topic for a macroeconomics book to take up. Recall the structure of the dating market we analyzed in Bumble. There are two sides to the market. One side—men—looks over many profiles and applies to those they are interested in. The other side of the market—women—reviews the application and reaches out if they deem the applicant to be sufficiently qualified. When the two match, they go on a date, which generates some value.

Now consider the structure of the following unrelated, but also two-sided market. On one side of the market, workers look over many job vacancies and apply to those they are interested in. On the other side, firms review applications and reach out to qualified applicants. When the two match, the firm hires the worker, which generates output.

1. When describing the market on Bumble, what market of interest to macroeconomists were we also describing?

In what follows we are going to reinterpret the variables in our model of the dating market as variables in the labor market.

2. What are the labor market analogues to men and women in the dating market?

3. In the dating market, θ was the fixed cost that a woman had to pay when joining the app. What is the analogous interpretation of θ in the labor market?

4. In the dating market, we showed that a match generates a surplus of $y - w$ for the woman and $w - b$ for the man, where y denoted the gross value of the date, w the amount of the bill covered by the woman, and b the value for a man of being on the app, but not getting a match. What do y, w, and b represent in the labor market?

5. Show that the total surplus, s, generated by a match in the labor market—a worker filling a vacancy—is $y - b$.

6. If the wage goes up, what happens to the share of the total surplus that goes to the worker? What if the wage goes down? What role does the wage play in the allocation of the total surplus?

7. Let β denote the fraction of the total surplus that goes to the worker. What range of values can β take?

8. Show that the wage can be written as a function of β:

$$w = (y - b)\beta + b \tag{9.1}$$

9. Show that the surplus of the firm can be written as a function of β:

$$y - w = (y - b)(1 - \beta) \tag{9.2}$$

10. What is the wage when $\beta = 0$? What is the wage when $\beta = 1$?

11. Given that β is about the share of the economic pie that goes to workers, what economic feature does β capture?

12. We defined k as the ratio of women to men in the dating market. In the labor market k is the ratio of jobs to workers; we call this ratio the *labor market tightness*. If the labor market is *tight* what is true of the relative abundance of jobs to workers?

References

Diamond, P. (1982). Wage determination and efficiency in search equilibrium. *Review of Economics Studies, 49*(2), 217–227.

Pissarides, C. (1985). Short-run equilibrium dynamics of unemployment, vacancies and real wages. *American Economic Review, 75*(4), 676–690.

Pissarides, C. (1990). *Equilibrium unemployment theory.* Oxford: Blackwell.

10 Search and Unemployment

Participants in the labor market must search; workers for jobs and firms for workers. A statistic that summarizes the state of this search is the ratio of jobs to workers: *labor market tightness*. In this chapter we will identify some features that affect labor market tightness, and show how labor market tightness translates into unemployment and vacancies in equilibrium.

10.1 A Simple Model of the Labor Market

Consider a labor market with search. Firms post jobs and search for workers; workers, in turn, search for firms. The fraction of workers that find jobs, p, is an increasing function of the labor market tightness—the ratio of jobs to workers—k:

$$p = A\mathrm{f}(k) \tag{10.1}$$

where $\mathrm{f}(\cdot)$ is an increasing function of k.

The fraction of jobs that are filled, q, is also a function of labor market tightness, k:

$$q = A\mathrm{g}(k) \tag{10.2}$$

where $\mathrm{g}(\cdot)$ is a decreasing function of k. A is the efficiency of matching in the labor market; it therefore affects both sides of the market, p and q.

1. The *unemployment rate* is the fraction of the workers in the labor market who have not matched to a job. Write down the unemployment rate, u, as a function of p.

2. Show that the unemployment rate can be written as the following function of how tight the job market is:

$$u = 1 - A\mathrm{f}(k) \tag{10.3}$$

3. Is u increasing or decreasing in k?

4. The *vacancy rate* is the fraction of jobs in the labor market that have not been filled. Write down the vacancy rate, v, as a function of q.

5. Show that the the vacancy rate can be written as the following function of how tight the job market is:

$$v = 1 - Ag(k) \tag{10.4}$$

6. Is v increasing or decreasing in k?

Posting a job, regardless of whether it is filled or not, requires firms to pay a fixed cost, θ. The total surplus that a filled job generates is $y - b$, where y is the value generated by the worker and b is the value to the worker of being unemployed. Finally, the worker keeps a fraction β of the total surplus.

7. What is the share of the total surplus that the firm keeps when a job is filled?

8. Show that the expected value of posting a job for a firm is:

$$q[(y - b)(1 - \beta) - \theta] - [1 - q]\theta$$

[Hint: The expected value is also the average payoff from posting a job.]

9. Explain why, if there are no barriers to entry, in equilibrium, the above expression will equal zero.

10. Set the expected value from posting a job equal to zero and derive the following *implicit* function for the labor market tightness, k:

$$g(k) = \left(\frac{\theta}{A}\right) \frac{1}{(y - b)(1 - \beta)} \tag{10.5}$$

11. We have already seen how the expression above is called the free entry condition. It is sometimes also called the *zero profit condition*. Briefly explain why we might give it this alternate name.

Unemployment is a function of job market tightness, equation (10.3), and job market tightness is determined in equilibrium by the zero profit condition, equation (10.5). It follows, therefore, that any variable that has an effect on job market tightness, must also have an effect on unemployment.

10. Consider equation (10.5). If the right-hand side of the equation increases, what must happen to the left-hand side?
[Hint: This is not a trick question.]

11. In order for the left-hand side of equation (10.5) to increase, must k increase or decrease?

12. If θ increases, what happens to k?

13. What does the change in k induced by the increase in θ then do to the unemployment rate, u?
[Hint: What equation relates job market tightness and the unemployment rate?]

14. Describe in economic terms the causal chain from an increase in θ to a change in the unemployment rate.

15. If b or β increases, what happens to k?

16. What does the change in k induced by the increase in b or β then do to u?

17. Describe in economic terms the causal chain from an increase in either b or β to a change in the unemployment rate.

18. If y increases, what happens to k?

19. What does the change in k induced by the increase in y then do to u?

20. Describe in economic terms the causal chain from an increase in y to a change in the unemployment rate.

21. Explain why A has a direct and an indirect effect on u.

22. Suppose only the direct effect of A matters. Is unemployment an increasing or decreasing function of A's direct effect.

23. If A increases what happens to k?

24. Suppose only the indirect effect matters. How does the change in k induced by the change in A affect u?

25. The overall effect of A combines both the indirect and direct effects. Is unemployment increasing or decreasing in A?

10.2   Job Markets

Table 10.1 displays changes to the unemployment rate over time (rows) and differences in the unemployment rates for workers with four different levels of educational attainment (columns): those without a high school diploma, those with a high school diploma, those with a bachelor's degree and those with a master's degree. The time period in each row corresponds to a business cycle phase. Unshaded rows are expansions while shaded rows are recessions.

We are going to develop explanations for the differences in the unemployment rates documented in table 10.1 that are consistent with our model of search. We are interested in whether our model can offer some plausible interpretations of the data. We are not conducting a quantitative exercise that uncovers causal relationships between the variables of our model and the rates of unemployment in table 10.1.

For the purposes of our analysis we will assume that each group of educational attainment constitutes a separate labor market, each having its own free entry condition, equation (10.5), with variables that are different across markets and that might also change through time within each market.

Table 10.1
Unemployment rates (percent) by educational attainment over the business cycle. Rows in white are expansions; shaded rows are recessions, dated by the National Bureau of Economic Research.

Business cycle dates	Educational attainment			
	No HS diploma	HS diploma	Bachelor's degree	Master's degree
Jan 92–Feb 01	8.6	4.8	2.3	-
Mar 01–Jun 01	7.2	4.2	2.3	2.2
Jul 01–Nov 07	7.9	4.8	2.5	2.3
Dec 07–Jun 09	10.6	6.7	3.1	2.7
Jul 09–Jan 20	9.7	6.6	3.2	2.9
Feb 20–Apr 20	13.4	10.5	5.1	4.1
Apr 20–Dec 23	7.3	5.5	2.8	2.5
1992–2023	8.8	5.6	2.8	2.6

Sources: Bureau of Labor Statistics and National Bureau of Economic Research.

1. Rank the four labor markets from highest to lowest average unemployment. Has this ranking changed through any of the phases of the business cycle over the past thirty years?

2. Which subsequent level of educational attainment leads to the lowest drop in the unemployment rate? Which leads to the largest drop?

Let's consider the differences in unemployment rates between those without and those with a high school diploma; the first two columns under "Educational attainment" in table 10.1.

3. Which group is likely to have more workers under the age of eighteen?

4. The alternative to being employed and receiving a wage is to be unemployed. The value of being unemployed, however, is not zero; it is b. How does the value of b compare for those who are under eighteen versus those who are legally adults?

5. Even if those with and those without a high school diploma are equally productive—have the same y—explain why those without a high school diploma likely generate a lower surplus when hired.

6. Choose another variable (not y or b) and explain how its value might differ in the two job markets. Does the difference you outlined help explain the difference in unemployment rates between those with and without a high school diploma?

Let's now focus on how the unemployment rate changes as the economy moves from expansions into recessions, and see whether those changes apply uniformly across the four different job markets.

7. Calculate the factor by which unemployment increased during the Great Recession (Dec 07–Jun 09) relative to the preceding expansion (Jul 01–Nov 09) in each of the four labor markets.

8. Group the four different markets into the two with the largest factors and the two with the smallest.

9. Calculate the factor by which unemployment increased during the Covid-19 recession (Feb 20–Apr 20) relative to the preceding expansion (Jul 09–Jan 20) in each of the four labor markets.

10. Group the four different markets into the two with the largest factors and the two with the smallest.

11. How does your groupings for the Covid recession compare to those for the Great Recession?

12. We can think of the Covid lockdowns as affecting the efficiency of matching, A, since they prevented firms and workers from forming productive relationships. According to the ratios you calculated in question 9, which two markets saw the smallest decreases in A? Which saw the highest?

13. Offer a brief explanation as to why A would have dropped by more in the job markets with middle levels of education, high school diploma and bachelor's degree, than in the two markets at the ends of the educational attainment ladder, no high school diploma and master's degree.

References

Diamond, P. (1982). Wage determination and efficiency in search equilibrium. *Review of Economics Studies, 49*(2), 217–227.

Katz, L., & A. Krueger (1999). The high-pressure US labor market of the 1990s. *Brookings Papers on Economic Activity, 30*(1), 1–88.

Pissarides, C. (1985). Short-run equilibrium dynamics of unemployment, vacancies and real wages. *American Economic Review, 75*(4), 676–690.

Pissarides, C. (1990). *Equilibrium unemployment theory.* Oxford: Blackwell.

11 The Beveridge Curve

The labor market has a peculiar feature: supply and demand are never equal. There is always excess supply—unemployed workers are supplying labor but have not found any demand for it. Strangely, there is also excess demand! Unfilled vacancies suggest firms are trying to hire labor yet not finding any suppliers. In the aftermath of the Covid pandemic, for example, many businesses found it hard to hire workers. And yet the unemployment rate was not zero. The statistical relationship between excess demand, *vacancies*, and excess supply, *unemployment*, is called the *Beveridge curve*. In this chapter we will examine this relationship.

11.1   The Beveridge Curve in Theory

Consider a labor market where workers find a job with probability p and firms find a worker with probability q. Some matches, however, are not stable. Conditional on a worker and a firm matching, there is a probability δ that they will separate.

1. Offer a brief economic interpretation of δ.

2. Write down the probability that a worker matches with a firm and remains matched. [Hint: The probability that two events happen in sequence is the product of their probabilities.]

3. Write down the probability that a worker matches with a firm, but separates. [Hint: Same as above.]

4. Write down the probability that a worker does not match with a firm.

5. Which of the three outcomes above leads to employment? Which leads to unemployment?

6. Given your answers above, show that the unemployment rate, u, is given by:

$$u = 1 - (1 - \delta)p \qquad (11.1)$$

Is u an increasing or decreasing function of the separation rate, δ?

7. Repeat questions 2–5 but for the firm.

8. Given your answers above show that the vacancy rate, v, is given by:

$$v = 1 - (1 - \delta)q \tag{11.2}$$

Is v an increasing or decreasing function of the separation rate, δ?

The probabilities of matching, p and q, are themselves functions of the job market tightness, k:

$$p = A\mathrm{f}(k) \qquad\qquad q = A\mathrm{g}(k)$$

where A is the efficiency of matching, $\mathrm{f}(\cdot)$ is an increasing function of k and $\mathrm{g}(\cdot)$ is a decreasing function of k.

9. Job market tightness is a ratio. What is its numerator? How about its denominator?

10. Rewrite the unemployment and vacancy rates, equations (11.1) and (11.2), as functions of k rather than functions of p and q.

11. Use your answer above to explain why the unemployment rate, u, is a decreasing function of k and why the vacancy rate, v, is an increasing function of k.

The unemployment and vacancy rates are both functions of the same variable, k, and both depend on the same parameters, A and δ. This suggests an implicit equilibrium relationship between the two. The relationship between unemployment and vacancies is called the *Beveridge curve*. Let's sketch it.

12. What is the range of values that u and v can take?

13. Consider broadly low, intermediate, and high values of k, u, and v. Suppose k is low; what are the corresponding values of u and v? Suppose k is intermediate; what are the corresponding values of u and v? Suppose k is high; what are the corresponding values of u and v?

14. Set up a large coordinate plane with v on the y axis and u on the x axis. Use your answers above to sketch a graph of the implied relationship between v and u. Note that while the graph is only qualitative, it should still exhibit certain features consistent with our analysis up to this point.

15. Draw the 45 degree line on your graph. On which part of the Beveridge curve—above or below the 45 degree line—would you expect to be when the economy is in a boom? How about when the economy is in recession?

16. Now suppose that the separation rate, δ, increases. What happens to the values of u and v for each k that you considered in question 13?

17. Given your answer above, does an increase in the separation rate shift the Beveridge curve up or down?

18. Draw this new Beveridge curve on your graph.

19. Now suppose that the efficiency rate, A, increases. What happens to the values of u and v for each k that you considered in question 13?

20. Given your answer above, does an increase in the matching efficiency shift the Beveridge curve up or down?

21. Draw this new Beveridge curve on your graph.

22. You should now have three Beveridge curves on your graph. What two possible causes could lead the curve to shift up? What two possible causes could lead the curve to shift down?

11.2   The Beveridge Curve in Practice

Our model of search predicts an inverse equilibrium relationship between vacancies and unemployment. In this section we verify that this relationship is indeed borne out in the data. Figure 11.1 plots the relationship between the monthly unemployment and vacancy rates in the United States from 2001 to 2023. While all three panels plot the same data, each panel highlights one of the three business cycles of the twenty-first century.

1. What seems to have happened to the Beveridge curve with each successive business cycle? What are the two possible explanations that our model of search offers for this shift?

2. Consider the Great Recession, figure 11.1(b). Would you say the Beveridge Curve shifted during the recession or in the subsequent expansion?

3. If the Beveridge curve did shift after the Great Recession and then remained stable, do the different positions of the shaded squares in figure 11.1(b) represent changes in k, A or δ?

4. If the Beveridge curve did shift after the Great Recession and then remained stable, do the differences between the black triangles and shaded squares in figure 11.1(b) represent changes in k, A, or δ?

5. The Great Resignation looks like an upside-down U, with time moving from right to left; the shaded triangles on the right branch correspond to months in 2021, while the shaded triangles on the left branch correspond to more recent months in 2022 and 2023. Would you say the two branches fall on the same Beveridge curve or do they represent a shift?

6. One of the explanations that has been put forward for the Great Resignation is that the pandemic saw an increase in payments to workers, including extended unemployment benefits and stimulus payments. This increase in benefits then led workers to quit their jobs

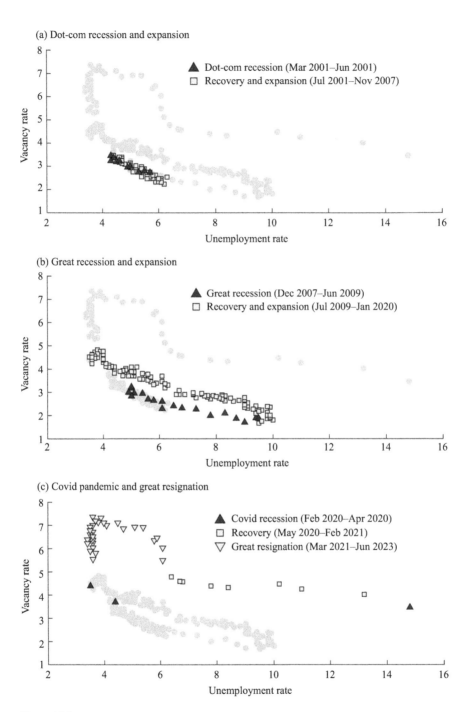

Figure 11.1
The Beveridge curve. The vacancy rate is calculated as the ratio of job openings to the sum of job openings plus total jobs. *Source*: Bureau of Labor Statistics.

at higher rates. Can we tell this story in our model? If yes, explain what variables would change and in what direction. If no, explain how we could expand our model to be able to tell this story.

7. If this story of the Great Resignation is true, do we expect the triangles on the left branch to be different because of differences in k or differences in A or δ?

8. If this story of the Great Resignation is true, does the movement across the top of the inverted U from right to left reflect changes in k, A, or δ?

References

Daly, M., B. Hobijn, A. Sahin, & R. Valletta (2012). A search and matching approach to labor markets: Did the natural rate of unemployment rise? *Journal of Economic Perspectives, 26*(3), 3–26.

Diamond, P. (1982). Wage determination and efficiency in search equilibrium. *Review of Economics Studies, 49*(2), 217–227.

Elsby, M., R. Michaels, & D. Ratner (2015). The Beveridge curve: A survey. *Journal of Economic Literature, 53*(3), 571–630.

Pissarides, C. (1985). Short-run equilibrium dynamics of unemployment, vacancies and real wages. *American Economic Review, 75*(4), 676–690.

Shimer, R. (2005). The cyclical behavior of equilibrium unemployment and vacancies. *American Economic Review, 95*(1), 25–49.

12 Choices as Optimization

Economics starts from the premise that agents make choices in pursuit of objectives given the constraints they face. Mathematically, this translates into solving *constrained optimization* problems: choosing among alternatives within a set of constraints in order to maximize (or minimize) some objective function.

When there are only two alternatives, the problem is trivial: choose whichever alternative achieves the higher value of your objective function. In this chapter we will generalize this intuition. We will derive a solution for a wide class of constrained optimization problems that we can then apply to all the specific problems we will encounter in this book.

Suppose you are choosing an amount of two options, *a* and *b*. We call any amounts (a_i, b_i) an *allocation*. The value of each allocation is given by your *objective function*:

$$U(a_i, b_i)$$

This is the function you are trying to maximize.

However, you cannot choose *any* allocation (a_i, b_i). Instead you can choose only allocations that also satisfy the following equation:

$$F(a_i, b_i) = X \tag{12.1}$$

where $F(a_i, b_i)$ is another function of the allocation. Loosely speaking, the function $F(\cdot)$ is a combination of a_i and b_i. Equation (12.1) defines your constraint because it *requires* that any allocation chosen, when combined—as defined by function $F(\cdot)$—must always equal X.

12.1 Improving Allocations

To find the best allocation we will exploit a simple fact: the value of the objective function under the best allocation is higher than under any other allocation. This allows us to make our search more manageable by dividing it into a sequence of trivial tasks; comparing only two allocations at a time.

1. Consider two allocations (a_1, b_1) and (a_2, b_2). Show that the difference in the value of the objective function can be written as:

$$U(a_2, b_2) - U(a_1, b_1) = [U(a_2, b_2) - U(a_1, b_2)] + [U(a_1, b_2) - U(a_1, b_1)] \qquad (12.2)$$

2. Write an economic interpretation for the left-hand side and each of the two bracketed terms on the right-hand side of equation (12.2).

[Hint: Think of (a_1, b_2) as an intermediate allocation between (a_1, b_1) and (a_2, b_2).]

3. Show that the change in the value of the objective function of switching to allocation (a_2, b_2) from (a_1, b_1) can be written as:

$$U(a_2, b_2) - U(a_1, b_1) =$$

$$\left[\frac{U(a_2, b_2) - U(a_1, b_2)}{a_2 - a_1} (a_2 - a_1) \right] + \left[\frac{U(a_1, b_2) - U(a_1, b_1)}{b_2 - b_1} (b_2 - b_1) \right] \qquad (12.3)$$

4. Suppose that your utility increases if you switch from allocation (a_1, b_1) to allocation (a_2, b_2). Will you make the switch? Will the right-hand side of equation (12.3) be greater than, less than, or equal to zero?

5. Now suppose there is a third allocation (a_3, b_3), so that your utility increases again if you switch from (a_2, b_2) to (a_3, b_3). Will you make the switch again? Will the right-hand side of equation (12.3) be greater than, less than, or equal to zero?

6. If you continue this process, at what point will you stop switching allocations? Write down what the right-hand side of (12.3) will be equal to when you stop switching allocations.

We will now define the following functions:

$$MU_a(a, b) \equiv \frac{U(a_2, b_2) - U(a_1, b_2)}{a_2 - a_1}$$

$$MU_b(a, b) \equiv \frac{U(a_1, b_2) - U(a_1, b_1)}{b_2 - b_1}$$

7. Write down the economic interpretation of $MU_a(\cdot)$ and $MU_b(\cdot)$.

8. Substitute the two expressions above into the equation from question 6 and show that when you stop switching allocations:

$$-\frac{b_2 - b_1}{a_2 - a_1} = \frac{MU_a(a, b)}{MU_b(a, b)} \qquad (12.4)$$

9. The ratio $MU_a(a, b)/MU_b(a, b)$ is called the *marginal rate of substitution*, or MRS. If a stands for apples and b for bananas, what are the units of this ratio?

10. Suppose the differences $a_2 - a_1$ and $b_2 - b_1$ can be made arbitrarily small (that is, closer and closer to zero). If the limit exists, what mathematical procedure can you use to find $MU_a(\cdot)$ and $MU_b(\cdot)$?

11. Given your answer above, describe an algorithm—the series of steps—to find the $MRS(a, b)$ of an objective function, $U(a, b)$.

12.2 Changing Allocations

In the previous section we examined the process of comparing two allocations in search of the one you *want*. The only potential allocations that you *can* choose from, however, are those that satisfy the constraint. We call any allocation that satisfies the constraint a *feasible* allocation. We now turn to the requirements that our search must satisfy in order to ensure that we consider only feasible allocations.

Consider the following function:

$$G(a_i, b_i, X) \equiv X - F(a_i, b_i)$$

1. Rewrite the constraint, equation (12.1), in terms of $G(\cdot)$ rather than $F(\cdot)$. We call $G(\cdot)$ the *constraint function*.

2. What is the change in $G(\cdot)$ equal to when comparing any two feasible allocations (a_1, b_1) and (a_2, b_2)?

3. Now consider an intermediate allocation (a_1, b_2). Show that:

$$G(a_2, b_2, X) - G(a_1, b_2, X) + G(a_1, b_2, X) - G(a_1, b_1, X) = 0$$

4. Show that the change in the value of the constraint function of switching to allocation (a_2, b_2) from (a_1, b_1) can be written as:

$$\frac{G(a_2, b_2, X) - G(a_1, b_2, X)}{a_2 - a_1}(a_2 - a_1) + \frac{G(a_1, b_2, X) - G(a_1, b_1, X)}{b_2 - b_1}(b_2 - b_1) = 0 \quad (12.5)$$

We will now define the following functions:

$$MC_a(a, b) \equiv \frac{G(a_2, b_2, X) - G(a_1, b_2, X)}{a_2 - a_1}$$

$$MC_b(a, b) \equiv \frac{G(a_1, b_2, X) - G(a_1, b_1, X)}{b_2 - b_1}$$

5. Write down the economic interpretation of $MC_a(\cdot)$ and $MC_b(\cdot)$.

6. Substitute the two expressions above into the equation 12.5 to show that any feasible switch must satisfy:

$$-\frac{b_2 - b_1}{a_2 - a_1} = \frac{MC_a(a, b)}{MC_b(a, b)} \quad (12.6)$$

7. The ratio $MC_a(a,b)/MC_b(a,b)$ is called the *marginal rate of transformation*, or MRT. If a stands for apples and b for bananas, what are the units of this ratio?

8. Suppose the differences $a_2 - a_1$ and $b_2 - b_1$ can be made arbitrarily small (that is, closer and closer to zero). If the limit exists, what mathematical procedure can you use to find $MC_a(\cdot)$ and $MC_b(\cdot)$?

9. Given your answer above, describe an algorithm—the series of steps—to find the $MRT(a,b)$ of the constraint function, $G(a,b,X)$.

12.3   Choice

A constrained optimization problem consists of solving for the pair (a^*, b^*) that

(i) maximizes the objective function: $U(a,b)$;

(ii) satisfies the constraint: $G(a,b) = 0$.

We are now in a position to derive the condition that this pair must satisfy.

1. Translate the mathematical term "pair" into its economic counterpart.

2. Translate the mathematical phrase "solving for the pair" into its economic counterpart.

3. Equation (12.4) describes the condition under which you are *willing to* exchange a for b at the chosen allocation. Equation (12.6) describes the condition under which you are *able to* exchange a for b at any feasible allocation. Explain why the chosen allocation (a^*, b^*) must satisfy both conditions.

4. Show that equations (12.4) and (12.6) imply the following *optimality condition:*

$$\underbrace{\frac{MU_a(a^*, b^*)}{MU_b(a^*, b^*)}}_{} = \underbrace{\frac{MC_a(a^*, b^*)}{MC_b(a^*, b^*)}}_{}$$

$$MRS(a^*, b^*) = MRT(a^*, b^*) \tag{12.7}$$

5. Explain what the optimality condition, equation (12.7), says in words.

13 Studying for the Final

The night before two final exams, you have to decide how much time to spend studying for each. Suppose you have already set a hard bedtime that you will stick to, so you have only a fixed number of hours, H, to devote to studying. Denote the amount of time you spend on the first subject by H_a and the amount of time you spend on the second by H_b.

13.1 Constraints

1. Write down the time constraint you face.

2. If the amount of time you spend studying is the *input*, what is the *output* of your efforts?

3. Does each additional hour of studying for a particular subject contribute the same amount to your ability to perform well on the exam the next morning?

4. Let $g_a(\cdot)$ denote the number of points you expect to earn in the first exam. Given your answer to the previous question, sketch a plot of $g_a(\cdot)$ *as a function* of the number of hours you dedicate to studying tonight, H_a. You do not need to write down an exact functional form, just a sketch of your answer to the previous question.

The *marginal return* of studying is the *increase* in $g_a(\cdot)$ that results from an additional—arbitrarily small—amount of time spent studying. Mathematically, it is the derivative of the function g_a with respect to H_a.

5. Are the marginal returns to studying positive or negative?

6. Are the marginal returns to studying increasing or decreasing?

13.2 A Linear Objective

Suppose that your objective is simply to maximize the *total* number of points you receive from *both* exams.

1. Explain why, if that is the case, your objective is to maximize the following function:

$$g_a(H_a) + g_b(H_b) \tag{13.1}$$

2. Write down the constrained optimization problem that you face the night before the final in deciding how much time to allocate to each subject.

3. What is the marginal rate of substitution between H_a and H_b?

4. What is the ratio of the marginal cost of spending time between the two subjects? [Hint: Recall that the ratio of the marginal costs is how much you have to give up of H_a in order to get one more unit of H_b, and vice versa.]

5. Write down the optimality condition of the constrained optimization problem.

6. What is the *economic* interpretation of this optimality condition?

13.3   A Concave Objective

1. When you are taking a test, what matters more: going from 0 to 10 or from 90 to 100? In other words, is each extra point on an exam as valuable to you as the previous point?

2. Let $u(g)$ denote the *value* you place on the total points you earn, g. Given your answer to the previous question, sketch a plot of $u(\cdot)$ *as a function* of the total number of points you earn, g.

Consider the following *objective* function for your performance in the two exams tomorrow:

$$u(g_a(H_a)) + u(g_b(H_b)) \tag{13.2}$$

3. Consider your sketch in question 2. What signs of the first and second derivative of $u(\cdot)$ are consistent with that sketch?

4. Write down the constrained optimization problem that you face the night before the final in deciding how much time to allocate to each subject.

5. Write down the optimality condition of this problem. [Hint: You'll need to use the chain rule.]

6. Isolate the terms with $u'(\cdot)$ on one side and the terms with $g'(\cdot)$ on the other, where the primes denote derivatives. What is the economic interpretation of this condition?

14 Beer

The Federal Reserve targets inflation as measured by the Personal Consumption Expenditures Price Index, or PCEPI. This measure of inflation is the growth rate of the deflator of the consumption component of aggregate demand. Many news outlets, however, report inflation as measured by the Consumer Price Index, or CPI. The Social Security Administration also uses the CPI to make cost-of-living adjustments to social security payments. The CPI measures the changes in the cost of buying a fixed basket of goods. What's the difference between these two alternative measures? And does the difference matter? Let's ask college students deciding which beer to buy.

14.1 Consumption and Prices

Consider a college student who consumes two kinds of beer—Sierra Nevada, C_s, and Goose Island, C_g—with the objective of maximizing the following utility function:

$$U(C_g, C_s) = u(C_g) + u(C_s)$$

where $u(C) \equiv C^\alpha$ and $0 < \alpha < 1$.

The student has a beer allowance, Y, the price of Sierra Nevada is P_s, and the price of Goose Island is P_g.

1. Write down the student's total beer expenditures.

2. Show that the student's budget constraint is given by:

$$P_g C_g + P_s C_s - Y = 0 \tag{14.1}$$

3. Write down the student's constrained optimization problem.

4. Write down the marginal rate of substitution between Goose Island, C_g, and Sierra Nevada, C_s.

5. Write down the marginal rate of transformation between Goose Island, C_g, and Sierra Nevada, C_s.

6. Show that the student's optimality condition is given by:

$$\left(\frac{C_g}{C_s}\right)^{\alpha-1} = \frac{P_g}{P_s} \tag{14.2}$$

7. We call the right-hand side of equation (14.2) the *relative price* of Goose Island. What are its units? Given your previous answer, what do we mean by relative?

Suppose that during junior year, a six-pack of both beers is the same price, $P_g = P_s$. We will graphically depict the student's chosen allocation.

8. Solve for C_g in the budget constraint, equation (14.1), to get the following slope-intercept form:

$$C_g = -C_s + B \tag{14.3}$$

where $B \equiv Y/P_g$.

9. What is the slope? What is the economic interpretation of the y intercept, B?
[Hint: What are the units of Y/P_g?]

10. Solve for C_g in the optimality condition, (14.2), to get the following slope-intercept form:

$$C_g = C_s \tag{14.4}$$

11. Set up a large coordinate plane with C_g on the y axis and C_s on the x axis. Graph the budget constraint and the optimality condition, equations (14.3) and (14.4), respectively.

12. Show that they intercept at (C_s, C_g):

$$\left(\left(\frac{1}{2}\right)B, \left(\frac{1}{2}\right)B\right)$$

What is the economic significance of this point?
[Hint: *Can* the student ever not be on the budget constraint? *Will* the student ever not satisfy the optimality condition?]

Now suppose that during senior year the price of Goose Island stays the same, but the price of Sierra Nevada increases by a factor of Π.

12. Is Π greater than or less than one?

13. Show that the budget constraint is now given by:

$$C_g = -\Pi C_s + B \tag{14.5}$$

14. Explain the economic reasoning for why the y intercept stays the same.

15. Show that the optimality condition is now given by:

$$C_g = \Pi^{1-\alpha} C_s \tag{14.6}$$

16. On the same diagram from junior year, graph the senior year budget constraint and optimality condition, equations (14.5) and (14.6), respectively.

17. Show that as a senior, the student will choose the allocation (C_s, C_g):

$$\left(\left(\frac{1}{\Pi^{1-\alpha} + \Pi} \right) B, \ \left(\frac{\Pi^{1-\alpha}}{\Pi^{1-\alpha} + \Pi} \right) B \right)$$

18. Does the student's consumption of Sierra Nevada increase or decrease during senior year? Does the student's consumption of Goose Island increase or decrease during senior year?

[Hint: Recall that $\Pi > 1$. Another hint: Recall that $0 < \alpha < 1$.]

19. Explain why changes in the relative price lead to your above result.

14.2   Cost of Living Adjustments

Since there was inflation between junior and senior years, the parents decide to increase the student's beer allowance, which recall was Y during junior year. By how much do they need to increase it in order to offset the effects of inflation?

One way to proceed is to increase the student's allowance until the new amount, Y^L, is enough to purchase the allocation from junior year $(B/2, B/2)$. This is what the Social Security Administration does. It holds the bundle of goods fixed, and increases the income required to buy the same bundle at the new prices.

1. To calculate the new allowance, Y^L, write down how much the original allocation, $(B/2, B/2)$, costs during senior year.

2. Manipulate your answer above to show that the gross rate of inflation of the allowance between junior and senior years must be:

$$\frac{Y^L}{Y} = \frac{1 + \Pi}{2} \tag{14.7}$$

3. This ratio can alternatively be interpreted as an *index*, with junior being the base year. The index we have calculated is called a *Laspeyres index*. *Laspeyres* indices measure the increase in the cost of buying a *fixed* basket of goods and services. Is the PCEPI a Laspeyres index? How about the CPI?

4. Does the allocation $(B/2, B/2)$ satisfy the student's optimality condition, equation (14.6), during senior year?

5. Given your answer above, will the student continue to buy the same amount of Sierra Nevada and Goose Island after receiving Y^L?

6. Write down the student's budget constraint during senior year with the increased allowance.

7. Combine your answer above with the student's optimality condition, equation (14.6), to show that with Y^L, the student's chosen allocation, (C_s, C_g), will now be:

$$\left(\frac{1+\Pi}{2} \left(\frac{1}{\Pi^{1-\alpha} + \Pi} \right) B, \; \frac{1+\Pi}{2} \left(\frac{\Pi^{1-\alpha}}{\Pi^{1-\alpha} + \Pi} \right) B \right)$$

There is another way to proceed. Instead of increasing the allowance until the student can buy the same allocation from junior year, the parents can increase the allowance until the student can buy an allocation during senior year that would have been affordable during junior year. Rather than increasing the allowance to make sure the student can afford the *same allocation*, they can increase the allowance to make sure the student can afford an allocation on the *same budget constraint*.

8. As a senior, the student will choose an allocation that satisfies equation (14.6). But the parents want to make sure the allocation chosen would have been affordable junior year, equation (14.3). Set up a large coordinate plane with C_g on the y axis and C_s on the x axis, and graph the two equations.

9. Show that the two equations intersect at (C_s, C_g):

$$\left(\frac{1}{1 + \Pi^{1-\alpha}} B, \; \frac{\Pi^{1-\alpha}}{1 + \Pi^{1-\alpha}} B \right)$$

10. Explain why the parents will give the student a beer allowance, Y^P, to purchase the allocation given by the intersection of the two curves.

11. To calculate the new allowance, Y^P, write down the cost of buying the above allocation during senior year.

12. Show that the gross rate of inflation of the allowance between junior and senior years must be:

$$\frac{Y^P}{Y} = \frac{\Pi + \Pi^{1-\alpha}}{1 + \Pi^{1-\alpha}} \tag{14.8}$$

13. This ratio can alternatively be interpreted as an *index*, with junior being the base year. The index we have calculated is called a *Paasche index*. *Paasche* indices measure the increase in the cost of buying the *current* basket of goods and services. Is the PCEPI a Paasche index? How about the CPI?

The parents now have two options to increase the beer allowance, Y^P or Y^L. How do these compare?

14. Notice that the gross rate of inflation under both methods can be written as the formula:

$$\frac{x + \Pi}{x + 1} \tag{14.9}$$

where x depends on whether the parents use a Paasche or a Laspeyres index. Write down the value of x for Y^L and Y^P.

15. Use your answer above to explain why $Y^L > Y^P$.

16. Let's reconsider the diagram from question 8 in this section. Add to that diagram the two possible senior-year budget constraints; one for each of the two possible increases, Y^L and Y^P. Make sure to draw these accurately. Be especially careful about where all the lines intersect.
[Hint: Both budget constraints have the same slope, $-\Pi$, the only difference is the y intercept.]

17. Explain what each of the allocations denoted by the three intersections in your diagram represents.
[Hint: You have already solved for all three allocations.]

18. Intuitively, if the price of Sierra Nevada goes up *relative* to the price of Goose Island, what does the student do?

19. If the parents increase the beer allowance to Y^L, do they take this behavioral change into account? How about if they increase the beer allowance to Y^P?

20. Given your answers above, which price index do you expect to measure a higher inflation rate, the CPI or the PCEPI? What information does the PCEPI incorporate that the CPI excludes?

21. Now suppose that C_g denotes goods, not Goose Island, and C_s denotes services, not Sierra Nevada. And instead of parents, it is Congress deciding which price index to use in order to determine the increase in retirement benefits. Which price index will retirees favor?

15 Dinner

The *production function* is a mapping from inputs (usually the factors of production) into output:

$$Y = F(K, L) \qquad (15.1)$$

where K is capital, L is labor—the factors of production—and Y is output. What are some sensible properties we would expect this mapping, $F(\cdot)$, to display? Let's consider the production of dinner, which requires the combination of two factors of production: the kitchen and the cook.

15.1   Essential Inputs

1. What factor of production is the kitchen? What factor of production is the cook?

2. How much dinner can the kitchen produce on its own without the cook?

3. What are the values of K, L, and Y in the example above?

4. Substitute the values from the previous question into expression (15.1). Discuss.

5. How much dinner can the cook produce without a kitchen?

6. What are the values of K, L, and Y in the example above?

7. Substitute the values from the previous question into expression (15.1). Discuss.

15.2   Positive but Decreasing Marginal Returns

1. You are making dinner by yourself when suddenly someone in your family offers to help. With two people cooking, will you be able to prepare *more* or *less* food than when it was just yourself?

2. A third family member joins; what happens to the amount of food that you can now make?

3. How does the *additional* amount of food that is now possible to cook with a third family member's help compare to the *additional* amount that became possible when the second family member began helping? How does it compare to the amount that you could cook if you were making dinner on your own?

4. Imagine that you are now joined by a bunch of family and friends as you cook dinner. At this point yet another friend joins and starts helping. How much more food do we expect this friend to contribute to the overall effort relative to the first, second, and third persons who began cooking?

5. If every helper's contribution is positive, the production function exhibits *positive marginal returns*. What is the sign of the first derivative of the production function?

6. If every additional helper's contribution is getting smaller, the production function exhibits *decreasing marginal returns*. What is the sign of the second derivative of the production function?

7. Given the two properties above, plot output, Y, on the y axis, as a function of labor, L, on the x axis, for a fixed kitchen size (that is, for a constant K).

15.3   Constant Returns to Scale

1. Imagine that one cook in one kitchen can cook dinner for four in an hour. If we get a second cook and put them in a second kitchen, for how many people can dinner be made in an hour?

2. How about a third cook in a third kitchen?

3. If we scale all of the factors production by the same factor n, what happens to total output?

4. Consider equation (15.1) above. If instead of K and L we now use a total of nK and nL factors of production, what will happen to output? This property is called *constant returns to scale*.

16 Cobb and Douglas Are Hiring

Consider a firm whose objective is to maximize its profits. The firm must choose how much output to produce and how much labor and capital to hire in order to produce given its production function:

$$Y = AF(K, L) \tag{16.1}$$

where Y is output, K is capital, and L is labor; A is a proportionality constant. Further, we assume that the firm takes all prices as given. We will denote the price output, capital and labor by P, R, and W, respectively.

1. What happens to output as A increases for a given amount of capital and labor?

2. Given your answer above, offer a brief economic interpretation of A.

3. Write down an expression for the firm's total revenue.

4. Write down an expression for the firm's total costs as a function of its inputs, L and K, and their respective prices, W and R.

5. Show that the profit function of the firm is:

$$\Pi(Y, K, L) = PY - (RK + WL) \tag{16.2}$$

6. How much output would the firm choose to produce and how many inputs would it choose to hire if it did not face *any* constraints?
[Hint: Recall the firm wants to make Π as large as possible... What values of output, capital and labor do the trick?]

7. Why are the values from your previous question unrealistic? What prevents the firm from choosing them?

8. We now have an objective and a constraint. Write down the firm's constrained optimization problem.

Now that we have a constrained optimization problem we turn to the firm's choice of how many inputs to hire.

9. Show that the marginal rate of substitution between labor and output is given by:

$$\frac{-W}{P}$$

10. The expression above is called the *real wage*. What are its units?

11. Show that the marginal rate of transformation between labor and output is given by:

$$-AF_L(K,L) \tag{16.3}$$

where the subscript, $F_L(\cdot)$, denotes the partial derivative of the production function, $F(\cdot)$, with respect to labor, L.

12. Explain why $AF_L(K,L)$ is called the *marginal product of labor*.

13. Write down the optimality condition. If the production function displays diminishing marginal returns, what happens to the firm's demand for labor if the real wage increases?

14. Show that the marginal rate of substitution between capital and output is given by:

$$\frac{-R}{P}$$

15. The expression above is called the *real rental rate*. What are its units?

16. Show that the marginal rate of transformation between capital and output is given by:

$$-AF_K(K,L) \tag{16.4}$$

where the subscript, $F_K(\cdot)$, denotes the partial derivative of the production function, $F(\cdot)$, with respect to capital, K.

17. Explain why $AF_K(K,L)$ is called the *marginal product of capital*.

18. Write down the optimality condition. If the production function displays diminishing marginal returns, what happens to the firm's demand for capital if the real rental rate increases?

Now assume that the firm's production function is *Cobb-Douglas*:

$$F(K,L) = K^\alpha L^{1-\alpha}$$

19. If $F(\cdot)$ displays positive, diminishing marginal returns with respect to capital and labor, what are the possible values of α?

20. Show that when the production function is Cobb-Douglas, the optimality condition between output and labor implies:

$$L = \frac{(1-\alpha)Y}{W/P} \tag{16.5}$$

21. Set up a coordinate plane with labor on the y axis and the real wage on the x axis and graph labor as a function of the real wage.

22. Show that when the production function is Cobb-Douglas, the optimality condition between output and capital implies:

$$K = \frac{\alpha Y}{R/P} \tag{16.6}$$

23. Set up a coordinate plane with capital on the y axis and the real rental rate on the x axis and graph capital as a function of the real rental rate.

24. Consider your diagrams for labor and capital as a function of their respective relative prices. Are capital and labor increasing or decreasing in their relative price? You have just graphed the *labor demand curve* and *capital demand curve.*

25. Given your derivations above, what condition determines demand functions?

26. Substitute your demand functions into the profit function to determine the firm's profits.

17 The Price of Leisure

One of the most important decisions that households make is how much to work and how much to consume. The two allocations are not independent, since we use our earnings from work to pay for our consumption. Consider a household that enjoys consumption but would rather dedicate its time to leisure instead of work. We will denote consumption by C and hours worked by H. To capture these preferences, we say that the household aims to maximize the utility function $U(C, H)$. We will assume that the *marginal utility of consumption* (the derivative of $U(\cdot)$ with respect to C) is positive and decreasing, whereas the *marginal utility of work* (the derivative of $U(\cdot)$ with respect to H) is negative and decreasing.

1. What are the signs of the first and second partial derivatives of $U(\cdot)$ with respect to C?

2. What are the signs of the first and second partial derivatives of $U(\cdot)$ with respect to H?

The household earns an hourly wage, W, which it can use to buy consumption, C, at a price, P. This implies that the household's budget constraint can be written as

$$PC \leq WH \tag{17.1}$$

3. Explain why the budget constraint (17.1) will actually hold with equality.
[Hint: What do the signs of the first partial derivatives of $U(\cdot)$ imply about the household's preferences?]

4. Write down the constrained optimization problem of the household.

5. Write down the marginal rate of transformation between hours worked, H, and consumption, C.

6. What are the units of the marginal rate of transformation?

7. Write down the marginal rate of substitution between hours worked, H, and consumption, C.

8. Write down the optimality condition for the household.

Now suppose the household has the following utility function:

$$U(C, H) = \log(C) - \frac{1}{1+\phi} H^{1+\phi} \tag{17.2}$$

9. Show that under the utility function above, the household will choose consumption and work to satisfy the following equation:

$$H = \left(\frac{1}{C}\right)^{\frac{1}{\phi}} \left(\frac{W}{P}\right)^{\frac{1}{\phi}} \tag{17.3}$$

[Hint: What is the MRS when the utility function is given by (17.2)?]

10. Are hours worked an increasing or decreasing function of the real wage? You have just derived the *labor supply function.*

11. Set up a coordinate plane with hours worked on the y axis and the real wage on the x axis, and graph hours worked as a function of the real wage.

Let $\phi = 2$ and $W/P = 1$.

12. Graph equation (17.3) with H on the y axis and C on the x axis.

13. In the same graph as above, plot equation (17.1).
[Hint: Recall that (17.1) will hold as an equality. Solve for H.]

14. What allocation of consumption and labor, (C, H), will the household choose at this real wage?

Let $\phi = 2$ and $W/P = 2$.

15. Plot equation (17.3) with H on the y axis and C on the x axis.

16. In the same graph as above, plot equation (17.1).
[Hint: Make sure you substitute in the real wage given above.]

17. What allocation of consumption and labor, (C, H), will the household choose at this real wage?

18. The household has a fixed amount of time that it can dedicate to either work or leisure. What does the household give up in order to enjoy leisure?

19. Given your answer above, explain why the household supplies more labor when the real wage increases.

18 Elasticity

Elasticities measure how sensitive one variable is with respect to another *locally*. The price elasticity of demand, for example, measures how sensitive the demand function is to changes in price *at a given price*. The same is true for the price elasticity of supply. In general, we define the elasticity, ε, of a variable, Y, with respect to another variable, X, as the percentage change of Y *over* the percentage change in X. In this chapter we will explore the relationship between the concept of elasticity and the natural log.

18.1 The Price Elasticity of Labor Demand

Recall the labor demand function we derived from the Cobb-Douglas production function:

$$L = \theta \left(\frac{W}{P} \right)^{-1/\alpha} \tag{18.1}$$

where θ is a constant and $0 < \alpha < 1$.

1. Let $\ell \equiv \log(L)$ and $w \equiv \log(W/P)$. Transform the demand function above, (18.1), to write the log of labor demand, ℓ, as a function of the log of the real wage, w.
[Hint: Begin by taking the log of both sides.]

2. Suppose that you start with a log real wage, w', and the log real wage changes to w''. Give an interpretation of the difference $w'' - w'$ when this difference is close to zero.

3. Let ℓ' be the log labor demand when the log real wage is w' and ℓ'' be the log labor demand when the log real wage is w''. Give an interpretation of the difference $\ell' - \ell''$ when $w'' - w'$ is close to zero.

4. Show that the log difference in labor demand can be written as the following function of the log difference in the real wage

$$\ell'' - \ell' = \left(-\frac{1}{\alpha} \right) (w'' - w') \tag{18.2}$$

5. Explain why the ratio $(\ell'' - \ell')/(w'' - w')$ is the *price elasticity of labor demand.*

6. Graph ℓ as a function of w. What is the interpretation of the slope of your graph?

18.2   The Price Elasticity of Labor Supply

Consider the labor supply function we derived in chapter 17:

$$H = \lambda \left(\frac{W}{P}\right)^{1/\phi} \tag{18.3}$$

where $\lambda \equiv (1/C)^{1/\phi}$.

1. Let $h \equiv \log(H)$ and $w \equiv \log(W/P)$. Transform the supply function above, (18.3), to write the log of labor supply, h, as a function of the log of the real wage, w.
[Hint: Begin by taking the log of both sides.]

2. Suppose you start with a log real wage, w', and this changes to w'' by Δ, so that $\Delta \equiv w'' - w'$. How do you interpret Δ as it approaches zero?
[Hint: Recall that Δ is a log difference.]

3. How do you interpret $h(w'') - h(w')$ as Δ approaches zero?

4. Consider the following ratio:

$$\frac{h(w'') - h(w')}{w'' - w'}$$

Suppose you let Δ approach zero. If the limit of the above ratio exists, what does that ratio become?

5. Combine your answers to the three previous questions to explain why

$$\frac{\partial}{\partial w} h(w)$$

is the price elasticity of labor supply. Does this principle generalize?

6. What is the price elasticity of labor supply if labor supply is given by (18.3)?

19 When Are Market Economies Efficient?

The truism "markets are efficient" is so vague as to cover all manner of sins. What does it mean by "markets"? What does it mean by "efficient"? Does it imply that *only* markets are efficient? In this problem we will address these questions. As we define an efficient allocation and contrast it to the market's allocation, keep the following questions in mind: What are the assumptions in the market economy we model? Are the conclusions that we draw robust to those assumptions?

19.1 The Invisible Hand

Consider an economy that produces only cookies with a homogeneous labor supply and fixed capital. There are two agents in this economy. Households buy cookies and sell labor; firms buy labor and sell cookies. We assume that the price of cookies, P, and the price of labor, W, are taken as given by both households and firms.

The representative household of this economy consumes cookies, C, and sells its labor, H, to maximize the following objective function:

$$U(C, H) = \log(C) - \frac{H^{1+\phi}}{1+\phi} \qquad (19.1)$$

1. Write down the household's budget constraint.
2. Write down the constrained optimization problem of the household.
3. Write down the marginal rate of substitution between hours worked and consumption.
4. Write down the marginal rate of transformation between hours worked and consumption.
5. What are the units of the real wage?
6. Show that the household's optimality condition is given by:

$$\frac{W}{P} = CH^{\phi} \qquad (19.2)$$

7. Equation (19.2) expresses the real wage as a function of how many hours the household works. It is called the *inverse supply of labor*. Why might it have this name?
[Hint: What would you end up with if you solved for H?]

The representative firm hires labor, L, to produce cookies, Y, with the objective of maximizing profits. The firm must decide how much labor to hire given the amount of cookies it wants to bake, subject to the following production function:

$$Y = AK^{\alpha}L^{1-\alpha} \tag{19.3}$$

For simplicity we will assume that the firm's capital stock is fixed so that the only input the firm must hire is labor.

8. Write down the profit function of the firm.

9. Write down the constrained optimization problem of the firm.

10. Write down the marginal rate of substitution between labor and output.

11. Write down the marginal rate of transformation between labor and output.

12. Show that the firm's optimality condition is given by:

$$\frac{W}{P} = (1 - \alpha)\frac{Y}{L} \tag{19.4}$$

13. Equation (19.4) expresses the real wage as a function of how many hours of work the firm hires. It is called the *inverse demand of labor*. Why might it have this name?
[Hint: What would you end up with if you solved for L?]

Denote the equilibrium allocations by L^*, H^*, Y^*, and C^*. The equilibrium allocations must satisfy the optimality conditions of the household and the firm, the constraints of the household and the firm, and the following *market-clearing* conditions:

$$L^* = H^* \qquad\qquad\qquad Y^* = C^*$$

14. Briefly explain what each of these two conditions impose.

15. Combine the optimality conditions of the household and the firm with the market-clearing conditions above. Show that the equilibrium allocation of labor is a function of only preferences, ϕ, and the production function, α:

$$L^* = (1 - \alpha)^{1/(1+\phi)} \tag{19.5}$$

16. In a diagram, graph equations (19.3) and (19.5). For your diagram assume that $0 < \alpha < 1$ and $\phi > 0$. What does the intersection of the two curves represent?
[Hint: Plot output on the y axis and labor on the x axis.]

17. Suppose that ϕ increases. Use your diagram to explain what happens to the equilibrium allocation of labor and output, $\{L^*, Y^*\}$.

18. Suppose that α increases. Use your diagram to explain what happens to the equilibrium allocation of labor and output, $\{L^*, Y^*\}$.

19. Suppose A decreases. Use your diagram to explain what happens to the equilibrium allocation of labor and output, $\{L^*, Y^*\}$.

20. Technological growth in the US has been around 2 percent per year over the past century. Given your answer above, how would this have changed the number of hours Americans work?

19.2   The Visible Hand

The previous section explores how labor and output are allocated in a competitive market. In this section we eschew the invisible hand of the market and consider an alternative way to allocate resources.

Consider a household with the same objective as in the previous section, expression (19.1). Rather than selling its labor to, and then buying cookies from, the same firm, the household produces the cookies at home. Its production technology is the same as the firm's, given by expression (19.3):

$$C = AK^\alpha H^{1-\alpha}$$

Notice that there is no equilibrium in this problem; there is only one agent—the household—choosing an allocation, $\{C, H\}$. We are interested in comparing the household's *chosen allocation* without a market to the *equilibrium allocation* generated by the market economy, analyzed in the previous section.

1. Write down the household's objective function.

2. Write down the household's constraint.
[Hint: What constrains the household's ability to make cookies from its own labor?]

3. We now have an objective and a constraint! Write down the household's constrained optimization problem.

4. Write down the marginal rate of substitution between hours worked and consumption.

5. Write down the marginal rate of transformation between hours worked and consumption.

6. Show that the household's optimality condition is

$$CH^\phi = (1-\alpha)\frac{C}{H} \tag{19.6}$$

How does the *optimality* condition of the household compare to the *equilibrium* condition in the market economy from the previous section?

7. Solve for the allocation of labor, H, that the household will choose. How does this compare to equation (19.5) in the previous section?

8. How does the allocation of cookies, C, that the household chooses in this case compare to the equilibrium allocation from the previous section?

9. We call the allocation the household would choose the *efficient allocation*. Given the production function of the economy, is it possible to find an alternative allocation that makes the household better off?

10. In light of your answer to the previous two questions, *briefly* discuss whether the type of market economy in the previous section is consistent with the following excerpt from *The Wealth of Nations* by Adam Smith.

He generally, indeed, neither intends to promote the public interest, nor knows how much he is promoting it... By directing his industry in such a manner as its produce may be of the greatest value, he intents only his own gain, and he is in this, as in many other cases, led by an invisible hand to promote an end which was no part of his intention... By promoting his own interest he frequently promotes that of the society.

References

Gali, J. (2008). *Monetary policy, inflation and the business cycle: An introduction to the new Keynesian framework.* Princeton: Princeton University Press.

King, R., C. Plosser, & S. Rebelo (1988a). Production growth and business cycles: I. The basic neoclassical model. *Journal of Monetary Economics, 21*(2), 195–232.

King, R., C. Plosser, & S. Rebelo (1988b). Production growth and business cycles: II. New directions. *Journal of Monetary Economics, 21*(3), 309–341.

Smith, A. (2002). *The wealth of nations.* Oxford: Bibliomania.com.

20 The Government Expenditure Multiplier

Governments often increase their own spending as a way to "stimulate" the economy. While we know that government spending is one of the components of aggregate demand, we also know that GDP is an *equilibrium* outcome. Equilibrium outcomes depend not only on what the government does, but also on the *optimal* responses of households and firms to government policy. We are interested, therefore, in the following policy question: How does an increase in government spending—a stimulus—affect the equilibrium allocations of labor, consumption, and output?

20.1 Agents

Our economy has three agents: households, firms, and now the government. The government maintains a balanced budget: it buys output from the firm, G, at price P by levying an equal amount of *lump-sum* taxes, T, on the household's income.

$$PG = T \tag{20.1}$$

Equation (20.1) is the government's budget constraint.

The household supplies its labor, H, and demands output to consume, C, to maximize the following objective:

$$U(C, H) = \log(C) - \frac{H^{1+\phi}}{1+\phi} \tag{20.2}$$

The household earns an hourly wage of W for its labor. Like the government, it also pays P for some of the output of the firm.

1. What is the household's income?

2. What are the household's expenditures?

3. Write down the household's budget constraint.

4. Write down the constrained optimization problem of the household.

5. Write down the marginal rate of substitution between hours worked and consumption.

6. Write down the marginal rate of transformation between hours worked and consumption.

7. Write down the household's optimality condition between hours worked and consumption.

The firm hires labor, L, and produces output, Y, to maximize profits subject to the following production function:

$$Y = AL \qquad (20.3)$$

8. Write down the firm's profit function.

9. Write down the constrained optimization problem of the firm.

10. Write down the marginal rate of substitution between labor and output.

11. Write down the marginal rate of transformation between labor and output.

12. Write down the firm's optimality condition between labor and output.

20.2   Equilibrium

Now that we have the decision rules of households and firms, we want to describe what the equilibrium allocations will be, *given* the government's spending policy. Notice that we are not interested in *how* the government makes choices. For policy analysis, we want to describe the equilibrium outcomes for *some* choice that the government makes. We can then compare the different equilibrium outcomes that arise from different policy choices.

1. Write down the market-clearing condition in the goods market. Label which side of your equation is output and which side is aggregate demand.
[Hint: How many agents are now buying the goods that the firm produces?]

2. Combine the market-clearing condition in the goods market with the production function to show that, in equilibrium, consumption is a linear function of labor:

$$C = AL - G \qquad (20.4)$$

What is the slope? What is the y intercept?

3. Write down the market-clearing condition in the labor market.

4. Combine the household's and government's budget constraints along with the market-clearing condition in the labor market to show that, in equilibrium:

$$\frac{W}{P}L = C + G$$

Which side of the equation above corresponds to income and which corresponds to aggregate demand?

5. Combine the market-clearing condition in the labor market with the optimality conditions of the firm and the household to derive the following equilibrium relationship between consumption and labor:

$$C = \frac{A}{L^\phi} \tag{20.5}$$

We have two equations, (20.4) and (20.5), and two unknowns, C and L. This system of equations, however, cannot be solved analytically. We will instead solve it graphically.

6. Set up the coordinate plane with C on the y axis and L on the x axis. Graph equation (20.4).

7. In the same diagram as above, graph equation (20.5).
[Hint: What value does C take when L is very close to zero? What value does C take when L is very large?]

8. Explain why the intersection of the two curves denotes the equilibrium allocation of consumption and labor as a function of government spending, G, productivity, A, and household preferences, ϕ.

20.3 The Multiplier

We are now in a position to consider the effects of a stimulus package. As in the previous section, we will examine the effect of the stimulus graphically, since we cannot solve for the equilibrium allocations using algebra. For simplicity, let $A = 1$. Suppose that the government is purchasing a baseline amount, $\bar{G}$, and it approves a stimulus $S > 0$. Denote the new level of government purchases by $G' \equiv S + \bar{G}$.

1. Recall that equations (20.4) and (20.5) define the equilibrium allocations of consumption and labor. Does (20.5) depend on the level of government purchases?

2. With C on the y axis and L on the x axis, graph equations (20.4) and (20.5) when $G = \bar{G}$.

3. When $G = \bar{G}$ we will denote the equilibrium allocations by $\bar{C}$, $\bar{L}$, and $\bar{Y}$. Label the equilibrium allocation $(\bar{L}, \bar{C})$ on your diagram.

4. On the same diagram as above, graph equation (20.4) when $G = G'$. Why don't you need to graph equation (20.5) again for this new level of government purchases?

5. When $G = G'$ we will denote the equilibrium allocations by C', L', and Y'. Label the equilibrium allocation (L', C') on your diagram.

6. Let $\Delta C \equiv C' - \bar{C}$ denote the change in the household's consumption as a result of the stimulus. Does consumption increase or decrease in response to the stimulus? This effect is often referred to as the *crowding out* of private expenditure.

7. Let $\Delta G \equiv G' - \bar{G}$. What is ΔG equal to? Explain why the vertical distance between the two lines on your diagram is equal to S.

8. In your diagram, which is larger: the vertical distance between the lines or the vertical distance between the points where the lines intersect equation (20.5)?

9. Given your answers to the three previous questions, explain why:

$$\Delta G + \Delta C > 0 \tag{20.6}$$

10. Given your answers to the the three previous questions, explain why:

$$S > \Delta G + \Delta C \tag{20.7}$$

11. Let $\Delta Y \equiv Y' - \bar{Y}$ denote the change in output as a result of the stimulus. Show that $\Delta Y = \Delta C + \Delta G$.

12. Combine inequalities (20.6) and (20.7) with your answer above to show that

$$S > \Delta Y > 0 \tag{20.8}$$

13. Does output increase or decrease as a result of the stimulus? Does output increase/decrease by more or less than the size of the stimulus?

The *government expenditure multiplier*, m, is the ratio of the *change* in output over the *change* in government purchases:

$$m \equiv \frac{\Delta Y}{\Delta G}$$

14. Explain why m is a measure of the effectiveness of the stimulus, S.

15. Is the multiplier in this economy greater than, less than, or equal to one? What does that suggest about the effectiveness of a stimulus package?
[Hint: manipulate inequality (20.8).]

16. If it were up to the household, would it support the stimulus?

Now suppose that the economy becomes more productive, so that $A = 2$.

17. In a new diagram, redo questions 2–5, for this higher level of productivity.

18. Compare ΔC in the case where $A = 1$ to the case where $A = 2$. Is the decrease in consumption as a result of the stimulus larger when $A = 1$ or when $A = 2$?

19. Given your answer above, how does the government expenditure multiplier change as the economy becomes more productive?

References

Hall, R. (2009). By how much does GDP rise if the government buys more output? *Brookings Papers on Economic Activity*, 183–231.

Woodford, M. (2011). Simple analytics of the government expenditure multiplier. *American Economic Journal: Macroeconomics*, 3(1), 1–35.

21 Why Do Americans Work So Much More than Europeans?

Ask Ed Prescott. Notwithstanding the somewhat irreverent transatlantic stereotypes of Europeans as lazy (by Americans) and Americans as workaholics (by Europeans), Prescott suggested that part of that difference might come down to tax policy. We will take up his argument here.

21.1 Taxes and Labor

We have an economy with a representative firm and a representative household. The household supplies labor and demands output for its own consumption. The firm demands labor and supplies output. Some of that output is purchased by the household and some by the government. In order to pay for the output, the government introduces marginal taxes. Labor income is taxed at a marginal rate τ_h, while consumption is taxed at a marginal rate τ_c.

The representative household supplies labor, H, and demands consumption, C, to maximize its utility function:

$$U(C,H) = \log(C) - \frac{H^{1+\phi}}{1+\phi}$$

The firm pays the household an hourly wage, W, which is subsequently taxed by the government. Similarly, the firm receives P for each unit of consumption sold, while the household pays P plus the consumption tax.

1. Show that the household's budget constraint is given by:

$$(1+\tau_c)PC - (1-\tau_h)WH = 0$$

2. How does the price that the household pays for consumption compare to the price that the firm receives?

3. How does the price that the firm pays for labor compare to the price that the household receives?

4. Write down the constrained optimization problem of the household.

5. Write down the marginal rate of substitution between hours worked and consumption.

6. Write down the marginal rate of transformation between hours worked and consumption.

7. Is the real wage that the household receives higher or lower than the real wage that the firm pays?

8. We define the *tax wedge*, ω, as the ratio between the real wage that the household earns and the real wage that the firm pays:

$$1 - \omega \equiv \frac{1 - \tau_h}{1 + \tau_c} \tag{21.1}$$

What is the range of values that ω can take? What is the value of ω if all taxes are abolished?

9. Explain why ω does not depend on whether taxes are levied on consumption, τ_c, or income, τ_h.

10. Show that the household's optimality condition implies the following inverse supply curve of labor:

$$\frac{W}{P} = \frac{CH^\phi}{1 - \omega} \tag{21.2}$$

Is the left-hand side of equation (21.2) the real wage that the household receives or the real wage that the firm pays?

The firm owns a fixed amount of capital, K. It hires labor, L, at the wage, W, and produces output, Y, which it sells at price, P, subject to a Cobb-Douglas production function,

$$Y = K^\alpha L^{1-\alpha}.$$

11. Write down the constrained optimization problem of the firm.

12. Write down the marginal rate of substitution between labor and output.

13. Write down the marginal rate of transformation between labor and output.

14. Show that the firm's optimality condition is:

$$\frac{W}{P} = (1 - \alpha)\frac{Y}{L} \tag{21.3}$$

15. Set up a coordinate plane with the real wage on the y axis and L and H on the x axis. Graph the inverse demand for labor, equation (21.3), and the inverse supply of labor, equation (21.2), in the case where there are no taxes.
[Hint: Make your diagram large enough to add more curves. Another hint: What is the tax wedge when the tax rates are zero?]

16. The intersection of the inverse demand and inverse supply curves satisfies the market-clearing condition $L = H$. Describe what this condition means. We will denote this intersection by $\left(L_0, \frac{W_0}{P_0}\right)$.

17. In the same diagram as above, graph the inverse labor supply when there are taxes.
[Hint: What inequality does the tax wedge satisfy when tax rates are not zero?]

18. Denote the new intersection by $\left(L_\tau, \frac{W_\tau}{P_\tau}\right)$. How do the equilibrium real wage and equilibrium labor supply change when taxes are introduced?

19. Does it matter whether the government taxes income or consumption?

21.2 Tax Policy

In the previous section we developed a model for the equilibrium allocation of labor in an economy with income and consumption taxes. In this section we will attempt to answer the motivating question of this chapter by taking our model to the data.

1. Combine the inverse demand and supply functions from the previous section with the market-clearing condition to show that the equilibrium allocation of labor, L, is given by the following equation:

$$L = \left((1 - \alpha)(1 - \omega)\left(\frac{1}{c}\right)\right)^{1/(1+\phi)} \qquad (21.4)$$

where $c \equiv C/Y$ is the fraction of aggregate demand that is allocated to consumption in equilibrium.

2. We are interested in taking our model to the data. List the unknowns that we need to measure in order to predict the equilibrium allocation of labor.

3. Manipulate the inverse demand for labor to show that $1 - \alpha$ is equal to the fraction of pretax income that goes to labor.

4. What data might we need in order to measure the tax wedge?

5. What data might we need in order to measure the fraction of aggregate demand that is consumed?

Table 21.1 shows Prescott's estimates of the tax wedge and hours worked for seven countries in two different time periods. Prescott defines labor supply as the average weekly hours worked per person aged 16–64. Column 2 reports hours worked by Europeans—as well as Canadians and Japanese—*relative* to Americans. For example, between 1993 and 1996 Germans worked only $\frac{3}{4}$ of what Americans did. The table also has data on the fraction of income that goes to labor and the fraction of aggregate demand that goes to consumption.

6. Since we are interested in the extent to which taxes can explain the differences in hours worked, we will follow Prescott and assume that ϕ is the same across countries and through time. There are various estimates for ϕ, but we will use the ones reported by Chetty, Guren, Manoli and Weber (2011) and set $\phi = 1.85$. What is the corresponding elasticity of labor supply implied by this value?

7. We now have values for all of the right-hand-side variables in equation (21.4). Choose two countries and calculate the hours worked relative to the US for both periods according

Table 21.1
Taxes and labor supply.

Country	Hours worked relative to the US	Labor share of income $1 - \alpha$	Consumption share of aggregate demand c	Tax wedge ω
Period: 1993–1996				
France	0.68	0.62	0.74	0.59
Germany	0.75	0.66	0.74	0.59
Italy	0.64	0.54	0.69	0.64
UK	0.88	0.55	0.83	0.44
Canada	0.88	0.69	0.77	0.52
Japan	1.04	0.60	0.68	0.37
USA	1.00	0.61	0.81	0.40
Period: 1970–1974				
France	1.04	0.66	0.66	0.49
Germany	1.05	0.67	0.66	0.52
Italy	0.82	0.59	0.66	0.41
UK	1.10	0.55	0.77	0.45
Canada	0.94	0.72	0.77	0.44
Japan	1.27	0.60	0.68	0.25
USA	1.00	0.64	0.74	0.40

Sources: Prescott (2004) and Penn World Tables (2015).

to our model. How do the model's predicted values compare to the actual values reported in column 2?

[Hint: You will need to calculate L for the US and then for the countries you choose.]

8. Within the framework of our model, what can explain the differences between our predictions and the data?

[Hint: Conditional on the assumption that our model is correct, what is the only additional assumption we have made?]

9. In chapter 18 we showed that $1/\phi$ is the elasticity of labor supply: the percent change in labor supplied by households given a one percent change in the real wage. Consider the 1993–1996 period. If our model describes the equilibrium allocation of hours, what can you say about elasticity of labor supply in the two countries you chose relative to the US?

So far we have compared the working habits of Americans to Europeans. But the tax wedge isn't merely different across the Atlantic; it has also changed in each country through time. How much of the difference in hours worked between the seventies and nineties can be explained by changes in tax policy?

10. Let $\ell_t^i \equiv L_t^i / L_t^{US}$ denote the entries in column 2. The t refers to the time period and i refers to the country. Let $\Lambda^i \equiv L_{90s}^i / L_{70s}^i$ denote the gross growth rate of hours worked in

country i. Show that you can calculate this growth rate using the entries in column 2 if you also know the growth rate of hours worked in the US:

$$\Lambda^i = \left(\frac{\ell_{90s}}{\ell_{70s}}\right) \Lambda^{US} \tag{21.5}$$

11. The gross growth rate of hours worked in the US between the two periods is 1.10. Choose two countries and calculate the gross growth rate of hours worked in each.

12. Once again, assume that $\phi = 1.85$ for all countries in both time periods. For the same two countries as above, calculate the growth rate of hours worked predicted by the model.

13. Now relax the assumption that ϕ is constant through time. For the predicted growth rates of the model to match the actual growth rates, how would the elasticity of labor supply have to have changed in each country between the seventies and the nineties?

References

Chetty, R., A. Guren, D. Manoli, & A. Weber (2011). Are micro and macro labor supply elasticities consistent? A review of evidence on the intensive and extensive margins. *American Economic Review, 101*(3), 471–475.

Feenstra, R., R. Inklaar, & M. Timmer (2015). The next generation of the Penn World Table. *American Economic Review, 105*(10), 3150–3182. Available at www.ggdc.net/pwt

Prescott, E. (2004). Why do Americans work so much more than Europeans? *Federal Reserve Bank of Minneapolis Quarterly Review, 28*(1), 2–11.

22 Market Power

So far we have considered economies where households and firms are price takers. Given the prevailing market prices, they choose how much labor and goods to buy and sell. While this is certainly a good description in some markets, it is also obvious from daily experience that some firms choose the prices they charge for the goods they sell. When agents are able to influence equilibrium prices we say they have *market power*. In this chapter we will analyze how firms with market power choose prices to maximize profits.

Consider a profit-maximizing firm that produces a final good, Y, with N intermediate inputs, $\{X_1, X_2, \ldots, X_N\}$, according to the production function:

$$Y = \sum_{i=1}^{N} X_i^{1-\alpha} \tag{22.1}$$

where $1 > \alpha > 0$. The price of each intermediate good, X_i, is R_i, while the price of the final good, Y, is P. The final goods firm maximizes profits subject to its production function taking all prices as given.

1. Write down the profit function of the final goods firm.

2. Write down the constrained optimization problem of the final goods firm.

3. Write down the marginal rate of substitution between an arbitrary intermediate good, X_i, and the final good, Y.

4. Write down the marginal rate of transformation between an arbitrary intermediate good, X_i, and the final good, Y.

5. Write down the optimality condition of the final goods firm to derive the following inverse demand function:

$$\frac{R_i}{P} = (1 - \alpha)X_i^{-\alpha} \tag{22.2}$$

All intermediate goods firms produce their good, X_i, using only labor as input according to the same production function:

$$X_i = L_i \tag{22.3}$$

where L_i denotes the total labor hired to produce good i.

We will consider the problem of the intermediate goods firms in two types of competitive markets. In the first, each type of intermediate good is produced by many firms, and so each individual firm is a price *taker*. In the second, each type of intermediate good is produced by a single firm. As the sole producer of good i, the firm has market power and is a price *setter*.

We begin with the case where the firm takes the price of labor, W, the price of its own good, R_i, and the price of the final good, P, as given.

6. Write down the profit function of the intermediate goods firm.

7. Write down the constrained optimization problem of the intermediate goods firm.

8. Write down the marginal rate of substitution between the intermediate good, X_i, and labor, L_i.

9. Write down the marginal rate of transformation between the intermediate good, X_i, and labor, L_i.

10. Show that the optimality condition implies:

$$\frac{R_i}{P} = \frac{W}{P} \tag{22.4}$$

11. In a diagram with R_i/P on the y axis and X_i on the x axis, graph equations (22.2) and (22.4). What does the intersection of the two curves represent?
[Hint: α and $\frac{W}{P}$ are both constants in your graph.]

12. Show that the equilibrium allocation of X_i is a function of the real wage:

$$X_i^* = \left(\frac{1}{\alpha}\frac{W}{P}\right)^{-1/\alpha} \tag{22.5}$$

[Hint: Think about the intersection of the curves in your diagram.]

We now turn to the case where the intermediate goods firm is the only producer of good i and can thus set the price. When a firm is the only producer of a good, we call it a *monopolist*. Importantly, the monopolist still takes the price of labor, W, and the price of the final good, P, as given.

13. Show that the profit function of the intermediate goods firm can be written as:

$$X_i(R_i - W)$$

14. The profit function is increasing in both the price the intermediate goods firm sets, R_i, and the amount it produces, X_i. Why is firm i not able to simultaneously charge an arbitrarily high price and sell an arbitrarily high amount of good X_i?

15. Given your answer above, explain why equation (22.2) constrains the monopolist.

16. We now have an objective and a constraint. Write down the constrained optimization problem of the monopolist.

17. Write down the marginal rate of substitution between the price it charges, R_i, and the quantity it produces, X_i.

18. Write down the marginal rate of transformation between the price it charges, R_i, and the quantity it produces, X_i.

19. Write down the optimality condition of the firm.

20. Combine the optimality condition you derived in the previous question with the inverse demand function, equation (22.2), to show that the firm's chosen price is a linear function of the real wage:

$$\frac{R_i}{P} = \mu \frac{W}{P} \qquad (22.6)$$

where $\mu \equiv 1/(1 - \alpha)$. Is μ greater than or less than one?

21. Economists call μ the price *markup*. Offer an educated guess as to why.
[Hint: What was the equilibrium relative price of good i when firms were price takers?]

22. In the diagram where you graphed equations (22.2) and (22.4), graph equation (22.6). How do the equilibrium price and quantity compare when producers are price takers versus when they are price setters?

23. Let X_i^* denote the equilibrium allocation of good i when the intermediate goods firm is a price *taker*, and let X_i^m denote the equilibrium allocation of good i when the intermediate goods firm is a price *setter*. Show that X_i^m is a function of X_i^*:

$$X_i^m = \mu^{-1/\alpha} X_i^*$$

Under which market structure does the intermediate goods firm produce more output, X_i?

Reference

Dixit, A., & J. Stiglitz (1977). Monopolistic competition and optimum product diversity. *American Economic Review, 67*(3), 297–308.

23 When Are Market Economies Inefficient?

In chapter 19, "When Are Market Economies Efficient?," we compared the equilibrium allocations that arise in a market economy with those that the household would choose if it had direct control over the factors and means of production. The market economy fared well in that comparison: its allocation was efficient. But that efficiency arose because price-taking firms set the marginal product of labor equal to the real wage, while price-taking households set the marginal rate of substitution equal to the real wage. As we will see in this problem, when firms have market power, the market will no longer equate households' marginal rate of substitution with firms' marginal rate of transformation, putting into question the efficiency of the market allocation.

23.1 The Visible Hand

Our household makes cookies, C. The recipe calls for N ingredients but rather than buying them, our household makes those, too. We index each ingredient by i, and denote by H_i the hours spent making each ingredient. The household's utility function is given by:

$$U(C, H_1, H_2, ..., H_N) = \log(C) - \frac{\left(\sum_{i=1}^{N} H_i\right)^{1+\phi}}{1+\phi} \tag{23.1}$$

The amount of each ingredient the household can make is directly proportional to how many hours the household spends making it. So we can write the production function of cookies as a function of the hours the household spends making each ingredient:

$$C = \sum_{i=1}^{N} H_i^{1-\alpha} \tag{23.2}$$

1. Write down the constrained optimization problem of the household.

2. Write down the marginal rate of substitution between consuming cookies, C, and hours spent making an ingredient, H_i.

3. Write down the marginal rate of transformation between consuming cookies, C, and hours spent making an ingredient, H_i.

4. Write down the optimality condition between consuming cookies, C, and hours spent making an ingredient, H_i.

5. Explain why the optimality condition derived above implies that the household will spend the same amount of hours on each ingredient, i.

6. Let $H \equiv NH_i$; rewrite the optimality condition in terms of H:

$$CH^\phi = (1 - \alpha) \left(\frac{H}{N} \right)^{-\alpha} \tag{23.3}$$

What is the economic interpretation of H?

7. Rewrite the production function in terms of H :

$$C = N^\alpha H^{1-\alpha} \tag{23.4}$$

8. Combine the optimality condition with the production function to derive the household's chosen labor allocation:

$$H^* = (1 - \alpha)^{1/(1+\phi)} \tag{23.5}$$

9. Write down the household's chosen allocation of cookies, C^*, as a function of N, α, and ϕ.

10. Graph the chosen allocation of cookies as a function of N. If, instead of cookies, we had interpreted C^* as output, what would be economic interpretation of N?

23.2   The Invisible Hand with Market Power

We now reconsider the production of cookies in a market setting with tiered production. We have three agents: households, final goods firms, and intermediate goods firms. The households sell their labor and buy cookies. The final goods firms buy the ingredients and sell cookies. Each of the N intermediate goods firms produces a single ingredient and is a monopolist in that market; this means they can set the price of their good. They all hire labor from households in a common labor market at a market-determined wage, W. For algebraic simplicity, we will normalize the price of cookies to one.

The household has the same objective function, (23.1), where H_i now denotes that total labor the household sells to intermediate goods firm, i.

1. Write down the household's budget constraint.

2. Write down the marginal rate of substitution between C and H_i.

3. Write down the marginal rate of transformation between C and H_i.

4. Let $H \equiv \sum_i^N H_i$ denote the total hours supplied by the household. Show that the optimality condition between C and H_i can be written as:

$$CH^\phi = W \tag{23.6}$$

The final goods firm produces cookies using ingredients, X_i, according to the following production function:

$$Y = \sum_{i=1}^N X_i^{1-\alpha} \tag{23.7}$$

5. Let P_i denote the price of each intermediate good; write down the profit function of the final goods firm.

6. Write down the marginal rate of substitution between each intermediate good, X_i, and output, Y.

7. Write down the marginal rate of transformation between each intermediate good, X_i, and output, Y.

8. Show that the optimality condition of the final goods firm:

$$(1-\alpha)X_i^{-\alpha} = P_i \tag{23.8}$$

Explain why this is the inverse demand function of good X_i.

All intermediate goods firms have an identical linear production technology: $X_i = H_i$. The firm sets the price and produces the quantity that is consistent with the demand for its good, X_i.

9. Show that the firm's profit function is: $X_i(P_i - W)$.

10. Why can't firm i choose to sell *any* quantity X_i at *any* price P_i?

11. Given your answer above, write down the constrained optimization problem of the intermediate goods firm.

12. Show that the marginal rate of substitution between quantity, X_i, and price, P_i, is:

$$\frac{P_i - W}{X_i}$$

13. Show that the marginal rate of transformation between quantity, X_i and price, P_i, is:

$$\alpha(1-\alpha)X_i^{-\alpha-1}$$

14. Write down the optimality condition and combine it with the inverse demand function for good i to get:

$$P_i = \mu W \tag{23.9}$$

where $\mu \equiv 1/(1-\alpha)$ is the markup over marginal cost.

Now that we have optimality conditions for the household, (23.6), final goods firm, (23.8), and intermediate goods firm, (23.9), we can combine them with the market-clearing conditions to derive the equilibrium allocations of labor supply, H and output, Y.

15. Explain why the final goods firm will demand the same amount for all intermediate goods.

16. Explain why the market-clearing condition in the intermediate goods market implies:

$$H = X_i N$$

17. Combine the optimality conditions of the final and intermediate goods firms to derive the following inverse labor demand function:

$$(1 - \alpha)H^{-\alpha}N^{\alpha} = \mu W \tag{23.10}$$

18. We now have an inverse labor demand function, (23.10), and an inverse labor supply function, (23.6). Use them to write down the market-clearing condition in the labor market.

$$(1 - \alpha)H^{-\alpha}N^{\alpha} = \mu C H^{\phi} \tag{23.11}$$

19. Write down the market-clearing condition in the final goods market.

20. Combine your answers above with the production function to write C as a function of N and H:

$$C = N^{\alpha}H^{1-\alpha} \tag{23.12}$$

21. We now have two equilibrium relationships: equations (23.11) and (23.12). Combine them to show that the equilibrium allocation of labor in the market economy is:

$$H^m = \left(\frac{1}{\mu}\right)^{1/(1+\phi)} H^* \tag{23.13}$$

where the efficient allocation, H^*, is given by (23.5). This is the allocation that the household would have chosen if it had direct control over the means of production without markets.

22. Is the market allocation, H^m, larger or smaller than efficient allocation?

23. Write down the market allocation of cookies, C^m, as a function of C^*, μ, α, and ϕ. Will this allocation be larger or smaller than the efficient allocation, C^*?

24. If some firms have market power and are able to choose their prices, do we expect the market allocation to be efficient?

References

Blanchard, O., & N. Kiyotaki (1987). Monopolistic competition and the effects of aggregate demand. *American Economic Review, 77*(4), 647–666.

Dixit, A., & J. Stiglitz (1977). Monopolistic competition and optimum product diversity. *American Economic Review, 67*(3), 297–308.

Gali, J. (2008). *Monetary policy, inflation and the business cycle: An introduction to the new Keynesian framework.* Princeton: Princeton University Press.

24 The Two Margins of Labor

When we say that labor is one of the factors of production, what do we mean by "labor"? The essential quality of labor is *time*—to complete the tasks that are required to produce goods and services, workers must spend time. The labor input of the production function, therefore, is the total amount of *human* hours dedicated to work.

1. Suppose that a firm wants to decrease its labor input. How can it do so without firing any workers?

2. Suppose that a firm wants to increase its labor input. How can it do so without paying any of its existing workers overtime?

3. When the firm changes the amount of hours it demands from each worker, we say it has adjusted along the *intensive* margin. When the firm changes the number of workers it employs, we say it has adjusted along the *extensive* margin. To illustrate this difference, suppose you are making orange juice. If you wanted to make more juice you could buy more oranges. Which margin would this adjust? If you could not buy more oranges, how else might you be able to get more juice? Which margin would this adjust?

Let Y denote output, L population, N number of workers, E number of employed workers, and H total human hours worked.

4. Which of the three variables related to labor—N, E, or H—is the relevant input in the production function?

5. Consider the ratio $\frac{Y}{L}$. Describe this ratio in words. Explain why this ratio is used to distinguish between developed and developing economies.

6. Consider the ratio $\frac{Y}{H}$. Describe this ratio in words. Explain why this ratio is a measure of productivity.

7. Consider the ratio $\frac{H}{E}$. Describe this ratio in words. Explain why this ratio is usually eight when the time scale of production is one day.

8. Let $U \equiv N - E$. What does U denote?

9. Explain why $\frac{U}{N}$ is the *unemployment rate*.

10. Consider the ratio $\frac{E}{N}$. Explain why this ratio is the *employment rate*. Show that the employment rate equals one minus the unemployment rate.

11. The ratio $\frac{N}{L}$ is called the *labor force participation rate*. Explain why this ratio is higher in countries with relatively young populations, like the United States, than in countries with aging populations, like Japan.

12. Show that income per capita can be decomposed into the product of four ratios:

$$\frac{Y}{L} = \frac{Y}{H}\frac{H}{E}\left(1 - \frac{U}{N}\right)\frac{N}{L} \tag{24.1}$$

13. Of the four ratios, one measures productivity; the other three relate to the two margins of adjustment. Which ratios measure adjustments along the intensive margin? Which ratios measure adjustments along the extensive margin?

Since linear relationships are easy to manipulate and interpret, we want to linearize equation (24.1). The first step in doing so requires that we define the following log variables. Denote log output by $y \equiv \log Y$, log population by $\ell \equiv \log L$, log productivity by $a \equiv \log(Y/H)$, log hours per worker by $h \equiv \log(H/E)$, the unemployment rate by $u \equiv U/N$, and log workforce by $n \equiv \log N$.

14. Rewrite equation (24.1) in terms of the logs:

$$y = a + h - u + n \tag{24.2}$$

15. One of the features of economic variables is that they tend to fluctuate around a trend. In what follows, we will focus on the deviations of the variables from their trends. The [log] trends of variables are often called their *natural rates*. Let $\bar{x}$ denote the natural rate of a variable, x. Rewrite equation (24.1) in terms of the natural rates of each variable.

16. Explain why the deviations from the trend, $\tilde{x} \equiv x - \bar{x}$, measure the fluctuations of that variable.

17. Subtract the trend equation you wrote in question 15 from (24.2) to get the following relationship in terms of the deviations from trend:

$$\tilde{y} = \tilde{a} + \tilde{h} - (u - \bar{u}) + \tilde{n} \tag{24.3}$$

18. The difference between output and its natural rate, $\tilde{y}$, is called the *output gap*. If the output gap is positive, would you describe the economy as being in a boom or a recession? How about if the output gap is negative?

19. Unemployment is never zero, even during booms. Offer an educated guess as to why economists find it useful to decompose the unemployment rate into its natural rate, $\bar{u}$, and its deviation from that rate, $\tilde{u}$.

Table 24.1
Long-run responses of labor productivity and labor inputs to the changes in the output gap.

Dependent variable	Okun estimates	Gordon estimates	
		1963–1986	1986–2009
Output per hour	0.33	0.22	0.03
Hours per employee	0.17	0.28	0.34
Unemployment rate	−0.33	−0.40	−0.64
Labor force participation rate	0.17	0.03	0.15
Total hours	0.67	0.74	1.27

Source: Gordon (2010).

20. If the output gap increases, do you expect the unemployment rate to increase or decrease? Is the sign on u in equation (24.3) consistent with your intuition?

21. Suppose that the unemployment rate, u, increases. Does this increase affect only $\tilde{y}$ or can it also affect other variables on the right-hand side of (24.3)?

22. Given your answers above, explain why we do not expect a one percent increase in the unemployment rate to translate into an equal one percent increase in the output gap.

Table 24.1 presents estimates of the long-run responsiveness of labor productivity and the different margins of labor inputs to a one percent increase in the output gap. We call them "long-run" because they capture the effect over a full year rather than the immediate impact in a single quarter.

23. The first four rows in table 24.1 correspond to a gap, $\tilde{x}$, from equation (24.3). Identify which gap corresponds to each row.

24. Okun (1965) was the first to estimate the relationship between the unemployment rate and the output gap. Column one in table 24.1 reports his original estimates. In addition to the long-run estimates, he also estimated the short-run response of unemployment to be −0.50. Is the long-run response higher or lower than the short-run response? Why might that be the case?

25. Okun's *estimates* of the equilibrium relationship between the unemployment rate and the output gap became known as *Okun's law*. Given Gordon's subsequent estimates, explain why the term "law" turned out to be an unfortunate misnomer for Okun's findings.

26. Since 1965, has the unemployment rate become more or less sensitive to changes in the output gap? How about hours worked? How about the labor force participation rate?

27. Since 1965, has labor overall become more or less sensitive to changes in the output gap?

28. Given your answers above, has labor become more or less volatile relative to output over the past sixty years?

References

Gordon, R. (2010). Okun's law and productivity innovations. *American Economic Review, 100*(2), 11–15.

Okun, A. (1965). The gap between actual and potential output. In E. Phelps (ed.), *Problems of the modern economy.* New York: Norton.

25 Having Your Cake, and Eating It, Too

Suppose you have a cake that stays equally fresh for exactly two days and then goes bad. The choice you face, therefore, is how much of the cake to eat today and how much to eat tomorrow. We will denote this allocation by $\{C_t, C_{t+1}\}$ where C_t is the amount of cake you eat today and C_{t+1} the amount of cake you eat tomorrow. Notice that this allocation is *dynamic*: rather than choosing an allocation of *several* goods at *one* time, you are choosing the allocation of *one* good over *several* time periods.

1. Write down the budget constraint when it comes to eating cake.
[Hint: How many cakes do you have?]

2. What is the marginal rate of transformation between eating some cake today, C_t, and eating some cake tomorrow, C_{t+1}?

Consider the following utility function:

$$U(C_t, C_{t+1}) = u(C_t) + \beta u(C_{t+1}) \tag{25.1}$$

3. Why might the utility function depend on the *allocation* of cake $\{C_t, C_{t+1}\}$ and not just on the *total amount* of cake?

4. Now consider the parameter β. If $\beta < 1$, what is true about the relative weights of $u(C_t)$ and $u(C_{t+1})$? What about if $\beta > 1$?

5. Given your answers to the previous question, what aspect of preferences does β capture? What does introspection suggest about your own β? Is it greater than, equal to, or less than one?

6. Write down the marginal rate of substitution between eating cake today, C_t, and eating cake tomorrow, C_{t+1}.

7. Show that the following is the optimality condition for the cake-eating problem:

$$\frac{u'(C_t)}{\beta u'(C_{t+1})} = 1 \tag{25.2}$$

where $u'(\cdot)$ is the derivative of $u(\cdot)$.

Now consider the specific function $u(\cdot) = \log(\cdot)$. The utility function can now be written:

$$U(C_t, C_{t+1}) = \log(C_t) + \beta \log(C_{t+1}) \tag{25.3}$$

8. Write down the optimality condition given the utility function (25.3) and solve for C_{t+1}.

9. With C_{t+1} on the y axis and C_t on the x axis, graph the optimality condition above when $\beta = \frac{1}{2}, \beta = 1$, and $\beta = 2$.

10. Solve for C_{t+1} in the budget constraint you wrote down in question 1 and graph it on the same diagram as above.

11. Explain why each of the intersections in your diagram is the chosen allocation, $\{C_t, C_{t+1}\}$, given the specific value of β.

12. What happens to C_t as β increases? Is this consistent with the interpretation of β that you offered in question 4?

26 Alexander and the National Debt

To pay for the American Revolution, all of the thirteen colonies went into debt. After independence, the now states all owed significant amounts to private creditors. In 1791, under Alexander Hamilton's leadership, the Department of the Treasury moved to federalize this debt.

Under Hamilton's plan, Congress chartered the Bank of the United States, which would then pay off the remaining balance on all of the debts that the States had incurred. To raise the funds needed for this operation the Treasury issued bonds and sold them through the newly chartered bank. These were the first bonds ever issued by the federal government. Thus, Hamilton consolidated the debts of the states into a single national debt. The plan was to pay it all off by 1811, and so the charter of the bank was set by law to expire that year. Without the bank, there was no mechanism in place for the Treasury to service the debt. To pay the debt, Hamilton simultaneously instituted a whiskey tax. His plan established the full faith and credit that the federal government enjoys today.

Why was Hamilton's plan successful? And what can his success teach us about government budgets? To answer these questions we will rebuild the budget constraint that Hamilton faced and examine how he was able to meet it. Let T_t denote the tax revenue in year t and B_t denote the value of the bonds issued by the Treasury in year t. To keep things simple we will assume that the Treasury issued bonds that lasted only one year; in year t it had to pay off all of the bonds, plus interest, issued in year $t - 1$. At the same time, in year t, the Treasury would issue a new set of bonds, B_t, that would come due in year $t + 1$. We will also assume that the bonds paid a constant, real rate of interest, $1 + r$. Finally, we will denote government purchases in year t by G_t.

26.1   1791

Let $\bar{B}$ denote the total value of the outstanding debts that the Treasury paid off in 1791 under Hamilton's plan. Recall that B_{1791} is the total value of the bonds issued by the Treasury in 1791, G_{1791} are total government purchases and T_{1791} is total revenues from the whiskey tax in 1791.

1. If Hamilton had announced the creation of the Bank of the United States, but had not announced any taxes, would creditors have been willing to buy the bonds that the Treasury issued, B_{1791}? Why?

2. Write down the two expenditures of the Treasury in 1791.

3. Write down the two sources of funding for the Treasury in 1791.
[Hint: If taxes could not cover all expenditures how else could the government raise funds?]

4. Write down the budget constraint for the Treasury in 1791.

26.2   1792, 1793, …

1. Explain why $B_{1791}(1+r)$ is the total amount that the Treasury had to pay back in 1792 for the bonds issued in 1791.

2. Write down the two expenses for the Treasury in 1792.

3. Write down the two sources of funding for the Treasury in 1792.

4. Combine your answers above to show that the government's budget constraint for 1792 can be written as:
$$B_{1791} = \frac{B_{1792}}{(1+r)} + \frac{T_{1792}}{(1+r)} - \frac{G_{1792}}{(1+r)} \tag{26.1}$$

5. Are there any terms that link the budgets of 1791 and 1792? If so, combine the two budgets into a single equation.

6. Write down the budget constraint for 1793 and solve for B_{1792}.
[Hint: This is the same process that led us to equation (26.1).]

7. Are there any terms that link the budget of 1793 with the *combined* budgets of 1791 and 1792 you found in question 5? If so, substitute the budget from 1793 into your answer from question 5 to create a combined budget for 1791, 1792, and 1793.

8. Write down the budget constraint for 1794 and solve for B_{1793}.

9. Substitute your answer above into your answer for question 7 in this section.

10. Use the pattern from the years above to explain why we can combine the budget constraints for n years after 1790 into the single *intertemporal budget constraint*:
$$\bar{B} = \frac{B_{1791+n}}{(1+r)^n} + \sum_{j=0}^{n} \frac{T_{1791+j}}{(1+r)^j} - \sum_{j=0}^{n} \frac{G_{1791+j}}{(1+r)^j} \tag{26.2}$$

[Hint: What would happen if you kept iterating the years forward to 1795, 1796, … and so on?]

11. The difference between tax income and government purchases in a given year is called the *primary surplus*, s_t.
$$s_t \equiv T_t - G_t \tag{26.3}$$

Substitute the definition of the primary surplus above into the intertemporal budget constraint, equation (26.2), to write the intertemporal budget constraint in terms of the primary surplus instead of government purchases and taxes.

26.3   1811

Recall that once the bank's charter expired in 1811, the Treasury would have no way of paying its outstanding bonds.

1. Given the impending expiration of the bank's charter, would anyone buy bonds from the Treasury in 1811?

2. Use your answer above to explain why creditors will satisfy the following inequality in 1811:

$$B_{1811} \leq 0 \tag{26.4}$$

[Hint: How much debt will creditors be willing to buy from the Treasury?]

3. Explain what it means for the Treasury to want to satisfy the following inequality in 1811:

$$B_{1811} \geq 0 \tag{26.5}$$

4. Given that inequalities (26.4) and (26.5) must both hold, what will be the equilibrium amount of debt outstanding in 1811? This is called the *transversality condition*.

5. Let $n = 20$, so that we iterate the intertemporal budget constraint all the way to 1811. Combine your answers above with your answer to question 11 in the previous section; show that the intertemporal budget constraint for Hamilton's plan can be simplified to the following equation:

$$\bar{B} - \left(\sum_{j=0}^{20} \frac{s_{1791+j}}{(1+r)^j} \right) = 0 \tag{26.6}$$

We say the government is *solvent* as long as the left-hand side of the equation above is less than or equal to zero.

6. The second term on the left-hand side of equation (26.6) is called the *present discounted value of primary surpluses* in 1791. At least how large must the present discounted value of all primary surpluses be in order for the government to remain solvent?

7. Suppose that for several years between 1791 and 1811 the federal government ran primary deficits: $s_t < 0$. Would this have necessarily implied that the federal government would become *insolvent* (i.e., not able to pay its debts)?

27 The Value of the Firm

Consider a pharmaceutical firm that has developed a new vaccine. The vaccine is protected by a patent that lasts $T + 1$ years: the current year and T more after that. While under patent protection, the firm expects to make a yearly profit, π, from selling the vaccine. When the patent expires, any competitor can produce the vaccine and profits will fall automatically to zero. There is a constant yearly net real interest rate, r.

1. Once the patent protection has expired, what is the maximum amount that you would be willing to pay to buy the patent?

2. Suppose it is the last year of patent protection. What is the maximum amount, v_1, that you would be willing to pay for the patent?

Now, suppose that there are two years left of patent protection. There are now two years' profits that you have the opportunity to buy *today*.

3. What is the maximum amount you would be willing to pay *this year* for *this year's* profits?
[Hint: This is not a trick question; it really is as simple as it sounds.]

You have an amount, x, *today* that you can use either to buy a one-year bond at the prevailing real interest rate, r, or buy next year's profits.

7. If you spend all of x on bonds, what amount will you earn next year for your investment?

8. If, instead, you spend x to buy next year's profits, what amount will you earn next year from your investment?

9. Given that you can always buy bonds, what are the *minimum* earnings that you must receive next year from buying the firm's profits?
[Hint: What relation must the answers to the two previous questions satisfy?]

10. Rewrite your answer above to show that you will buy *next year's* profits *today* as long as the x satisfies the following inequality:

$$x \leq \frac{\pi}{1+r} \tag{27.1}$$

11. The right-hand side of (27.1) is the *present discounted value* of next year's profits. What do we mean by *present*, what do we mean by *discounted*?

12. Explain why the following expression is called the present discounted value *of all profits* when there are only two years left of patent protection:

$$\pi + \frac{\pi}{1+r}$$

13. Suppose that you can't buy the firm's profits one year at time, you can only buy the entire firm. What is the *maximum* amount, v_2, that you would be willing to pay for the firm when there are two years left of patent protection?
[Hint: Note that buying the firm is equivalent to buying the profits for this and next year.]

14. How much more are you willing to pay for the firm when it has two years left of patent protection, v_2, versus during its last year of patent protection, v_1? Twice as much, more than twice, or less than twice? Briefly explain your answer.

Now, suppose there are three years left of patent protection. We already know how much you would be willing to pay for the current and next year's profits. All we have to do is derive how much you would be willing to pay *today* for profits *two years* in the future.

15. Once again, you can spend x on bonds today. What amount will you earn next year for your investment?

16. If you take next year's earnings and reinvest them in bonds, how much will you earn in two years' time?

17. If, instead, you spend x to buy the profits two years from now, how much will you earn in two years' time?

18. Given that you can always buy bonds and reinvest your earnings year after year, what are the *minimum* earnings that you must receive in two years' time if you decide to buy the firm's profits?

19. Rewrite your answer above to show that you will spend x today and the profits two years from now only if the following inequality holds:

$$x \le \frac{\pi}{(1+r)^2} \qquad\qquad (27.2)$$

where the right-hand side is the present discounted value of profits two years in the future.

20. Inequality (27.1) gives us the maximum, x, you would be willing to pay today for profits one year into the future; inequality (27.2) gives us the maximum, x, you would be willing to pay today for profits two years into the future. There is a pattern emerging. What is the maximum amount, x, you would be willing to pay today for profits t years into the future?

21. What is the *maximum* amount, v_3, that you would be willing to pay for the entire firm when it has three years left of patent protection?

22. Use the pattern above to explain why the present discounted value of all profits when there are $T + 1$ years left of patent protection—the current year plus T *more*—is given by:

$$\sum_{j=0}^{T} \frac{\pi}{(1+r)^j}$$

23. What is the *maximum* amount, v_{T+1}, that you would be willing to pay for the firm when it first receives patent protection?

24. What is the *minimum* offer for which the owner will agree to sell the firm?

25. Given your answers above, show that, in *equilibrium*, the value of the firm is equal to the present discounted value of all profits:

$$v_{T+1} = \sum_{j=0}^{T} \frac{\pi}{(1+r)^j}$$

Developing new vaccines is expensive. For simplicity, suppose that if the firm invests a fixed amount, it immediately develops the vaccine. That is, once it pays the fixed cost, the firm can take the vaccine to market and begin earning profits that same period.

26. What is the maximum investment that the firm is willing to make in order to develop the vaccine?

27. If r goes up, how does the maximum investment that the firm is willing to make change?

28. If T goes up, how does the maximum investment that the firm is willing to make change?

28 The Efficient Market Hypothesis

In chapter 27, "The Value of the Firm," we showed that the value of the firm is *forward-looking* and equal to the present discounted value of all future profits. Many firms, especially the largest ones in the world, are publicly traded, so their value is determined by the equilibrium price of their stocks. How does the stock market valuation of the firm compare to the value of the firm that we derived in chapter 27?

Consider a publicly traded firm with a total number of shares, S_t, that trade at a price, p_t. We will further assume that the firm is expected by all market participants to make profits, π, for the next $T + 1$ periods, including the current one. It follows that the present discounted value of all future profits is given by

$$v_{T+1} \equiv \sum_{j=1}^{T} \frac{\pi}{(1+r)^j}$$

where r is the net real interest rate.

1. What fraction of the firm can the owner of one share claim?

2. Let v_{T+1}^s denote the owner's valuation of the present discounted value of all profits. What is the minimum price at which the owner of stock is willing to sell one share?

3. Let v_{T+1}^b be the buyer's valuation of the present discounted value of all profits. What is the maximum price that a buyer is willing to pay for one share?

The *efficient market hypothesis* states that stock markets reveal all of the relevant, available information. This implies that both buyers and potential sellers know the correct present discounted value of all profits:

$$v_{T+1}^s = v_{T+1}^b = v_{T+1}$$

4. In the United States, insider trading is illegal: it is a felony to trade stocks based on information about a firm that is not known to the public. If shareholders engage in insider

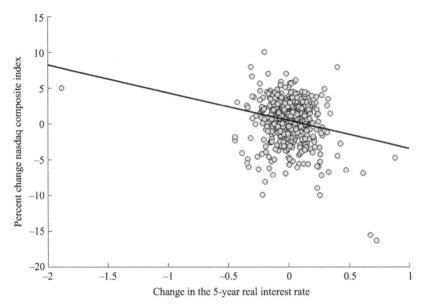

Figure 28.1
Percentage change of NASDAQ Composite index and change in the five-year real interest rate. Biweekly frequency. The change in the real interest rate is computed as the difference in the yield in the secondary market of five-year, inflation-protected government bonds (TIPS). *Sources:* NASDAQ OMX Group and Board of Governors of the Federal Reserve System.

trading, what might be true about the minimum price at which they are willing to sell and the maximum price that buyers are willing to pay?

5. Show that under the efficient market hypothesis, the *equilibrium* share price will be:

$$p_t = \frac{1}{S_t} \sum_{j=0}^{T} \frac{\pi}{(1+r)^j} \qquad (28.1)$$

[Hint: Under the efficient market hypothesis, what is true about the maximum price that a buyer will offer and the minimum offer that seller will accept?]

6. Suppose you want to buy the entire firm. If the efficient market hypothesis is correct, how much will you pay for all of the shares? How does this compare to the value of the firm, v_{T+1}?

7. Suppose that a firm buys back its stock so that the number of shares, S_t, drops. What will happen to the price of the stock? Has the value of the firm changed?

8. Suppose that the market expects the firm's future profits to increase. What will happen to the price of the stock? Has the value of the firm changed?

9. If a firm has negative profits today but a positive stock price, what must be true about its future profits?

10. If the market expects real interest rates to drop in the future, what happens to the price of the stocks today?

11. Figure 28.1 plots the percentage change of the NASDAQ Composite Index, a broad measure of stock prices, against changes in the five-year real interest rate. The trend line has a a slope of −3.9. Explain whether the slope of the trend line is consistent with equation (28.1).

Reference

Fama, E. (1970). Efficient capital markets: A review of theory and empirical work. *Journal of Finance, 25*(2), 383–417.

29 The Current Account

Consider a small open economy with a representative household that both produces output, Y_t, and consumes, C_t. The household has access to international asset markets and can either save or borrow from abroad at the world real interest rate, r_t.

1. Let A_t denote the net foreign assets that the household owns in period t. Explain why $r_t A_t$ is the total income from those assets in period t.

2. In addition to the value of its production, Y_t, the household also receives net remittances from abroad, NR_t. Net remittances are transfers without any reciprocal obligations. Give an example of a remittance.

3. Write down the total revenues of the household in period t.
[Hint: There are three sources.]

4. What are the two things that the household can do with its income?

5. Combine your answers above to show that the household's budget constraint is:

$$0 = Y_t + r_t A_t + NR_t - (C_t + S_t) \tag{29.1}$$

where S_t denotes the amount of income that the household saves.

6. Write down the household's net foreign asset position in period $t+1$, A_{t+1}, as function of its current assets, A_t, and how much of its current income it saves, S_t.

7. Combine your answer above with the household's budget constraint, equation (29.1), to show that the change in assets, $\Delta A_{t+1} \equiv A_{t+1} - A_t$, is equal to the household's income minus its consumption:

$$\Delta A_{t+1} = Y_t + r_t A_t + NR_t - C_t \tag{29.2}$$

8. The *trade balance*, TB_t, is the value of exports minus the value of imports. It is sometimes also called *net exports*. Write down the market-clearing condition in the goods market. Label the side of the equation that corresponds to output and the side that corresponds to aggregate demand.
[Hint: There is no domestic investment and no government in this economy.]

9. Use the market-clearing condition to rewrite the household's budget constraint, equation (29.2), in terms of the trade balance, TB_t, rather than consumption and output.

10. The *current account*, CA_t, is the net income from abroad.

$$CA_t \equiv TB_t + r_t A_t + NR_t \qquad (29.3)$$

Explain why each of these three sources is net, rather than gross, income from abroad and give an example of each.

11. Substitute the definition of the current account into the household's budget constraint you derived in question 9 to show that the current account is equal to the change in the net foreign asset position in the economy:

$$CA_t = \Delta A_{t+1}$$

Figure 29.1 plots the current account and trade balance as a percent of output in three very different countries: China, Ireland, and El Salvador. In what follows, we will analyze the very different relationships between the trade balance and current account in all three countries.

12. Define the lowercase of each variable as a percent of GDP, $x_t \equiv X_t / Y_t$, for any variable, X, and show that we can redefine the current account relationship as:

$$ca_t = tb_t + r_t a_t + nr_t \qquad (29.4)$$

13. Which of the variables above corresponds to the black lines in figure 29.1? Which corresponds to the dotted lines? What two variables above are not plotted?

14. What is the main determinant of the current account in China?

In the 1980s, Ireland adopted a development strategy based on bringing foreign capital by lowering its corporate taxes. Today, Ireland has one of the lowest tax burdens of any industrialized economy at 20.9 percent, 13 percent below the OECD average. Low corporate taxes, an English-speaking population, and membership in the European Union proved to be a winning combination—the European headquarters of Airbnb, Facebook, Google, Microsoft, and PayPal are all in Dublin.

15. What does Ireland's economic model suggest about its net foreign asset position?

16. Explain why Ireland has a relatively low current account while at the same time having a large, positive trade balance.

The 1980s was a bloody decade for El Salvador; civil war erupted in 1979 and raged until 1992. The war precipitated an exodus of Salvadorans, many of whom emigrated to the US. According to US immigration services, 34,000 Salvadorans migrated legally to the US during the seventies. That number jumped to a quarter million in the eighties, and remained

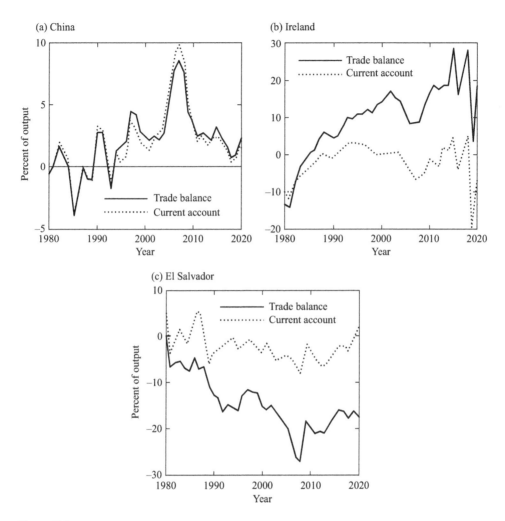

Figure 29.1
Current account and trade balance as a percentage of output. *Sources:* International Monetary Fund and World Bank.

at a quarter million during the nineties. The 2020 census counted 2.3 million Salvadoran Americans. By comparison, El Salvador had a population of 6.3 million that same year.

17. As Salvadorans moved to the US, what happened to the remittances from the US to El Salvador?

18. Sketch a graph of net remittances as a percentage of GDP for El Salvador between 1980 and 2020.

[Hint: Assume that $r_t a_t$ is a negligible component of ca_t for El Salvador.]

19. Calculate the percentage of Salvadorans who lived in the US in 2020. Use your sketch to estimate the total net remittances as a percentage of GDP for El Salvador in 2020. How do the two estimates compare?

[Hint: The total population of Salvadorans includes those who live abroad.]

30 Trade Deficits

The United States has run trade deficits for several decades. These deficits have translated into negative current accounts and a deterioration of the US net foreign asset position. Today the US is a net *debtor* to the rest of the world. From time to time, usually during elections, the trade deficit is treated as a cause for alarm. Yet the rest of the world seems more sanguine and continues lending to the US to finance its purchases of foreign goods. Why?

To answer this question we will consider an open economy with a representative household producing output, Y_t, with labor as its only input (i.e., no capital and hence no investment). The household consumes, C_t, and trades with the rest of the world. We denote the household's trade balance, exports minus imports, by TB_t. The household also gives and receives remittances from abroad; we denote the *net* remittances by NR_t. Finally, the household also has access to world asset markets and can lend or borrow from the the world at the constant real interest rate, r.

1. Let D_t denote the net foreign debt the household owes at the beginning of period t. Show that if the household still owes $D_{t+1}/(1+r)$ at the end of period t, after receiving income and incurring expenses, then D_{t+1} is the net foreign debt the household will owe at the beginning of period $t+1$.

2. Show that the household's budget constraint in period t can be written as:

$$Y_t - C_t + NR_t + \frac{D_{t+1}}{1+r} \geq D_t \tag{30.1}$$

3. Write down the household's budget constraint in period $t+1$.

4. Substitute the $t+1$ budget constraint into the t budget constraint to get the following intertemporal budget constraint:

$$\frac{Y_{t+1} - C_{t+1}}{1+r} + Y_t - C_t + \frac{NR_{t+1}}{1+r} + NR_t + \frac{D_{t+2}}{(1+r)^2} \geq D_t \tag{30.2}$$

5. Write down the household's budget constraint in period $t+2$ and substitute it into the intertemporal budget constraint above.

6. Show that if we keep writing budget constraints up to period $t + T$ we will get the following intertemporal budget constraint:

$$\sum_{j=0}^{T} \left(\frac{1}{1+r} \right)^j (Y_{t+j} - C_{t+j} + NR_{t+j}) + \frac{D_{t+T}}{(1+r)^T} \geq D_t \qquad (30.3)$$

When does the final period T actually happen? In any given period we can always imagine the possibility of the period to come. To incorporate this idea we will keep iterating (30.3) indefinitely by taking the limit as T goes to infinity.

7. Will the rest of the world ever be willing to lend the household an *infinite* amount? By the same token, will the household ever be willing to lend the rest of the world an infinite amount? Given your answers, show that:

$$\lim_{T \to \infty} \frac{D_{t+T}}{(1+r)^T} = 0 \qquad (30.4)$$

This is the *transversality condition*.

8. Write down the market-clearing condition in the final goods market. Label the side that corresponds to output and the side that corresponds to aggregate demand.
[Hint: There are only two components of aggregate demand in this economy.]

9. Substitute the market clearing and the transversality conditions into the intertemporal budget constraint, equation (30.3), to get the following infinite-horizon intertemporal budget constraint:

$$\sum_{j=0}^{\infty} \left(\frac{1}{1+r} \right)^j (TB_{t+j} + NR_{t+j}) \geq D_t \qquad (30.5)$$

10. Describe in words the right-hand side of equation (30.5).

11. The US is a net donor of foreign aid and many of its immigrant workers send part of their income to their families abroad. What does that imply about the sign of the present discounted value of net remittances for the US?

12. The United States currently has a net foreign debt position, $D_t > 0$, while at the same time running trade deficits. Given your answer above, do you expect the US to continue running trade deficits indefinitely, or will those deficits eventually turn into surpluses?

31 Fifty Days

On October 25, 2022, Liz Truss's premiership became the shortest in UK history at just fifty days. Her position became untenable when the interest rates on UK sovereign debt increased sharply after her government laid out its fiscal policy proposals. On October 14, *The Daily Star*, a British tabloid, published a live online feed of a head of lettuce and infamously asked: Will this head of lettuce still be fresh when the prime minister resigns? The lettuce outlasted Truss.

31.1   The Government's Budget Constraint

We begin by building the government's intertemporal budget constraint. To simplify our analysis of Liz Truss's predicament we will focus on a two-period economy; we can interpret period one as the present and period two as the long-term future.

Each period, t, the government can raise revenue either through levying taxes or by issuing bonds that will be due the following period, $t+1$, at the net real interest rate, q. Its expenditures can be divided into three categories. Government purchases, G_t, are the component of aggregate demand that comes from the government. The government must also repay the bonds, with interest, that were issued in the previous period. Finally, there are transfers. Transfer payments are negative taxes; while taxes are payments from households to the government, transfers are payments from the government to households. Since transfers and taxes are analogous, we will denote *net* taxes, tax revenue minus transfer payments, by T_t.

1. If the government issues a total of $B_t/(1+q)$ bonds in period $t-1$, at the gross real interest rate, $1+q$, write an expression for the total amount due in period t.

2. Write down an expression for government expenditures in period one.

3. Write down an expression for government revenue in period one.

4. Write down the government's budget constraint in period one.

5. Write down an expression for government expenditures in period two.

6. Given that the economy lasts for only two periods, will the markets buy government bonds in period two?

7. Considering your answer above, write down the government's budget constraint in period two.

8. The two budget constraints have one term in common: the bonds issued in period one. Combine the two constraints to derive the following *intertemporal budget constraint*:

$$B_1 \leq (T_1 - G_1) + \left(\frac{1}{1+q}\right)(T_2 - G_2) \tag{31.1}$$

9. The *primary surplus* is the difference between tax revenues and government spending in period t. We call the right-hand side of inequality (31.1) the *present discounted value of the primary surplus*. To what period does the term *present* refer?

10. In order for the government to satisfy its budget constraint, what must be true of the present discounted value of primary surpluses relative to its outstanding debt?

11. The above budget constraint is expressed in *levels*, yet government finances are usually expressed as a fraction of output. Rather than quote the level of debt, for example, it is common to instead quote the debt-to-GDP ratio. Why might this practice be useful?

12. Let $\tau_t \equiv T_t/Y_t$ denote the fraction of income that the government garnishes as net taxes. Rewrite the-right hand side of the intertemporal budget constraint in terms of τ.

$$B_1 \leq (\tau_1 Y_1 - G_1) + \left(\frac{1}{1+q}\right)(\tau_2 Y_2 - G_2)$$

τ is called the *average tax burden*. Briefly explain what this term means.

13. Let $g_t \equiv G_t/Y_t$ denote the ratio of government purchases to aggregate demand. Rewrite the right-hand side of the intertemporal budget constraint in terms of g_t.

$$B_1 \leq (\tau_1 Y_1 - g_1 Y_1) + \left(\frac{1}{1+q}\right)(\tau_2 Y_2 - g_2 Y_2)$$

Briefly explain why g_t is used as a measure of the size of the government.

14. Let $b_t \equiv B_t/Y_t$ denote the ratio of government debt to output. Divide both sides of the intertemporal budget constraint by Y_1 to express it in terms of the debt-to-GDP ratio, b_1.

15. Suppose that output is expected to grow at the gross rate $(1+\gamma)$. Rewrite output in period two, Y_2, as a function of output in period one, Y_1, and the expected growth rate.

16. Substitute your answer above into the right-hand side of the intertemporal budget constraint to get the following:

$$b_1 \leq (\tau_1 - g_1) + \left(\frac{1+\gamma^e}{1+q}\right)(\tau_2^e - g_2^e) \tag{31.2}$$

Since the present is denoted in period one, period two outcomes have not yet been realized. To distinguish between actual outcomes and expectations of those outcomes, notice that future values have a superscript ^{e} for *expected*.

17. Most OECD countries offer public-funded pensions that become available at a certain age. Since these pensions—and the age eligibility cutoff—were first introduced, life expectancy has increased by several years and we expect that increase to continue, even if at more modest rates. Use inequality (31.2) to explain why the continued increase in life expectancy can pose a risk to the solvency of the government.
[Hint: What happens to the right-hand side of the inequality (31.2) if the size of transfer payments goes up? Remember that if transfer payments increase, τ decreases.]

18. Many countries in Europe and Asia have seen their birth rates fall below the population replacement rate. Although these countries are very densely populated, their governments do not seem very keen on the impending population drop. Use inequality (31.2) to explain why governments worry about decreasing populations.
[Hint: Recall that output, Y, is a function of capital and labor, $F(K, L)$. What happens when L falls?]

31.2   The Government and the Bond Market

In the previous section we derived the government's budget constraint; any government that remains *solvent* must satisfy inequality (31.2). We will now examine how bond markets interact with governments when they issue debt.

The UK is an open economy and it sells its sovereign bonds in international financial markets. Consider the European bond market, where Germany is the safest debtor. So safe, in fact, that we will assume there is zero chance of Germany defaulting on its debt. A trader in this market must decide whether to invest in a completely safe German bond or the slightly riskier, if still very safe, British bond. We will denote the net real interest rate of the German bonds by r. We call r the *riskless rate*. We will assume that traders have the objective of maximizing their expected returns.

1. Let μ denote the probability that the UK government remains solvent and is able to pay its debts in the future. If the UK remains solvent, it pays off the bond and its interest. If it defaults, it pays off nothing. Show that the expected payment on a British bond is:

$$B_t(1+q)\mu$$

[Hint: The expected payment is the weighted sum of outcomes, where the probabilities of each outcome correspond to the weights.]

2. If $(1+q)\mu > 1+r$, will traders buy German or British bonds? What will happen to the rate of return on British bonds? What if the inequality is reversed?

3. Use your answers above to explain why, in equilibrium, the following must hold:

$$(1+q)\mu = (1+r) \tag{31.3}$$

This equilibrium condition is called a *no arbitrage* condition.

4. Substitute the no arbitrage condition above with inequality (31.2) to express the UK government's budget constraint in terms of the riskless rate, r, and the risk of default, $1 - \mu$:

$$b_1 \le (\tau_1 - g_1) + \left(\frac{\mu}{1+r}\right)(1+\gamma^e)(\tau_2^e - g_2^e) \tag{31.4}$$

Does the riskless rate depend on the domestic conditions of the UK? How about the risk of default?

5. If the probability of default goes all the way to zero, what happens to the interest rate at which the UK government can borrow?

6. If the probability of default goes all the way to one, what happens to expression (31.4)? What is the economic interpretation of this result?

7. Explain why μ captures "market confidence" in the UK government. What happens to the right-hand side of inequality (31.4) when market confidence is high?

8. Given that the UK cannot control the riskless rate, r, which is set in the international markets, or its current debt-to-GDP ratio, b_1, list the four domestic components that determine whether inequality (31.4) continues to hold.

31.3   Resignation

We now have all the pieces in place to understand why the policies of the Truss government wreaked havoc in the bond markets and forced her resignation. The government introduced deep tax cuts and argued that these cuts would lead to higher output growth. The tax policy did not affect future taxes or government spending so that g_1, g_2 and τ_2 remain unchanged. Let τ_1 and γ^e denote the original tax code and the corresponding expected growth rate of UK output, respectively. Let $\hat{\tau}_1$ and $\hat{\gamma}^e$ denote the tax code under Truss and the corresponding growth rate of UK output, respectively. The following two inequalities summarize Truss's argument: $\tau_1 > \hat{\tau}_1$ and $\gamma^e < \hat{\gamma}^e$. The question is: by how much does economic growth have to increase to make up for the decrease in tax revenue?

1. Write down the right hand side of (31.4) under Truss's plan, $(\hat{\tau}_1, \hat{\gamma}^e)$, and again under the original tax policy, (τ_1, γ_e). Write down the inequality between the two that is consistent with Truss's argument.

2. Manipulate your answer above to show that Truss's tax plan would be fiscally sound only if the following inequality holds:

$$\left(\frac{\mu}{1+r}\right)(\hat{\gamma}^e - \gamma^e)(\tau_2^e - g_2^e) \ge \tau_1 - \hat{\tau}_1 \tag{31.5}$$

3. Is the right hand side of (31.5) positive or negative?

4. Notice that the right-hand side of inequality (31.5) is determined in the present whereas the left-hand side depends on the future, and hence on present expectations of future outcomes. If the market expected the growth rate of the UK economy under the Truss tax cuts to satisfy (31.5), would the probability of the UK defaulting on its debt rise or drop? How would that be reflected in (31.5)? What would happen to the interest on UK bonds?
[Hint: Recall that the interest on UK bonds is given by the no arbitrage condition (31.3).]

5. If the market disagreed with Truss's assessment of her policy, how would inequality (31.5) change?

6. If the market believed that the right-hand side of (31.5) was, in fact, larger than the left hand side, what would happen to the probability of the UK defaulting on its debt? How would that be reflected in (31.5)? What would happen to the interest on UK bonds?

7. The interest rates on UK bonds rose sharply after Truss introduced her tax cuts. What does this sharp rise imply about the market's assessment of the UK government's claim that the tax cuts would be offset by the increase in output growth?

8. Consider the intertemporal budget constraint, inequality (31.4), once more. Offer a brief, qualitative explanation as to how a deterioration in the budget constraint—say a drop in expected output growth or an increase in expected future government spending—can be exacerbated by a decrease in market confidence.

32 Misdiagnoses

From time to time newspapers publish stories about patients who were misdiagnosed with terminal illnesses, proceeded to live lavish lifestyles, and found themselves bankrupt when their diagnoses were corrected and their life expectancy suddenly jumped by several years, if not decades. These stories are all about the transversality condition.

Consider a consumer who lives for two periods and earns the same amount of income, Y, in each period. The consumer begins period one with no assets and no debt. Each period, she can either borrow or save at the constant real interest rate, r. She gets utility from consuming each period.

1. Write down the consumer's budget constraint in period one. Which term from the first period's budget constraint will also be in period two's budget constraint?

2. Write down the consumer's budget constraint in period two.

3. Assuming that the consumer has no children and does not care about any future periods, does she want to save in period two?

4. If the consumer *could*, would she want to borrow in period two?
[Hint: This is blue-sky thinking. Don't let constraints stop you!]

5. Let S denote savings. Given your answers to the previous two questions, what does the consumer want S to be less than?

6. Will anyone in the market be willing to lend to the consumer in period two?

7. Write down the mathematical inequality that the above constraint imposes on the consumer's choice of S.

8. You now have an inequality that arises from what the consumer *wants* to do and an inequality that arises from what she *can* do. Show that the two imply the following transversality condition:

$$S_2 = 0 \tag{32.1}$$

9. Combine the transversality condition above with the per-period budget constraints to derive the following intertemporal budget constraint:

$$C_1 + \frac{C_2}{1+r} = Y + \frac{Y}{1+r} \tag{32.2}$$

10. Let $D \equiv C_1 - Y$. What is the economic interpretation of D?

11. Show that debt can be written as a function of the consumer's period two consumption:

$$D = \frac{Y}{1+r} - \frac{C_2}{1+r} \tag{32.3}$$

12. Set up a coordinate plane with D on the y axis and C_2 on the x axis, and graph equation (32.3). What is the maximum amount of debt that the consumer can incur in period one? This is called the *natural debt limit*.

13. Suppose the consumer borrows up to her natural debt limit. How much will she be able to consume in period two?

14. Is she likely to borrow up to her natural debt limit given its implications for future consumption?

Now suppose the consumer is diagnosed with a terminal illness in period one and will now live only up to the end of period one.

15. Will the consumer want to save or borrow in period one?

16. If the consumer goes to the bank and the bank knows her prognosis, what is the maximum amount the bank will be willing to loan her? What is the consumer's natural debt limit in this case?

17. If the consumer goes to the bank, but the bank doesn't know about her illness and expects her to be around in period two, what is the maximum amount the bank will be willing to loan her? What is the consumer's natural debt limit in this case?

18. Will the consumer borrow anything less than her natural debt limit after her diagnosis?

19. Suppose the bank cannot tell that the consumer has a terminal illness—as is always the case in the newspaper stories of misdiagnoses—and so lends her $Y/(1+r)$. If the consumer was misdiagnosed, how much will she be able to consume in period two?

20. Would she have chosen this consumption allocation if she had known she would live for two periods?

33 The Euler Equation

Consider a household that lives for two periods, consumes a single good, and provides a fixed amount of labor independent of the real wage. We denote the household's real income in periods one and two by Y_1 and Y_2, respectively. The household can either save some of its income or borrow in each period at the same real gross interest rate, $(1+r)$. We denote the household's savings (or borrowing) decisions in periods one and two by B_1 and B_2, respectively. As a convention, we let $B > 0$ denote borrowing. We also assume that the household begins its life with no savings and no debt. Finally, we denote the household's decision of how much to consume in periods one and two by C_1 and C_2, respectively.

33.1 The Intertemporal Budget Constraint

1. Write down the household's budget constraint in period one and solve for B_1.
[Hint: Remember that the household starts period one with no debt and no savings.]

2. If $B_1 > 0$ implies the household is *borrowing*, use your budget constraint above to explain why $B_1 < 0$ implies the household is *saving*.

3. Write down the household's budget constraint in period two and solve for B_1.

4. Set the two budget constrains equal to each other and show that the resulting *intertemporal budget constraint* can be written as:

$$C_1 + \frac{1}{1+r}C_2 = \frac{B_2}{1+r} + Y_1 + \frac{1}{1+r}Y_2 \tag{33.1}$$

5. What is the name for the left-hand side of equation (33.1)?

6. Suppose the household's utility is increasing in how much it consumes. Explain why this implies that the household wants $B_2 \geq 0$.
[Hint: What happens to the left-hand side of equation (33.1) when B_2 increases?]

7. Explain why creditors would require that the household satisfy $B_2 \leq 0$.
[Hint: What does $B_2 > 0$ mean for creditors?]

8. Given your answers above, explain why, in equilibrium, $B_2 = 0$. Then substitute this result into the intertemporal budget constraint (33.1).

9. Solve for C_2 and plot your equation with C_2 on the y axis and C_1 along the x axis. Make sure you label the intercepts correctly. Do not make this graph too small, you will be adding to it in the following section.

10. What is the slope of this graph?

11. What is the *relative price* between consuming today, C_1, and consuming tomorrow, C_2?

12. What is the x-intercept of this graph?

33.2   The Household's Problem

We assume that the household has a *time separable* intertemporal utility function:

$$U(C_1, C_2) = u(C_1) + \beta u(C_2) \qquad (33.2)$$

where $\beta < 1$ is the discount factor, and $u(\cdot)$ is the *per-period* utility function. Further, we assume that the first derivative of $u(\cdot)$ is positive and the second derivative is negative.

1. Use the budget constraint you derived in the previous section to write down the household's constrained optimization problem.

2. Write down the marginal rate of substitution between C_1 and C_2.

3. Write down the marginal rate of transformation between C_1 and C_2.

4. Write down the optimality condition for this problem. This condition is called the *Euler equation*.

Now consider a specific per-period utility of consumption:

$$u(C) = \log(C) \qquad (33.3)$$

5. Show that when household preferences are given by (33.3), the Euler equation can be written as:

$$C_2 = (1+r)\beta C_1 \qquad (33.4)$$

6. What happens to the slope of the equation you derived above if β increases? Give an economic interpretation.

7. What happens to the slope of the equation you derived above if r increases? Give an economic interpretation.

8. In the same graph where you sketched out the intertemporal budget constraint, sketch three different cases of the Euler equation: when the slope is greater than one, equal to one, and less than one.

9. What does the intersection of the *intertemporal budget constraint* and the *Euler equation* tell us?

10. Consider the case in your graph where the slope of the Euler equation is equal to one. If β decreases, what must happen to the real interest rate, r, in order for the allocation $\{C_1, C_2\}$ to remain unchanged? Offer an economic intuition for this result.

34 Capital Markets

One of the many roles financial markets play is the allocation of capital. When we say that firms "raise capital," we mean to say that they raise liquid funds that they can use to acquire the capital—either physical or intangible—that is one of the inputs in their production function. Here we develop a simple model of how capital markets operate.

34.1 Stocks and Bonds

A firm goes to the markets to raise capital. The investor can either invest V_t in the firm or buy government bonds. If she invests, the *expected value* of the dividend she receives the following period is $E_t[D_{t+1}]$, where $E_t[\cdot]$ denotes the mathematical expectation evaluated at time t. Another name for the expected value is the *mean*. If she buys a government bond, the following period she receives a gross return $(1 + r_t)$ for sure.

1. Explain why

$$\frac{E_t[V_{t+1} + D_{t+1}]}{V_t}$$

is the expected gross return of buying the stock.

2. Suppose the investor's objective is to maximize her expected return. If the return from bonds is higher than the expected return from stocks, will she buy stocks or bonds? How about the other way around?

3. Since investors hold both stocks and bonds, what must be true about the expected return of stocks and bonds in equilibrium? Show that this implies the following *no arbitrage* condition:

$$V_t = \frac{E_t[D_{t+1} + V_{t+1}]}{1 + r_t} \tag{34.1}$$

4. If equation (34.1) describes the stock market, what three variables determine its value?

34.2   The Demand for Capital

In the previous section we took the firm at its word, so to speak. We accepted that it pays dividends and trades at some value. But what generates the dividends and the value? We will answer these questions by analyzing two cases. In both cases the firm operates in competitive markets and uses capital, K, and labor, L, as inputs to produce output, Y, according to a Cobb-Douglas production function:

$$Y = AK^{\alpha}L^{1-\alpha}$$

In both cases the firm must pay a wage, W, and since only relative prices matter, we normalize the price of output to one. Capital depreciates at a constant rate, δ. The difference arises in their capital structure; in the first case, the firm rents its capital, while in the second case, it owns it.

Suppose the firm rents its capital at the rate R. In addition to paying for the rental of the capital it hires, the firm must also repay any capital depreciation.

1. Show that the firm's total capital bill is $(R + \delta)K$.

2. Write down the profit function of the firm.

3. Write down the marginal rate of substitution between output and labor.

4. Write down the marginal rate of transformation between output and labor.

5. Show that the optimality condition is given by:

$$(1 - \alpha)Y = WL \qquad\qquad (34.2)$$

6. Explain why W is a relative price.

7. Write down the marginal rate of substitution between output and capital.

8. Write down the marginal rate of transformation between output and capital.

9. Show that the optimality condition is given by:

$$R = MPK - \delta \qquad\qquad (34.3)$$

where MPK denotes the *marginal product of capital*.

10. Show that the marginal product of capital is $\alpha Y/K$.

11. Suppose that output and capital are the same good. What are the units of R?

12. Show that, in equilibrium, the firm's total capital bill will be αY.

13. After paying for capital and labor, does the firm have any income left over to pay dividends?

[Hint: Substitute the optimality conditions in the firm's profit function.]

Now suppose that instead of renting, the firm owns its capital. We will consider the simple case where the firm maintains a fixed amount of capital. Because capital depreciates, the firm must invest δK to keep its capital stock constant.

14. Write down the profit function of the firm.
[Hint: How many factors of production does the firm have to hire?]

15. Explain why the optimality condition between output and labor is the same as in equation (34.2).

16. The firm pays out as dividends, D, any revenue that is left over after paying its costs. Combine equation (34.2) with the profit function to derive the following expression for dividends:

$$D = \alpha Y - \delta K \tag{34.4}$$

17. Compare your answer above with the net payment that the owners of capital got in the case where the firm leased, rather than owned, its capital to explain why dividends are not profits.
[Hint: What are the dividends really compensating?]

18. Show that dividends can be rewritten as $D = (MPK - \delta)K$.

19. Explain why buying the firm is equivalent to buying all of its capital stock.

20. Combine your two previous answers with the no arbitrage condition, equation (34.1), to show that:

$$K = \frac{(MPK - \delta)K + K}{1 + r} \tag{34.5}$$

21. Show that, in equilibrium, the real interest rate is equal to the marginal product of capital minus the depreciation rate:

$$r = MPK - \delta \tag{34.6}$$

22. What does the real interest rate reflect in equilibrium?

23. Explain why, in equilibrium, the real interest rate is equal to the real rental rate of capital.

Table 34.1 displays income per worker, capital per worker, and the marginal product of capital for ten countries in 2007. This is a subsample from the estimates by Caselli and Feyrer (2007); their full sample includes 53 countries.

24. What does the table suggest about the differences in the real interest rate across the world?

25. Caselli and Feyrer estimate that the average MPK in high-income countries is 0.08 while the average MPK in low-income countries is 0.07. Given their findings and the data in

Table 34.1
Income per worker, capital per worker, and the marginal product of capital. Income and
capital per worker are in 2005 International US dollars.

Country	Income per worker	Capital per worker	MPK
Australia	46,436	118,831	0.08
Botswana	18.043	27,219	0.14
Colombia	12,178	15,251	0.06
Egypt	12,670	7,973	0.05
Italy	51,060	139,033	0.07
Mexico	21,441	44,211	0.09
Philippines	7,801	12,197	0.09
Spain	39,034	110,024	0.09
South Korea	34,382	98,055	0.10
United States	57,259	125,583	0.09

Sources: Caselli & Feyrer (2007)

table 34.1, explain whether there is evidence for unexploited arbitrage opportunities across
countries. Do you expect the net capital flow from high-income to low-income countries to
be positive, negative, or zero?

26. Use the data from the table to plot income per worker on the x axis against capital per
worker on the y axis. How are the two related?

27. Use the data from the table to plot income per worker on the x axis against the marginal
product of capital on the y axis. How are the two related?

28. What might account for countries with very different capital stocks per worker nonetheless having a very similar marginal product of capital?
[Hint: What other factors help determine the MPK?]

34.3   The Supply of Capital

We have seen that in equilibrium investors are indifferent between buying capital or bonds.
Investors, after all, are households interested in saving—in capital or bonds—only to
maximize their utility of consumption across time:

$$U(C_t, C_{t+1}) = \log(C_t) + \beta \log(C_{t+1})$$

subject to the intertemporal budget constraint:

$$C_t + \frac{C_{t+1}}{1+r} = Y_t + \frac{Y_{t+1}}{1+r}$$

1. Write down the marginal rate of substitution between current and future consumption.

2. Write down the marginal rate of transformation between current and future consumption.

3. Show that the optimality condition is given by:

$$\frac{C_{t+1}}{C_t} = \beta(1+r)$$

4. Suppose that consumption grows at a constant gross rate, $(1+\gamma)$. Show that:

$$r = \gamma + \rho \tag{34.7}$$

where $\rho \equiv -\log\beta$ is called the *rate of time preference*.

5. What determines the real interest rate in equilibrium?

We now have an inverse supply and an inverse demand function for capital.

6. Substitute the expression for the marginal product of capital into equation (34.6) to get:

$$r = \alpha\frac{Y}{K} - \delta \tag{34.8}$$

7. Set up a coordinate plane with r on the y axis and K on the x axis. Graph equations (34.8) and (34.7).

8. Label which curve in your diagram represents inverse supply and which one represents inverse demand.

9. What is the economic significance of the intersection in your diagram?

References

Caselli, F., & J. Feyrer (2007). The marginal product of capital. *Quarterly Journal of Economics, 122*(2), 535–568.

King, R., C. Plosser, & S. Rebelo (1988a). Production growth and business cycles: I. The basic neoclassical model. *Journal of Monetary Economics, 21*(2), 195–232.

35 The Marginal Propensity to Consume

The *marginal propensity to consume*, often called simply the MPC, is the marginal change in consumption that results from a marginal change in income. As we shall see in this problem, the marginal change in consumption depends on the type of income.

Consider a household that lives for two periods, t and $t+1$. The household receives income in each period, Y_t and Y_{t+1}, and must choose its dynamic consumption allocation, $\{C_t, C_{t+1}\}$. For simplicity, we assume that the household begins its life in period t with no assets and no debt. However, it can borrow or save between periods at the gross real interest rate, R.

1. Write down the household's budget constraint in period t.

2. Given that there is no period $t+2$, will the household be *able* to borrow in period $t+1$?

3. Given that there is no period $t+2$, will the household be *willing* to save in period $t+1$?

4. Given your answers to the two previous questions, write down the household's budget constraint in period $t+1$.
[Hint: Recall that R is a gross rate.]

5. Combine the two per-period budget constraints above to derive the household's intertemporal budget constraint. Label the side that corresponds to the present discounted value of consumption and the side that corresponds to the present discounted value of income.

6. Now suppose the household has the following utility function:

$$U(C_t, C_{t+1}) = \log(C_t) + \beta \log(C_{t+1})$$

where $\beta < 1$ is the discount factor of the future. Write down the constrained optimization problem of the household.

7. Write down the marginal rate of substitution between C_t and C_{t+1}.

8. Write down the marginal rate of transformation between C_t and C_{t+1}.

9. Write down the optimality condition.

10. Combine the optimality condition with the intertemporal budget constraint to solve for C_t as a function of the present discounted value of all income:

$$C_t = \left(\frac{1}{1+\beta}\right)\left(Y_t + \frac{Y_{t+1}}{R}\right) \tag{35.1}$$

11. You have just derived the *consumption function*. What is consumption a function of?

We can decompose income in two. *Permanent income* is the component of income whose changes persist forever into the future. *Transitory income* is the component of income whose changes die down over time. How does consumption react to each? We will begin by decomposing income into its two constituent parts:

$$Y_t = Y_t^P + Y_t^T \tag{35.2}$$

where Y_t^P denotes permanent income and Y_t^T denotes transitory income. Since one persists over time while the other one does not, we will suppose they behave according to the following laws of motion

$$Y_{t+1}^P = Y_t^P + \varepsilon_{t+1} \qquad\qquad Y_{t+1}^T = e_{t+1}$$

where ε_{t+1} and e_{t+1} are both two random variables whose expected value is zero: $E_t[\varepsilon_{t+1}] = E_t[e_{t+1}] = 0$.

12. Give an example of transitory income and an example of permanent income.

13. At time t the household does not yet know Y_{t+1}. However, we know from equation (35.1) that the household takes future income into account when choosing how much to consume today. Since it cannot make consumption choices on the *known* value of its future income, we will assume that it instead considers the *expected value* of its future income. Show that the expected value of the household's future income is:

$$E_t[Y_{t+1}] = Y_t^P$$

[Hint: Write down future income, Y_{t+1}, in terms of its two components and take the expected value.]

14. Use your answer above to rewrite equation (35.1) in terms of *current* permanent and transitory income:

$$C_t = \left(\frac{1}{1+\beta}\right)Y_t^T + \left(\frac{1}{1+\beta}\right)\left(\frac{1+R}{R}\right)Y_t^P \tag{35.3}$$

15. Take the derivative of consumption with respect to transitory income, Y_t^T. Is the marginal propensity to consume out of transitory income greater than, or less than one? Offer a brief explanation for this result.

16. Take the derivative of consumption with respect to permanent income, Y_t^P. Is the marginal propensity to consume out of permanent income higher or lower than transitory income? Give a brief economic explanation for this result.

17. Show that if $R\beta = 1$, the marginal propensity to consume out of permanent income is one. How does this compare the the marginal propensity to consume out of transitory income?

18. Let $\Delta X_t \equiv X_t - X_{t-1}$, where X_t can be consumption, temporary, or permanent income. Subtract the consumption function at time $t-1$ from the consumption function at time t to get the following function for the *change* in consumption:

$$\frac{\Delta C_t}{Y_t} = \left(\frac{1}{1+\beta}\right)\frac{\Delta Y_t^T}{Y_t} + \left(\frac{1}{1+\beta}\right)\left(\frac{1+R}{R}\right)\frac{\Delta Y_t^P}{Y_t} \tag{35.4}$$

19. If we want to take our model to data, explain why we can use either equation (35.3) or equation (35.4).
[Hint: What is true about the coefficients in both equations?]

20. Why might it be easier to rescale the data as a *share* of income, as in (35.4), than to look simply at *levels* of consumption and income, as in (35.3)?
[Hint: What do levels of consumption and income do over time?]

Figure 35.1 plots $\Delta C_t/Y_t$ and $\Delta Y_t/Y_t$ over time for three countries: Switzerland, Mexico and the US. As per your answers to the two previous questions, we will analyze these graphs using equation (35.4).

20. If transitory income is the largest component of income, will consumption change by more or less than changes in income?

21. As permanent income becomes a larger portion of income, will consumption begin responding more or less to changes in income?

22. So far we have supposed that the real rate of return is fixed. If we relax this assumption and allow R_t to change, how will that affect the marginal propensity to consume out of permanent income?

23. Mexico and Switzerland are small, open economies. The real interest rate they face is set in world capital markets; so we can assume that the real interest rate is *unrelated* to any changes in temporary or permanent income. What does figure 35.1 suggest about the relative size of transitory income to permanent income in Switzerland versus Mexico?

24. The United States is a large, open economy; since the US affects world markets, the real interest rate in the US is sensitive to domestic economic conditions. What does figure 35.1 suggest about the relative size of transitory to permanent income in the US?

25. What other variable can be co-moving with income to affect the empirical relationship between changes in consumption and income growth? Explain how that co-movement would manifest itself in the US data plotted in figure 35.1(c).

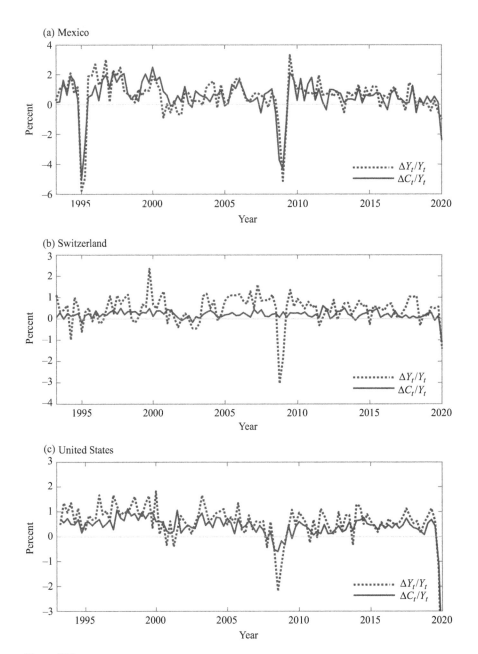

Figure 35.1
Output growth and change in consumption as a fraction of output. *Source*: World Bank

Reference

Deaton, A. (1992). *Understanding consumption*. Oxford: Oxford University Press.

36 The Invisible Hand across Time

In chapter 19, "When Are Market Economies Efficient?," we analyzed an economy where households and firms interacted in two markets—goods and labor—at a single point in time. What happens when we allow for the reasonable possibility that the economy lasts more than one period? We will consider the simplest extension that allows for such a possibility: households and firms will now live for two periods instead of one.

36.1   The Household

The household must now choose *four* allocations: how much to consume in both periods, $\{C_1, C_2\}$, and how many hours to work in both periods, $\{H_1, H_2\}$. The household's *intertemporal* utility function is given by:

$$u(C_1, H_1) + \beta u(C_2, H_2) \tag{36.1}$$

where β is the discount factor. The *per-period* utility function for consumption and labor, $u(C_t, H_t)$, is the same as in chapter 19, and is restated below:

$$u(C_t, H_t) = \log(C_t) - \frac{H_t^{1+\phi}}{1+\phi} \tag{36.2}$$

The household's intertemporal budget constraint is:

$$C_1 + \left(\frac{1}{1+r}\right)C_2 = \frac{W_1}{P_1}H_1 + \left(\frac{1}{1+r}\right)\frac{W_2}{P_2}H_2 \tag{36.3}$$

where W_t/P_t is the real wage in period t.

1. What is the name of the right-hand side of the intertemporal budget constraint?

2. What is the name of the left-hand side of the intertemporal budget constraint?

3. Write down the marginal rate of substitution between hours worked and consumption in both periods.

4. Write down the marginal rate of transformation between hours worked and consumption in both periods.

5. Argue that the optimality condition in both periods is identical and can be written as:

$$C_t H_t^\phi = \frac{W_t}{P_t}$$

6. Write down the marginal rate of substitution between consumption in period one, C_1, and consumption in period two, C_2.

7. Write down the marginal rate of transformation between consumption in period one, C_1, and consumption in period two, C_2.

8. Write down the optimality condition for consumption in period one and consumption in period two. What is the name of this equation?

36.2   The Firm

The firm also lives for two periods and must hire labor to produce output in each period subject to the production function:

$$Y_t = A_t L_t \tag{36.4}$$

Each period, the firm chooses an allocation, $\{Y_t, L_t\}$, to maximize the profits in that period given the real wage $\frac{W_t}{P_t}$.

1. Write down the profit function of the firm in an arbitrary period, t.

2. Write down the firm's constrained optimization problem in period t. Does the firm's constrained optimization problem change depending on the period?

3. Write down the marginal rate of substitution between output and labor in period t.

4. Write down the marginal rate of transformation between output and labor in period t.

5. Show that the optimality condition in both periods can be written as:

$$\frac{W_t}{P_t} = A_t \tag{36.5}$$

36.3   Equilibrium

We now consider a competitive equilibrium in this economy. A competitive equilibrium consists of *allocations*, $\{Y_1^*, Y_2^*, L_1^*, L_2^*\}$, and *relative prices*, $\left\{\frac{W_1}{P_1}, \frac{W_2}{P_2}, r\right\}$, such that markets clear and the firm and household satisfy their optimality conditions and their respective constraints.

1. Write down the market-clearing condition for the goods market in both periods.

2. Write down the market-clearing condition for the labor market in both periods.

3. Show that the equilibrium allocation of labor is the same in both periods and can be written as:

$$L_t^* = 1 \tag{36.6}$$

4. Combine equations (36.6) and (36.5) to derive the income of the household *in equilibrium*.

5. Show that the equilibrium allocation of output has the same form in both periods and can be written as:

$$Y_t^* = A_t \tag{36.7}$$

6. Show that, *in equilibrium*, output and income are equal.
[Hint: In the previous questions you have derived expressions for equilibrium output and equilibrium income.]

Let productivity grow at the rate $(1 + \gamma)$:

$$\frac{A_2}{A_1} = (1 + \gamma)$$

7. Is γ a net or a gross rate of growth?

8. Combine the market-clearing condition in the goods market with the Euler equation to show that, in equilibrium, the real interest rate is determined by the growth rate of productivity and the household's discount factor:

$$\frac{1 + \gamma}{\beta} = 1 + r \tag{36.8}$$

9. Suppose that the productivity growth rate increases. What happens to the growth rate of consumption? What happens to the equilibrium real interest rate?

10. Recall that β is a parameter that determines the household's *preferences* over the timing of consumption. Given equation (36.8), what data would we need to measure β? Explain what condition those data would need to satisfy in order to conclude that households discount the future.

References

Gali, J. (2008). *Monetary policy, inflation and the business cycle: An introduction to the new Keynesian framework*. Princeton: Princeton University Press.

King, R., C. Plosser, & S. Rebelo (1988a). Production growth and business cycles: I. The basic neoclassical model. *Journal of Monetary Economics, 21*(2), 195–232.

King, R., C. Plosser, & S. Rebelo (1988b). Production growth and business cycles: II. New directions. *Journal of Monetary Economics, 21*(3), 309–341.

37 Ricardian Equivalence

In all three recessions of the twenty-first century—the dot-com bubble, the Great Recession, and the Covid pandemic—the US government has mailed out checks to households in hopes of stimulating consumption, one of the components of aggregate demand. In this problem, we will analyze a two-period economy with two agents, households and the government. We are interested in how changes in lump-sum taxation affect household consumption.

37.1 The Household

The household begins the first period with no assets and no debt. Each period it receives an exogenous income, Y_t. The household has to pay a lump-sum tax, T_t, and can spend its after-tax income on consumption, C_t, or save it, S_t, at a fixed real interest rate, r.

1. Write down the household's budget constraint for period one.

2. Write down the household's budget constraint for period two.

3. Explain why, in equilibrium, the household will not save in period two: $S_2 = 0$.

4. Combine your answers to the previous three questions into the following intertemporal budget constraint:

$$C_1 + \frac{C_2}{1+r} = Y_1 - T_1 + \frac{Y_2 - T_2}{1+r} \tag{37.1}$$

The household allocates its consumption in the two periods to maximize the utility function:

$$U(C_1, C_2) = \log(C_1) + \beta \log(C_2)$$

5. Write down the household's constrained optimization problem.

6. Write down the household's marginal rate of substitution between C_1 and C_2.

7. Write down the household's marginal rate of transformation between C_1 and C_2.

8. Write down the household's optimality condition. What is the name of this equation?

9. Combine the household's optimality condition with its budget constraint to get the following expression for consumption in the current period, C_1:

$$C_1 = \frac{1}{1+\beta}\left(Y_1 - T_1 + \frac{Y_2 - T_2}{1+r}\right) \tag{37.2}$$

37.2   The Government

The government also begins the first period with no assets and no debt. Each period it can raise revenue through either taxes on the households, T_t, or by issuing bonds, B_t, at the fixed real interest rate, r. The government uses its funds to either pay the outstanding bonds, $B_{t-1}(1+r)$, or for government purchases, G_t.

1. Write down the budget constraint for the government in period one.

2. Write down the budget constraint for the government in period two.

3. Will the household buy any government bonds in period two? What does that imply for the equilibrium value of B_2?

4. Combine your answers to the previous three questions into the following intertemporal budget constraint:

$$G_1 + \frac{G_2}{1+r} = T_1 + \frac{T_2}{1+r} \tag{37.3}$$

The government is considering a tax rebate to stimulate consumption in the current period (period one). Importantly, there is no change to government purchases in any period. Denote the change in taxes if the rebate is approved by Δ_1 so that taxes in period one would be $T_1 - \Delta_1$, if the rebate is approved. Does the change in taxes today have an effect on taxes tomorrow? Let Δ_2 denote the—possibly zero—change in taxes in the second period that must go into effect if the rebate is approved.

5. Write down the budget constraint for the government in period one under the rebate.

6. Write down the budget constraint for the government in period two under the rebate.

7. Explain why, in equilibrium, it is still the case that $B_2 = 0$ even if the rebate is approved.

8. Combine the two budget constraints into the following intertemporal budget constraint:

$$G_1 + \frac{G_2}{1+r} = T_1 - \Delta_1 + \frac{T_2 + \Delta_2}{1+r} \tag{37.4}$$

9. Use the two intertemporal budget constraints to show that:

$$\Delta_1 = \frac{\Delta_2}{1+r} \tag{37.5}$$

What is the economic interpretation of this equation?

10. Equation (37.2) says that consumption is a function of the present discounted value of all income minus the present discounted value of all taxes. How does the present discounted value of all taxes change when the rebate is introduced?

11. What happens to consumption in the current period, C_1, if the rebate is approved?

12. Would your answer change if instead of a rebate the government had announced a tax increase?

13. What do your answers above suggest about the *timing* of lump-sum taxes' effect on consumption? This result is called *Ricardian equivalence*.

14. In equilibrium, what do households end up buying with the tax rebate?

Reference

Barro, R. (1974). Are government bonds net wealth? *Journal of Political Economy, 82*(6), 1095–1117.

38 Tax Rebates and Financial Frictions

In response to the 2008 Great Recession, the federal government issued stimulus payments to households. These were distributed according to the last four digits of taxpayers' social security numbers, which are random. Since distributing the payments took several months, this created a randomized control trial similar to those used to test the effectiveness of a new drug. Parker, Souleles, Johnson and McClelland (2013) compared the consumption of those who had received the stimulus (the treatment group) to those who were still waiting for it (the control group) and found that consumers spent between 12 and 30 percent of their stimulus payment.

1. Is the Parker et al finding consistent with Ricardian equivalence? If yes, explain why. Otherwise, explain what finding would have been consistent with Ricardian equivalence.

In light of their findings, we will develop a model for the stimulus payments during the Covid lockdowns of 2020, where Ricardian Equivalence doesn't hold. Consider a household that lives for two periods and derives utility from consumption:

$$U(C_1, C_2) = \log(C_1) + \beta \log(C_2)$$

where $\beta < 1$ is the discount factor.

The household finds itself quarantined in the first period, and therefore unable to earn any income. The quarantine will be lifted in the second period at which point the household will earn income, Y. The household starts the first period with no assets or debt and similarly ends the second period with no assets or debt. However, the household can transfer resources across periods either by borrowing or saving at the fixed real interest rate, r.

2. Will the household borrow or save in period one?

3. Write down the household's budget constraint in period one.

4. Write down the household's budget constraint in period two.

5. Combine your two budget constraints to show that the intertemporal budget constraint for the household can be written as:

$$C_1 + \frac{C_2}{1+r} = \frac{Y}{1+r} \tag{38.1}$$

6. Solve for C_1 and graph equation (38.1) with C_1 on the y axis and C_2 on the x axis. Make sure to label the intercepts. What is the economic significance of the x intercept?

7. Write down the household's constrained optimization problem.

8. Write down the marginal rate of substitution between C_1 and C_2.

9. Write down the marginal rate of transformation between C_1 and C_2.

10. Show that the household's optimality condition implies that consumption in period one can be written as the following function of consumption in period two:

$$C_1 = \frac{1}{\beta(1+r)} C_2 \tag{38.2}$$

11. Graph the household's optimality condition above in the same diagram as the budget constraint. What is the economic significance of the intersection of the two lines?

Now suppose the government decides to send the household a stimulus payment, S, in the first period. To finance the stimulus, the government issues debt, which it will repay in the second period through a tax, T. Unlike the household, which pays an interest r, however, the government can borrow at a reduced rate, $r - \delta$.

12. Why might economists refer to δ as a financial friction?

13. Show that the government's intertemporal budget constraint is:

$$S = \frac{T}{1+r} \tag{38.3}$$

[Hint: How much will the government have to pay in period two?]

14. Write down the household's budget constraint in period one.

15. Write down the household's budget constraint in period two.

16. Show that the household's intertemporal budget constraint is given by:

$$C_1 + \frac{C_2}{1+r} = \frac{S\delta + Y}{1+r} \tag{38.4}$$

17. If there were no financial frictions, how would the household's budget constraint with a stimulus payment compare to the household's budget constraint without a stimulus payment?

18. Solve for C_1 and graph equation (38.4) with C_1 on the y axis and C_2 on the x axis. Make sure to label the intercepts.

19. In the same diagram as above, graph the household's budget constraint without a stimulus payment ($S = 0$).

20. Why are the two budget constraints different? Does the household's scope for consumption increase or decrease with the stimulus?

21. Now graph the household's optimality condition, equation (38.2). How does consumption during the quarantine, C_1, change if the government sends the household a stimulus check?

22. Is the above result consistent with Ricardian equivalence?

References

Barro, R. (1974). Are government bonds net wealth? *Journal of Political Economy, 82*(6), 1095–1117.

Parker, J., N. Souleles, D. Johnson, & R. McClelland (2013). Consumer spending and the economics stimulus payments of 2008. *American Economic Review, 103*(6), 2530–2553.

39 The Great Capitol Hill Babysitting Co-op

In 1977, Joan and Richard Sweeney published an article titled "Monetary theory and the great Capitol Hill babysitting co-op crisis." The story started in the early 1970s with a group of young parents who lived on Capitol Hill, in Washington DC, and worked in Congress. Some 150 couples formed a co-op, in which they babysat each other's children. In order to manage the co-op, they came up with a simple solution: they issued vouchers that could be traded for hours of babysitting. Each couple received a number of vouchers upon joining; after that, the only way for a couple to get more vouchers was to babysit other couples' children. In what follows we are going to focus on the monetary theory and skip the crisis.

39.1 Real and Nominal

In any given period, t, we denote the total amount of hours of babysitting by H_t, the total number of vouchers in circulation by M_t, and the total number of vouchers that had to be exchanged for one hour of babysitting by P_t.

1. What is the factor of production in the co-op?

2. What is the output of the co-op?

3. Let Y_t denote output. Write down the production function of the co-op.
[Hint: Recall that output is a function of the factors of production.]

4. Which variables in the co-op are *nominal*?

5. Which variables in the co-op are *real*?

6. What coordination problem do the vouchers solve in this economy?

7. Why would a couple be willing to accept a voucher instead of a promise of future babysitting from another couple?

8. List three uses that the vouchers fulfill in the co-op.

39.2   The Grants

Organizing and running the co-op fell to one couple; let's call them the Grants. Their main job was to issue the vouchers. In exchange for running the co-op, the Grants did not have to babysit. Whenever they needed a babysitter, they would simply print new vouchers with which to pay. This type of funding scheme—printing vouchers to pay for babysitting—is called *seigniorage*.

Let G_t denote the total hours of babysitting that the Grants used each month and let Δ_t denote the total number of vouchers that they printed each month.

1. Explain why $M_t = \Delta_t + M_{t-1}$. What does Δ_t measure?

2. Explain why the following is the Grant's budget constraint in any given period:

$$\Delta_t = P_t G_t \tag{39.1}$$

What are the units of this budget constraint?

3. Explain why the total vouchers in circulation ultimately depends on how much babysitting the Grants need.

4. Show that the budget constraint (39.1) can be rewritten as:

$$\frac{M_t}{P_t} - \left(\frac{P_{t-1}}{P_t}\right)\frac{M_{t-1}}{P_{t-1}} = G_t \tag{39.2}$$

What are the units of this budget constraint?

5. Which of the two budget constraints above is nominal? Which is real?

6. We call M_t/P_t *real cash balances*. What are its units?

7. Given your answers above, describe the Grant's source of income (39.2) in terms of real cash balances.

39.3   The Sweeneys

Since they wrote the paper, we will let the Sweeneys stand in as the *representative household* of the co-op. There are three allocations that the Sweeneys choose at each point in time: how many vouchers to hold, M_t, how many hours to babysit, H_t, and for how many hours they want to get a babysitter, C_t. Finally, to simplify our analysis, we will model the co-op as lasting for only two periods.

Suppose the Sweeneys maximize the following utility function:

$$u(C_t, H_t) + \beta u(C_{t+1}, H_{t+1})$$

where the per-period utility, u($\cdot$), is given by:

$$u(C_t, H_t) = \log(C_t) - \frac{H_t^{1+\phi}}{1+\phi}$$

where $\phi > 0$.

1. Write down the budget constraint for the Sweeneys in period t.

2. Write down the budget constraint for the Sweeneys in period $t+1$.
[Hint: If the Sweeneys hold on to vouchers in period t, what can they do with those vouchers in period $t+1$?]

3. Combine the two budget constraints above into the following intertemporal budget constraint:

$$H_t + \left(\frac{P_{t+1}}{P_t}\right) H_{t+1} = C_t + \left(\frac{P_{t+1}}{P_t}\right) C_{t+1}$$

Is this constraint real or nominal?
[Hint: What are its units?]

4. Write down the Sweeneys' constrained optimization problem.

5. Write down the marginal rate of substitution and the marginal rate of transformation between C_t and H_t.

6. Write down the optimality condition between C_t and H_t. Show that the optimality condition is given by:

$$C_t H_t^{\phi} = 1 \tag{39.3}$$

Is the optimality condition different in period $t+1$?

39.4   The Classical Dichotomy

The co-op has both real and nominal variables; how are the two related in equilibrium? A *competitive equilibrium* in the co-op consists of *allocations* $\{H_{t+j}^*, C_{t+j}^*, G_{t+j}^*, M_{t+j}^*\}_{j=0,1}$ and *prices* $\{P_{t+1}^*\}_{j=0,1}$ such that the markets clear and all couples in the co-op satisfy their respective optimality conditions and budget constraints.

1. Write down the market-clearing condition in the babysitting market. Which side corresponds to aggregate demand? Which side corresponds to output?

2. Is there another market in the co-op?

Notice that we have not said anything about how the Grants choose how many hours of babysitting to use. Because the Grants can simply print vouchers every time they need a babysitter, their choices are driven by factors that are entirely *external* to the co-op economy. We will therefore consider G_t^* and G_{t+1}^* *exogenous* variables.

3. You now have the two equilibrium conditions. The first is the *optimality condition* of the Sweeneys, equation (39.3). The second is the *market-clearing condition* you wrote down above. Combine the two equilibrium conditions to derive the following equilibrium expression for output:

$$Y_t = (H_t^*)^{-\phi} + G_t^* \tag{39.4}$$

Is the condition above different in period $t+1$?

4. Explain why it is also the case that:

$$Y_t = H_t^* \tag{39.5}$$

5. Although it looks like a simple identity, the equation above is, in fact, a *function*. What is the name of this function?

Equations (39.4) and (39.5) cannot be manipulated until we can write equilibrium hours, H_t^*, as a function of G_t^*. So we will instead solve the system of equations graphically.

6. In a coordinate plane with Y_t on the y axis and H_t^* on the x axis graph equations (39.4) and (39.5).
[Hint: Recall that we are taking G_t^* as given. Another hint: Recall that $\phi > 0$.]

7. Explain why the intersection of your graph denotes the equilibrium allocation of output and hours in the co-op.

8. How does the intersection of your graph change if you change M_t or P_t?

9. Do the equilibrium allocations of any real variables change when the nominal variables change? The answer to this question is called *the classical dichotomy*.

References

Sweeny, J., & R.J. Sweeny (1977). Monetary theory and the great Capitol Hill baby sitting co-op crisis: Comment. *Journal of Money, Credit and Banking, 9*(1), 86–89.

Krugman, P. (1999). *The return of depression economics.* New York: Norton.

40 The Printing Press

In chapter 39, "The Great Capitol Hill Babysitting Co-op," we analyzed an economy that produced a single service: babysitting. Although relatively simple, this economy developed its own currency. The co-op printed and distributed vouchers that its members could exchange for hours of babysitting. Our model had two couples. The Grants stood in for the couple that organized the co-op and printed the vouchers. The Sweeneys stood in for all of the other couples in the co-op. Chapter 39 focused on the Sweeneys and the decisions they faced as participants in the co-op. This chapter is about the Grants; as the only couple in the co-op with the power to print new vouchers, it is natural to wonder whether they might abuse it and to what might be the scope of that abuse. Wouldn't an unscrupulous couple print and unlimited number of vouchers?

40.1 The Demand for Money

In chapter 39 we showed that the babysitting market in the co-op is independent of the number of vouchers in circulation. What determines the value and number of vouchers that circulate in equilibrium? To answer this question we now turn to the market for *real cash balances*, $\frac{M_t}{P_t}$, where M_t is the number of vouchers in circulation and P_t is the price of one hour of babysitting.

1. Which of the two agents in our model demands real cash balances?
2. Which of the two agents in our model supplies real cash balances?

Let H_t denote the total number of hours of babysitting that the Sweeneys supply, C_t the total number of hours of babysitting that the Sweeneys demand, and M_t the total number of vouchers that the Sweeneys hold, all in period t. Notice that the number of vouchers the Sweeneys hold is equivalent to the number of vouchers in circulation since all vouchers in circulation must be held by *someone*. As in chapter 39, we simplify our task by assuming that the co-op lasts for only two periods, t and $t + 1$.

The Sweeneys maximize the following utility function:

$$u(C_t, H_t) + \beta u(C_{t+1}, H_{t+1})$$

where the per-period utility, $u(\cdot)$, is given by:

$$u(C_t, H_t) = \log(C_t) - \frac{H_t^{1+\phi}}{1+\phi}$$

and $\phi > 0$, subject to the following sequence of *intratemporal* budget constraints:

$$P_t C_t = H_t P_t - M_t$$

$$P_{t+1} C_{t+1} = H_{t+1} P_{t+1} + M_t$$

3. Explain why the Sweeneys do not hold any vouchers at the end of period $t+1$ so that $M_{t+1} = 0$.

4. Are the budget constraints above real or nominal?

5. Combine the budget constraints into a real, intertemporal budget constraint.

6. Write down the marginal rate of substitution between C_t and C_{t+1}.

7. Write down the marginal rate of transformation between C_t and C_{t+1}.

8. Write down the optimality condition and show that the Euler equation can be written as:

$$C_{t+1} P_{t+1} = \beta C_t P_t$$

9. Substitute the right-hand side of each intratemporal budget constraint into your answer above to derive the *demand for real cash balances*:

$$\frac{M_t}{P_t} = \left(\frac{1}{1+\beta}\right)\left(\beta H_t - H_{t+1}\frac{P_{t+1}}{P_t}\right) \qquad (40.1)$$

10. Notice that the demand for real cash balances in period t depends on outcomes from period $t+1$. The Sweeneys must make choices in period t based on outcomes that have not yet occurred. List the two variables for which the Sweeneys must form *expectations* in period t. Add the superscript ^{e} to both of those variables in equation (40.1) to denote *expectations* in period t rather than *outcomes* in period $t+1$.

11. What is the economic interpretation of the following ratio?

$$\frac{P_{t+1}^e}{P_t}$$

How would the economic interpretation change if you take the log?

12. Let $\beta = 1$, $H_t = 2$ and $H_{t+1}^e = 1$. Substitute those values into equation (40.1) and graph the demand for real cash balances as a function of *inflation expectations*.

13. What happens to the demand for real cash balances if inflation expectations increase?

14. For any given number of vouchers in circulation, M_t, what variable must increase for real cash balances to decrease?

15. Given your two previous answers, what happens to current inflation when inflation *expectations* increase?

16. What happens to the demand for real cash balances if the expected gross inflation rate is higher than two?
[Hint: Can there be negative vouchers? Another hint: Use this answer to potentially fix your graph of the demand for real cash balances.]

17. Given your answer above, what happens to the co-op members' willingness to use vouchers as currency if they expect inflation to be too high in the future?

40.2   The Supply of Money

Suppose that the Grants print new vouchers according to the following rule:

$$M_{t+1} = (1 + \mu)M_t \tag{40.2}$$

1. Is μ a net or a gross growth rate?

2. How does μ capture the degree to which the Grants might abuse their position?

3. Is equation (40.2) real or nominal?

4. Rewrite equation (40.2) into the following *supply of real cash balances*:

$$\frac{M_t}{P_t} = \left(\frac{1}{1+\mu}\right)\left(\frac{M_{t+1}}{P_{t+1}^e}\right)\left(\frac{P_{t+1}^e}{P_t}\right) \tag{40.3}$$

[Hint: Begin by dividing both sides of (40.2) by P_{t+1}^e.]

5. Explain why M_{t+1} is known at time t and therefore does not require the superscript ^{e} to denote an expectation.
[Hint: All members of the co-op know μ.]

We now have expressions for the supply and demand—equations (40.3) and (40.1), respectively—of real cash balances in the co-op. We have two equations but three unknowns: the demand for real cash balances today, M_t/P_t, the *expected* demand for real cash balances tomorrow, M_{t+1}/P_{t+1}^e, and the *expected* inflation, P_{t+1}^e/P_t. How to proceed?

Notice that the Grants' rule, (40.2), makes it possible for the Sweeneys to work out today how many vouchers will be in circulation tomorrow. This makes it possible, in principle, for the Sweeneys to work out today what the price of one hour of babysitting will be tomorrow. Specifically, we have the following relationship between expected and actual prices:

$$P_{t+1}^e = P_{t+1} \tag{40.4}$$

We call this a *perfect foresight* equilibrium because the members of our economy do not face any uncertainty and are able to correctly anticipate the values of all future equilibrium outcomes.

To solve the perfect foresight equilibrium we will use the tried and true method of guess and check. We will first guess the equilibrium value of real cash balances in the the market and then solve for the perfect foresight inflation expectations implied by our guess.

6. Guess that the equilibrium allocation of real cash balances is constant:

$$\frac{M_t^*}{P_t^*} = \frac{M_{t+1}^*}{P_{t+1}^*} = \lambda$$

Substitute this guess into the supply of real cash balances to show that expected inflation is also constant and equal to $1 + \mu$.

7. To verify that our guess is correct, it must be the case that when inflation expectations are $1 + \mu$, the demand for real cash balances is constant. Combine your answer above with (40.1) to show that the equilibrium allocation of real cash balances is indeed constant and given by:

$$\lambda = \frac{1 - \mu}{2} \tag{40.5}$$

where $\beta = 1$, $H_t = 2$, and $H_{t+1}^e = 1$, as before.

8. Derive an expression for the *equilibrium price level*, P_t^*. Show that it depends on the number of vouchers in circulation, M_t^*, and *expected inflation*, μ.

40.3   Seigniorage

Recall that the Grants' budget constraint is given by:

$$P_t G_t = M_t - M_{t-1} \tag{40.6}$$

Since they can choose both M_t and M_{t-1}, it follows that their ability to pay for babysitting depends on the *equilibrium* price level, P_t^*. Now that we have an expression for the equilibrium price level we can answer explore the extent to which the Grants can abuse their position by increasing the rate at which they print new vouchers.

1. Combine the Grants' budget constraint with their voucher-printing rule—equation (40.2)—to show that the amount of babysitting the Grants can buy is a function of real cash balances, M_t/P_t, and the voucher growth rate μ.

$$G_t^* = \frac{M_t^*}{P_t^*} \left(\frac{\mu}{1 + \mu} \right) \tag{40.7}$$

2. Seigniorage—paying for real goods and services by printing currency—is also known as *the inflation tax*. Why?

3. Holding the demand for real cash balances constant, is the level of seigniorage increasing or decreasing in the growth rate of vouchers?

4. Combine equation (40.7) with the equilibrium demand for real cash balances, equation (40.5), to show that the total seigniorage the Grants can extract is, in equilibrium, a function only of the rate at which they print vouchers:

$$G_t^* = \frac{1}{2}\left(\frac{\mu(1-\mu)}{1+\mu}\right) \tag{40.8}$$

5. Suppose $\mu = 0$. What is G_t^*? What is the rate of inflation?

6. Suppose $\mu = 1$. What is G_t^*? What is the rate of inflation?

7. Use your answers above to help you graph G_t^* as a function of μ.
[Hint: G_t^* should be on the y axis and μ on the x axis.]

8. Can the Grants buy an unlimited amount of babysitting by printing an unlimited number of vouchers?

9. What happens to inflation expectations if the Grants try to print an unlimited number of vouchers? What happens to inflation?

10. What lesson can the Grants teach governments who try to pay for their expenses by printing money?

40.4 The Importance of Expectations

Suppose the Grants have been printing vouchers at a constant, known rate, μ, and hiring a constant and modest amount of babysitting, G. Then, in period t news gets out that they will need a lot more babysitting in the *future*—perhaps their boss became the Speaker of the House—and hence will have to increase the rate at which they print vouchers going forward.

1. Have the Grants actually changed their behavior at time t?

2. Denote the future [net] rate of money growth by μ', where $\mu' > \mu$. Is the rate of money growth *at time t* given by μ or by μ'?

3. We have shown that, in equilibrium, prices grow at the same rate as vouchers. If the growth rate of money at time $t+1$ will be μ', what must be true about inflation *expectations* today, P_{t+1}^e/P_t?

4. Explain why *yesterday's expectations* about *today's* inflation, P_t^e/P_{t-1}, was equal to $(1+\mu)$.

5. Let λ denote the equilibrium allocation of real cash balances in period $t-1$ and λ' denote the equilibrium allocation in period t. Substitute the different inflation expectations into the demand for real cash balances; which is higher, demand in period $t-1$ or in period t?

6. Substitute the equilibrium demand for real cash balances into the Grants' budget constraint and show that

$$G^*_{t-1} = \lambda \left(\frac{\mu}{1+\mu} \right) \tag{40.9}$$

[Hint: $P_{t-1} = (1/\lambda)M_{t-1}$ and $M_{t-1} = (1+\mu)M_{t-2}$.]

7. Substitute the equilibrium demand for real cash balances into the Grants' budget constraint and show that

$$G^*_t = \lambda' \left(\frac{\mu}{1+\mu} \right) \tag{40.10}$$

[Hint: $P_t = (1/\lambda')M_t$ and $M_t = (1+\mu)M_{t-1}$]

8. Consider the ratio G^*_t/G^*_{t-1}. Although the Grants have yet to change their behavior in period t, what happens to the amount of babysitting they can afford by virtue of the *news* that they will, *in the future*, increase the rate at which they will print new vouchers?

Let's consider the opposite case. Suppose the Grants have been working for the Speaker of the House, and so have been very busy at work. They have been printing new vouchers at a very high and constant rate, μ, to pay for a constant but high amount of babysitting, G. Then, in period t, their party loses control of the House. In period $t+1$, their boss will no longer be Speaker, and they will require a lot fewer hours of babysitting. Subsequently, they will print new vouchers at a much lower rate.

9. Have the Grants actually changed their behavior at time t?

10. Denote the future [net] rate of money growth μ', where $\mu' < \mu$. Given your answer above, is the rate of money growth *at time t* given by μ or by μ'?

11. We have shown that, in equilibrium, prices grow at the same rate as vouchers. If the growth rate of money at time $t+1$ will be μ', what must be true about inflation *expectations* today, P^e_{t+1}/P_t?

12. Explain why *yesterday's expectations* about *today's* inflation, P^e_t/P_{t-1}, was equal to $(1+\mu)$.

13. Let λ denote the equilibrium allocation of real cash balances in period $t-1$ and λ' denote the equilibrium allocation in period t. Substitute the different inflation expectations into the demand for real cash balances; which is higher, demand in period $t-1$ or in period t?

14. Substitute the equilibrium demand for real cash balances into the Grants' budget constraint and show that

$$G^*_{t-1} = \lambda \left(\frac{\mu}{1+\mu} \right) \tag{40.11}$$

[Hint: $P_{t-1} = (1/\lambda)M_{t-1}$ and $M_{t-1} = (1+\mu)M_{t-2}$.]

15. Substitute the equilibrium demand for real cash balances into the Grants' budget constraint and show that

$$G_t^* = \lambda' \left(\frac{\mu}{1+\mu} \right) \tag{40.12}$$

[Hint: $P_t = (1/\lambda')M_t$ and $M_t = (1+\mu)M_{t-1}$]

16. Consider the ratio G_t^*/G_{t-1}^*. Although the Grants have yet to change their behavior in period t, what happens to the amount of babysitting they can afford by virtue of the *news* that they will, *in the future*, decrease the rate at which they will print new vouchers?

17. What lesson does the above scenario offer a country that finds itself in a hyperinflationary spiral?

References

Blanchard, O., & M. Watson (1982). Bubbles, rational expectations and financial markets. In P. Wachtel (ed.), *Crises in the economic and financial structure: Bubbles, bursts, and shocks*. Lexington, MA: Lexington.

Sargent, T. (1993). *Bounded rationality in macroeconomics*. Oxford: Oxford University Press.

Sargent, T., N. Williams, & T. Zha (2009). The conquest of South American inflation. *Journal of Political Economy, 117*(2), 211–256.

Sweeny, J., & R.J. Sweeny (1977). Monetary theory and the great Capitol Hill baby sitting co-op crisis: Comment. *Journal of Money, Credit and Banking, 9*(1), 86–89.

41 Fisher and Prices

The Treasury borrows by issuing two types of bonds: T-Bills and TIPS. These bonds have different payment structures at the time of maturity, when the Treasury repays them. Given that both of these bonds trade in the market, it must be that, in equilibrium, traders are happy to hold both. Consider a risk-neutral trader whose objective is to maximize the expected return on her investment. Under what conditions will she buy both types of bonds?

41.1   T-Bills

T-Bills sold in period t have a *dollar* face value of B that the Treasury pays out in period $t+1$. As a result, investors who buy a T-Bill in period t buy them at *a discount*. They only pay:

$$\frac{B}{Q_t} \qquad (41.1)$$

1. Would the trader ever be willing to pay *more* than the face value for a T-Bill?

2. In light of your answer above, what must be the lower bound on Q_t?

3. Divide the amount the trader receives at $t+1$ by the amount the trader pays at t to show that the gross rate of return on T-Bills is Q_t.

4. Explain why Q_t is a *nominal* rate of return.
[Hint: What are the units of the bond?]

5. When does the trader find out about the nominal return on the bond: in period t or in period $t+1$?

6. When does the trader find out how much consumption the T-bill can buy when it pays out: in period t or in period $t+1$?

41.2   TIPS

TIPS stands for *Treasury Inflation Protected Securities*. TIPS sold in period t have a face value of A. Unlike T-Bills, however, A is *not* the total amount that is paid out in period $t + 1$. Since TIPS are protected against inflation, in period $t + 1$, the Treasury will pay out:

$$A\frac{P_{t+1}}{P_t} \tag{41.2}$$

As with T-bills, traders do not pay A in period t but also buy them at a discount; they pay only:

$$\frac{A}{R_t} \tag{41.3}$$

1. Is A—the face value of the TIPS—known to the trader at time t when she decides whether to buy it?

2. Suppose that the amount the trader spends on purchasing TIPS at time t, A/R_t, buys a total of consumption C at price P_t. Show that

$$A = R_t C P_t$$

3. Suppose that, instead of consuming C, the trader decides to spend A/R_t on TIPS. In terms of C and R_t, how much consumption could the trader purchase in $t + 1$ with the payout from the TIPS?

[Hint: Recall that (41.2) is the total amount of dollars the Treasury will pay in $t + 1$. Use the equation above to rewrite expression (41.2) in terms of C and R_t instead of A.]

4. Divide the consumption that the trader will be able to purchase tomorrow, the answer to the previous question, by the consumption, C, that the trader gives up today when buying TIPS to show that the the gross *real* rate of return on TIPS is R_t.

5. Given your answer above, what is the relative cost to a trader of consuming C today instead of buying TIPS?

6. When the Treasury sells TIPS, it is promising to adjust the face value by the *realized* rate of inflation when the bond is redeemed (in period $t + 1$). Can the trader know *for sure* beforehand (in period t) what that rate of inflation is going to be?

7. Divide the amount the investor receives at $t + 1$ over the amount the investor pays at t to show that the gross *nominal* rate of return on TIPS is:

$$R_t\frac{P_{t+1}}{P_t} \tag{41.4}$$

8. Given your answers to the two previous questions, explain why the gross nominal rate of return on TIPS can be known only at the time that the bond is redeemed, $t + 1$, not at the time the bond is purchased, t.

The trader must *guess* in period t what the rate of inflation will be in $t+1$ to come up with an *expected rate of return*. To distinguish between actual inflation in $t+1$ and expected inflation, we denote the *expected* future prices by P^e_{t+1}, where the superscript ^{e} stands for "expected." It follows that the trader's *expected nominal* rate of return on TIPS is:

$$R_t \frac{P^e_{t+1}}{P_t} \tag{41.5}$$

9. We have shown that a trader who buys TIPS is uncertain about the *nominal* rate of return. Are they uncertain about the *real* rate of return?
[Hint: Consumption is real.]

41.3 The Fisher Equation

Both TIPS and T-Bills are sold with different maturities—the length of time before they come due and the federal government must repay them. Figure 41.1 plots the annualized rates of return on TIPS (solid) and T-Bills (dashed) with a five-year maturity between 2003 and 2023. The shaded regions denote recessions, as dated by the National Bureau of Economic Research (NBER). Although distinct, these two rates are clearly related. In this section we derive that relationship.

1. Explain why traders can make investment decisions about TIPS based only on their *expected nominal* rate of return.

2. Suppose that traders *expect* the nominal rate of return on TIPS—equation (41.5)—to be higher than the *known* nominal return on T-bills, Q_t. Will any trader buy T-bills?

3. As traders divest from T-bills, what will happen to Q_t if the Treasury wants to continue selling T-bills?
[Hint: Recall that equation (41.1) is what traders pay for T-bills.]

4. At what point will this process stop?

5. Suppose that traders *expect* the nominal rate of return on TIPS—equation (41.5)—to be lower than the *known* nominal return on T-bills, Q_t. Will any trader buy TIPS?

6. As traders divest from TIPS, what will happen to R_t if the Treasury wants to continue selling TIPS?
[Hint: Recall that equation (41.3) is what traders pay for TIPS.]

7. Given your answers above, explain why the following relationship must hold in equilibrium:

$$Q_t = R_t \frac{P^e_{t+1}}{P_t} \tag{41.6}$$

Since Q_t and R_t are *gross* rates, let i_t and r_t denote their *net* counterparts, respectively, and define the net expected inflation rate by $\pi^e_{t+1} \equiv \log P^e_{t+1} - \log P_t$.

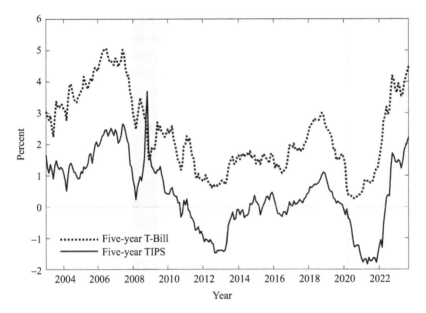

Figure 41.1
Yields of T-Bills and TIPS at a five-year constant maturity. *Source*: Board of Governors of the Federal Reserve System.

8. Take the logs of equation (41.6) and show that in equilibrium:

$$i_t = r_t + \pi_{t+1}^e \tag{41.7}$$

Equation (41.7) is called *the Fisher equation*. Explain in *English* what the Fisher equation says.

9. Refer to figure 41.1. Note that the yield on T-bills never goes negative while the yield on TIPS does. Explain why the yield on T-bills cannot be negative.

10. Refer to figure 41.1. Use the Fisher equation to offer an economic interpretation of the gap between the two rates.

11. If possible, draw a qualitative graph of inflation expectations at a five-year horizon over the past twenty years. Otherwise, explain what additional information not provided by figure 41.1 you would need in order to produce a graph of inflation expectations.

42 The Price of Money

The relative price of an allocation is the alternative allocation that was given up. The relative price of consumption, for example, is the gross real interest rate, $1 + r$, since one unit of consumption today requires us to give up $1 + r$ units of consumption tomorrow. Another example: the relative price of leisure is the real wage, W/P, since we forego W/P units of consumption for every hour we don't work. What, if anything, do we give up when we hold on to cash?

42.1 Cash or Cookies?

Suppose you have enough cash, M_t, to buy one cookie. You are deciding whether to buy—and eat!—the cookie, or keep the cash in your wallet.

1. Let P_t denote the price of the cookie. Show that:

$$\frac{M_t}{P_t} = 1 \tag{42.1}$$

2. What are the units of the left-hand side of equation (42.1)?

3. Explain why economists call the left-hand side of equation (42.1) *real cash balances*.

The relative price of 100 pennies is obviously the same as the relative price of four quarters or one dollar. Since money is both a store of value and a unit of account, we are interested in the relative price of *real cash balances* rather than the relative price of cash itself. In what follows, we will derive the relative price of M_t/P_t.

4. Suppose you decide to keep the cash in your wallet instead of buying the cookie today. How much cash will you have tomorrow?
[Hint: This is not a trick question.]

5. Let C denote the total amount of cookies that you will be able to buy *tomorrow* with the cash that you kept today. What is the present discounted value of tomorrow's consumption?

6. If you hold on to one unit of real cash balances today, you give up one cookie today. Given your answer to the previous questions, explain why this does not mean that the relative price of real cash balances is one. Is it higher or lower than one?

7. By holding on to the cash instead of buying the cookie do you give up or do you gain the present discounted value of tomorrow's consumption?

8. Combine your answers above to show that the relative price of real cash balances is given by:

$$1 - \frac{C}{1+r_t} \tag{42.2}$$

9. Show that $C = M_t/P_{t+1}$.

10. Combine your answer above with equation (42.1) to show that the total amount of cookies that you can buy tomorrow is the inverse of the gross inflation rate:

$$C = \frac{P_t}{P_{t+1}}$$

[Hint: Don't forget that $P_t/P_t = 1$.]

11. The Fisher equation is in terms of net rates, but it can also be written in terms of gross rates: $1 + i_t = (1+r_t)(P_{t+1}/P_t)$. Combine your answer above with the gross rate version of the Fisher equation to show that:

$$\frac{C}{1+r_t} = \frac{1}{1+i_t} \tag{42.3}$$

12. Substitute the equation above in equation (42.2) to show that the relative price of real cash balances is a function, $f(i_t)$, of the nominal interest rate only:

$$f(i_t) \equiv 1 - \frac{1}{1+i_t} \tag{42.4}$$

13. What is the relative price of real cash balances when the nominal interest rate is zero? Offer a brief economic explanation of this result.

14. What happens to the relative price of real cash balances when the nominal interest rate blows up and goes to infinity? Offer a brief economic explanation of this result.

15. Given your answers above, is the relative price or real cash balances an increasing or decreasing price of the nominal interest rate? Offer a brief economic explanation as to why.

16. Before the 1980s the Fed used to conduct monetary policy by targeting the money supply. If the supply of real cash balances increases, what happens to the nominal interest rate? [Hint: Is the demand for real cash balances increasing or decreasing in the nominal interest rate?]

17. Explain why the Fed can either target the nominal interest rate, as it does today, or the money supply, as it did before the 1980s, but not both.

42.2   The Approximate Price of Money

We showed in the previous section that the relative price of money is a nonlinear function of the nominal interest rate bounded between zero and one. While in principle the nominal interest rate can take any nonnegative value, in low-inflation environments, the nominal interest rate is very small.

1. Draw a detailed graph of the relative price of real cash balances—expression (42.4)—as a function of the nominal interest rate, i_t.
[Hint: You already know its value at $i_t = 0$]

2. We are interested in approximating the relative price around $i_t = 0$ since that is the value around which i_t usually hovers. Take the derivative of $f(i_t)$ and evaluate it at $i_t = 0$.

3. What is the slope of the line tangent to $f(0)$?

4. You have a point and you have a slope. Write down the equation of the line tangent to $f(i_t)$ at $i_t = 0$.

5. Do an online search for the current effective federal funds rate, the nominal interest rate that banks charge for overnight loans. Is i_t in this case close to zero?
[Hint: Recall that interest rates are often quoted as a percentage; don't forget to convert it to a decimal.]

6. Evaluate $f(i_t)$ and the tangent line you derived in question 4 using the federal funds rate you found above. How close are the two values?

7. What is the relative price of real cash balances when the nominal interest rate is small?

43 A Simple Model of Inflation

Since 2012 the Federal Reserve has had an explicit inflation target of 2 percent. This means that the Fed chooses monetary policy with the aim of keeping inflation at 2 percent. Of course, the Fed cannot control inflation perfectly. Because inflation is subject to random fluctuations—i.e., inflation is a random variable—some months it will be higher than 2 percent while some months it will come in lower. Assume that the Fed's inflation target means that inflation follows the following process:

$$\pi_t = \alpha + \sigma \varepsilon_t \tag{43.1}$$

where α and σ are constants, while ε_t is a random variable. ε_t captures the random factors that affect inflation and that are beyond the Fed's control. For simplicity, we assume that ε_t can take only two values, with equal probability:

$$\varepsilon_t = \begin{cases} 1 & \text{with probability } 0.5 \\ -1 & \text{with probability } 0.5 \end{cases}$$

1. What is the average value of ε_t? This is also called the *expected value* of ε_t or the *expectation* of ε_t. We denote the expectation of ε_t as $\mathrm{E}[\varepsilon_t]$.

2. We write $\Pr(\varepsilon_t = 1) = 0.5$ to say that "the probability that $\varepsilon_t = 1$ is one half." If, instead of one half, $\Pr(\varepsilon_t = 1) = 0.6$, how would the expected value of ε_t change?
[Hint: Think of a rigged coin that is now more likely to land "heads."]

3. Write down the two possible values that inflation can take as a function of α and σ.

4. What happens to these two values as σ increases?

5. Consider original case, where $\Pr(\varepsilon_t = 1) = 0.5$. What is the expected value of inflation as a function of α and σ?

6. Given your answer above, what is the economic interpretation of α?

7. Given your answer above, what numerical value should we assign to α?

44 A Not-So-Simple Model of Inflation

We showed in chapter 40, "The Printing Press," that today's expectations about *future* inflation can affect today's inflation rate. In the simple model of inflation from chapter 43 this was not the case: inflation depended only on the Fed's inflation target and a random component. Let's amend equation (43.1) from that model by including an expectations term:

$$\pi_t = \alpha + \theta \pi^e_{t+1} + \sigma \varepsilon_t \tag{44.1}$$

where π_t is the [net] inflation rate, α, θ, and σ are constants, π^e_{t+1} is expected inflation, and ε_t is a random component.

44.1 Expectations

In order to make progress we need to take a stand on how agents form expectations. During the 2010 Fifa World Cup, for example, an octopus called Paul would predict the winner ahead of each match in the knockout round by eating from the bowl marked with the flag of one of the teams. His predictions were so accurate that many fans actually placed bets based on Paul's choices. "Paul the Octopus," however, is hardly a sensible way to model expectations for the whole economy. The standard assumption in economics, which we will adopt in this problem, is that expectations are *rational*:

$$\pi^e_{t+1} = \mathrm{E}[\pi_{t+1}]$$

where $\mathrm{E}[\cdot]$ is the *mathematical* expectations operator. In words, the *rational expectations hypothesis* says that agents form their expectations about future variables by calculating the *expected value* of those variables *in equilibrium*.

1. Offer a brief interpretation of θ in equation (44.1).

2. Offer a brief interpretation of the difference:

$$\pi^e_{t+1} - \pi_{t+1} \tag{44.2}$$

3. Offer a brief interpretation of the expectation:

$$E[\pi_{t+1}^e - \pi_{t+1}] \tag{44.3}$$

4. The *law of iterated expectations* says that the expectation of the expectation is simply the expectation: $E[E[\pi_{t+1}]] = E[\pi_{t+1}]$. Apply the law of iterated expectations to show that under the hypothesis of *rational expectations* expression (44.3) is equal to zero. Offer a brief interpretation of this result.

5. What data would you need, and how would you proceed with those data to test the result you derived above?

Figure 44.1 displays inflation and inflation expectations according to two different methods of eliciting expectations. The top two panels display inflation expectations according to the Michigan Survey. This survey asks a representative sample of American consumers every month to forecast the inflation rate over the following year. They then report the *median* response as the aggregate expected inflation rate. The bottom two panels display inflation expectations according to the Federal Reserve Bank of Cleveland's market-based measure. Economists at the Cleveland Fed infer the expected inflation rate by looking at the difference between the market yields of nominal and real bonds.

Panel (a) plots expected inflation according to the Michigan Survey and actual inflation as measured by the PCEPI. Panel (b) plots the difference between the two. Panel (c) plots expected inflation according to the Cleveland Fed and actual inflation as measured by the PCEPI. Panel (d) plots the difference between the two.

6. What expression from the previous questions is plotted in panels (b) and (d)?

7. If possible, use figure 44.1 to qualitatively assess whether the forecast errors are, on average, zero. Otherwise, explain what additional data you would need to make your assessment.

44.2   Guess

The difficulty in solving equation (44.1) under the rational expectations hypothesis is that expectations about future inflation will affect how inflation behaves in equilibrium. Yet, at the same time, the behavior of inflation in equilibrium determines how expectations are formed. To overcome this apparent circularity, we will solve this problem using the method of guess and check. Assume that ε can take only the following two values:

$$\varepsilon_t = \begin{cases} 1 & \text{with probability } 0.5 \\ -1 & \text{with probability } 0.5 \end{cases}$$

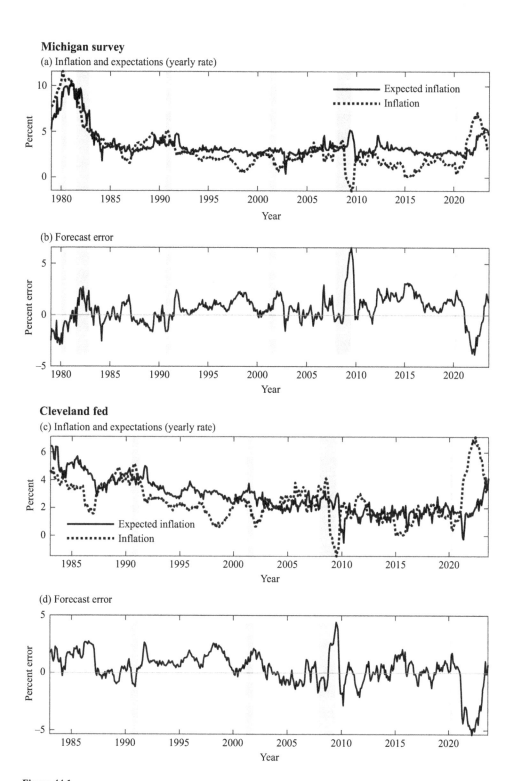

Figure 44.1
Inflation, inflation expectations, and forecast errors. *Sources*: University of Michigan Survey Research Center, Federal Reserve Bank of Cleveland, and US Bureau of Economic Analysis.

In everything that follows we will make two assumptions. The first is that expectations are rational; when we refer to expectations we mean the mathematical mean. The second is that θ can only take values between zero and one.

1. Does knowing anything about ε_t today help us in predicting ε_{t+1} tomorrow?
[Hint: Think of consecutive coin tosses.]

2. Evaluate $E[\varepsilon_{t+1}]$.

3. Consider how inflation tomorrow π_{t+1} will be determined:

$$\pi_{t+1} = \alpha + \theta \pi_{t+2}^e + \sigma \varepsilon_{t+1} \tag{44.4}$$

Take the expectations of both sides to show that the expected inflation tomorrow depends on the expected inflation the day after tomorrow according to the following equation:

$$E[\pi_{t+1}] = \alpha + \theta \, E[\pi_{t+2}^e] \tag{44.5}$$

4. Write down what the term $E[\pi_{t+2}^e]$ means *in words*.
[Hint: This is the expectation of an expectation. Think of it as the forecast of a forecast.]

We will now guess that inflation expectations are constant across time and we denote that constant by λ.

$$\pi_{t+j}^e = E[\pi_{t+j}] = \lambda$$

for *any* horizon j.

5. Substitute our guess about inflation expectations into equation (44.5) and solve for λ.

6. What happens to λ as θ gets closer to zero?

7. What happens to λ as θ gets closer to one?

44.3   Check

We will now check our solution for what inflation expectations are, given our guess. To do this we must verify that when inflation expectations are given by

$$\lambda = \frac{\alpha}{1 - \theta} \tag{44.6}$$

the *expected value* of inflation is also equal to $\frac{\alpha}{(1-\theta)}$.

1. Combine the solution to our guess, equation (44.6), with equation (44.1) to show that inflation is given by:

$$\pi_t = \frac{\alpha}{1 - \theta} + \sigma \varepsilon_t \tag{44.7}$$

2. Take the expectations of both sides of equation (44.7) to show that the average rate of inflation is

$$E[\pi_t] = \frac{\alpha}{1-\theta}$$

How does this compare to the expected inflation rate?

We have verified that our guess is correct. The mathematical expectations that are implied by our guess that inflation expectations are constant are *the same* as the expected inflation that constant expectations imply.

3. Graph the average rate of inflation as a function of θ.

4. On *average* what happens to inflation as θ gets closer to zero?

5. On *average* what happens to inflation as θ gets closer to one?

6. Recall that θ determines how sensitive inflation is to expectations. If inflation becomes more sensitive to expectations, what happens to its average value?

References

Bray, M. (1982). Learning, estimation and stability of rational expectations. *Journal of Economic Theory, 26*(2), 318–339.

Sargent, T. (1993). *Bounded rationality in macroeconomics*. Oxford: Oxford University Press.

45 Logs and Expectations

We showed in chapter 3, "What's so Natural About the Natural Log?," that when a net rate, r, is small, the log of the gross rate, $R \equiv 1 + r$, is approximately equal to the net rate:

$$\log(R) = r$$

Oftentimes, these rates are random variables. Think of the inflation rate, the growth rate of output or the real interest rate—all random variables. When rates are random, we can't take the log of R; the best we can do is take the log of its *expected value*, $E[R]$. Which gives rise to the question: Does the log of the expected value of the gross rate, $\log(E[R])$, equal the expected value of the net rate, $E[r]$? We will show here that when the expected value of the net rate is small, the answer is *yes*.

Suppose that net real interest rate, r, is a random variable that can take two values, high or low:

$$r = \begin{cases} r_h & \text{with probability } p \\ r_\ell & \text{with probability } 1 - p \end{cases}$$

where $r_h > r_\ell$ and r_h is small enough so that $\log(1 + r_h) = r_h$.

1. Write down the two values that the gross real interest rate, R, can take and their respective probabilities.

2. Write down the *expected value* of the gross real interest rate as a function of p, r_h, and r_ℓ.

3. Rearrange your answer above to show that:

$$E[R] = 1 + E[r] \tag{45.1}$$

4. What is the upper bound on $E[r]$? What is the lower bound on $E[r]$?
[Hint: Consider the extreme values of the probabilities.]

5. Given your answer above, explain why, if $\log(1 + r_h) = r_h$, then:

$$\log(E[1 + r]) = E[r] = E[\log(1 + r)]$$

46 The Taylor Principle

Modern central banks conduct conventional monetary policy by setting a short-term nominal interest rate. Among them are the Federal Reserve, the European Central Bank, the Bank of England, and the Bank of Japan. In this chapter, we will trace the transmission mechanism from monetary policy—the nominal interest rate—to inflation.

46.1 From the Real to the Nominal Interest Rate

We begin with two equilibrium relationships from previous results. The first is a no arbitrage condition in the bond market between real and nominal bonds:

$$i_t = r_t + \pi_{t+1}^e \tag{46.1}$$

The second is the household's optimality condition between present and future consumption:

$$\frac{u'(C_t)}{\beta u'(C_{t+1})} = 1 + r_t \tag{46.2}$$

where $u'(C)$ denotes the derivative of the per-period utility of consumption and β is the discount factor.

1. What is the name of equation (46.1)?

2. What is the name of equation (46.2)?

3. What is the name of the left-hand side of equation (46.2)?

4. What is the name of the right-hand side of equation (46.2)?

We now assume that per period utility is logarithmic $u(C) = \log C$.

5. Show that under logarithmic utility, we can rewrite equation (46.2) as

$$(1 + r_t)\beta = \frac{C_{t+1}^e}{C_t} \tag{46.3}$$

Note that we have replaced future consumption, C_{t+1}, with *expected* future consumption C^e_{t+1} since the future is uncertain.

6. What is the right-hand side of equation (46.3)?

7. Take the log of both sides of equation (46.3).

Now suppose that the net growth rate of consumption is given by

$$\log(C^e_{t+1}) - \log(C_t) \equiv \gamma + \chi \varepsilon_t \tag{46.4}$$

where γ and χ are constants and ε_t is a random variable that can take two values:

$$\varepsilon_t = \begin{cases} 1 & \text{with probability } 0.5 \\ -1 & \text{with probability } 0.5 \end{cases}$$

8. Offer a few reasons why the expected growth rate of consumption might be a random variable.

9. Offer a brief economic interpretation of γ.

10. Offer a brief economic interpretation of χ.

11. If χ increases, what happens to possible values that the expected growth rate of consumption can take?

12. Let $\rho \equiv -\log(\beta)$ denote the rate of time preference and show that we can rewrite the equilibrium net real interest rate as a function of only ρ and the expected net growth rate of consumption:

$$r_t = \rho + \gamma + \chi \varepsilon_t \tag{46.5}$$

[Hint: You have already taken the log of the Euler equation.]

13. If households discount the future, is ρ positive or negative?

14. Combine equations (46.5) and (46.1) to show that the nominal interest rate is a function of households' discount rate, expected consumption growth, and inflation expectations:

$$i_t = \rho + \gamma + \chi \varepsilon_t + \pi^e_{t+1} \tag{46.6}$$

15. If ε_t is a random variable, what is also be true of the nominal interest rate?

46.2 From the Nominal Interest Rate to Inflation

The central bank conducts monetary policy by setting the nominal interest rate. We assume that the central bank sets the nominal interest rate in *response* to the inflation rate according to the following rule:

$$i_t = \phi \pi_t \tag{46.7}$$

We call equation (46.7) the central bank's *monetary policy rule*.

1. Offer an economic interpretation of ϕ.

2. Equations (46.6) and (46.7) are both equilibrium relationships of the nominal interest rate. Show that this implies the following equilibrium expression of inflation:

$$\pi_t = \left(\frac{\rho + \gamma}{\phi}\right) + \left(\frac{1}{\phi}\right)\pi_{t+1}^e + \left(\frac{\chi}{\phi}\right)\varepsilon_t \qquad (46.8)$$

3. What variable determines the influence that *inflation expectations* have on inflation? Can this variable be adjusted by policymakers?

The equation you derived above should look a lot like equation (44.1) in "A Not-So-Simple Model of Inflation":

$$\pi_t = \alpha + \theta\pi_{t+1}^e + \sigma\varepsilon_t$$

Recall that, under the rational expectations hypothesis, we showed that in equilibrium inflation expectations are constant and equal to:

$$E_t[\pi_{t+1}] = \frac{\alpha}{1 - \theta}$$

We can draw on these results to solve for the rational expectations equilibrium in the current model.

4. What is the relationship between ϕ in equation (46.8) and θ in equation (44.1)? [Hint: We want to write θ as a function of ϕ.]

5. Write α in (44.1) as a function of ϕ, ρ, and γ. [Hint: Which terms in equation (46.8) corresponds to α in equation (44.1)?]

6. Given your answers above, explain why inflation expectations from the "Not-So-Simple Model of Inflation" must apply to this model as well.

7. Show that under the rational expectations hypothesis, inflation expectations in this model are given by:

$$E_t[\pi_{t+1}] = \frac{\rho + \gamma}{\phi - 1}$$

8. Show that under the rational expectations hypothesis, equilibrium inflation is given by:

$$\pi_t = \frac{\rho + \gamma}{\phi - 1} + \left(\frac{\chi}{\phi}\right)\varepsilon_t \qquad (46.9)$$

9. Graph inflation expectations $E_t[\pi_{t+1}]$ as a function of the Fed's policy stance, ϕ. What happens to inflation expectations when ϕ gets closer to one? What about when ϕ gets unboundedly large? [Hint: Expectations should be on the y axis while ϕ should be on the x axis.]

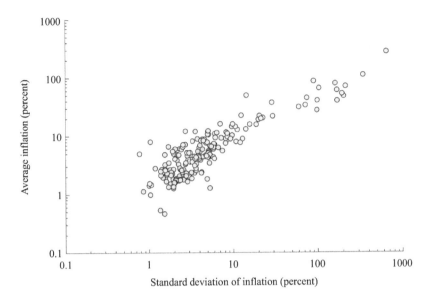

Figure 46.1
Average inflation and the standard deviation of inflation across the world (log scale). *Source*: World Bank.

10. What happens to the sensitivity of inflation to *expected inflation* as ϕ increases?

11. One of the mandates of the Federal Reserve is to maintain *price* stability in the United States. If the Federal Reserve follows a monetary policy rule similar to (46.7), would you recommend that it choose a ϕ that is close to one or very large? Use your answer to the previous question to justify your recommendation.

12. What is the lower bound on ϕ that is required for inflation to remain finite? This inequality is called the *Taylor Principle*.

13. Graph inflation, π_t, as a function of the Fed's policy stance, ϕ, for each of the two possible values of ε_t: when $\varepsilon_t = 1$ and when $\varepsilon_t = -1$. What happens to the two possible inflation outcomes when ϕ gets closer to one? What about when ϕ gets unboundedly large? [Hint: You are graphing *two* curves. Inflation should be on the y axis while ϕ should be on the x axis.]

14. Equation (46.9) and your graph from the previous question imply a relationship between *average* inflation and how variable inflation is. What is the effect of choosing a high ϕ on the variability of inflation?

15. Figure 46.1 plots the average inflation between 1960 and 2022 of several countries against the standard deviation—a measure of variability—of inflation. Is the correlation in figure 46.1 consistent with equation (46.9)? If no, explain what correlation is implied by

equation (46.9). If yes, explain what variable in equation (46.9) causes the correlation in the data.

16. The average [net] growth rate of consumption in the US over the past 150 years has been around 2 percent. The discount factor, β, is around 0.99. In 2012, the Fed announced that it would target 2 percent average inflation. Assuming that inflation behaves according to equation (46.9) calculate the value of ϕ that the Fed must choose in order to meet its inflation target.

References

Taylor, J. (1993). Discretion versus policy rules in practice. *Carnegie-Rochester Conference Series on Public Policy, 39*, 195–214.

Woodford, M. (2003). *Interest and prices*. Princeton: Princeton University Press.

47 Fiscal Shocks

Government purchases fluctuate from year to year. Random factors—sometimes large like Covid, sometimes small like cost overruns on a new weapons system—affect the government's expenditures on goods and services. Despite these fluctuations, however, "core" government purchases remain stable. In this chapter we want to understand how fluctuations of government purchases affect output, consumption, and inflation.

Consider a competitive economy with a representative firm, a representative household, and the government. The firm hires labor, L_t, from the household and produces output, Y_t. The household sells labor to the firm and buys some of the firm's output, C_t. The firm sells the remaining output, G_t, to the government.

While the level of government purchases is random, it fluctuates around its average value, $\bar{G}$. This implies a corresponding average value of consumption, $\bar{C}$, and output, $\bar{Y}$. We will refer to these values as the steady-state values of government purchases, consumption, and output, respectively.

47.1   The Real Impact of Fiscal Shocks

1. Let $\gamma \equiv \bar{G}/\bar{Y}$ denote the steady-state fraction of output purchased by the government. Write down the fraction of output purchased by the household in terms of γ.

2. For $X = Y$, C, G define the fluctuations around the steady-state, $\tilde{x}$, implicitly as:

$$X_t = (1 + \tilde{x}_t)\bar{X}$$

Give an economic interpretation of $\tilde{x}_t$. What are its units?

3. Write the market-clearing condition in the goods market. Label which side corresponds to output and which side corresponds to aggregate demand.

4. Subtract the steady-state market-clearing condition from your market-clearing above and divide both sides by the steady-state level of output.

5. Show that you can write your equation above in terms of the fluctuations terms as:

$$\tilde{y}_t = (1-\gamma)\tilde{c}_t + \gamma\tilde{g}_t \tag{47.1}$$

We now turn to the labor market.

6. The firm produces output according to the following production function:

$$Y_t = AL_t$$

Write down the firm's marginal product of labor.

7. The household's marginal rate of substitution between consumption and labor is $C_t L_t^{1/\varepsilon}$, where $\varepsilon > 0$ is the *Frisch elasticity* of labor supply. Write down the market-clearing condition in the labor market.

8. Combine the market-clearing condition with the production function to get the following equilibrium relationship between consumption and output:

$$C_t Y_t^{1/\varepsilon} = A^{(\varepsilon+1)/\varepsilon} \tag{47.2}$$

9. The condition above holds in all cases, in particular at the steady state. Substitute the steady-state values into (47.2) to derive an expression for the steady state level of output:

$$(1-\gamma)\bar{Y}^{(1+\varepsilon)/\varepsilon} = A^{(1+\varepsilon)/\varepsilon} \tag{47.3}$$

[Hint: After substituting the steady-state values, $\bar{Y}$ and $\bar{C}$, divide both sides by $\bar{Y}$.]

10. Rewrite equation (47.2) in terms of the fluctuation terms $\tilde{c}_t$ and $\tilde{y}_t$. Show that when $\tilde{c}_t$ and $\tilde{y}_t$ are close to zero, we can write the fluctuations of consumption as a function of the fluctuations in output:

$$\tilde{c}_t = -\left(\frac{1}{\varepsilon}\right)\tilde{y}_t \tag{47.4}$$

[Hint: Begin by combining equations (47.2) and (47.3). Another hint: What does $\log(1+x)$ equal when x is close to zero?]

We now have an equilibrium condition from the goods market, equation (47.1), and from the labor market, (47.4).

11. Combine the two equilibrium conditions to get an expression for $\tilde{y}_t$ as a function of $\tilde{g}_t$.

12. We call $\tilde{g}_t$ *fiscal shocks*. Offer an educated guess as to why.

13. We can define the fiscal expenditure multiplier, μ, *at the steady state* as the deviations in output from its steady state over the deviations in government purchases from their steady state:

$$\mu \equiv \frac{Y_t - \bar{Y}}{G_t - \bar{G}}$$

Rewrite μ in terms of $\tilde{y}_t$ and the fiscal shock, $\tilde{g}_t$.

14. We have the equilibrium relationship between $\tilde{y}_t$ and $\tilde{g}_t$, and the definition of the government expenditure multiplier. Combine the two to show that:

$$\mu = \frac{\varepsilon}{\varepsilon + 1 - \gamma} \tag{47.5}$$

15. μ is bounded above and below, what is the maximum value it can take? How about the minimum value?

16. Set up a coordinate plane with μ on the y axis and ε on the x axis. Graph the fiscal expenditure multiplier, μ, as a function of the elasticity of labor supply, ε.

17. Is μ increasing or decreasing in ε? Offer an economic explanation for this result.

18. Set up a coordinate plane with μ on the y axis and γ of the x axis. Graph the fiscal expenditure multiplier, μ, as a function of the relative fraction of aggregate demand due to government purchases, γ.

19. What happens to the multiplier as γ increases? Offer a brief economic explanation for this result.

47.2   The Nominal Impact of Fiscal Shocks

To analyze the nominal effects of fiscal shocks we need to introduce another agent , the central bank, and another market, the bond market.

No arbitrage between the nominal and real bond markets in equilibrium gives us the Fisher equation:

$$i_t = r_t + E_t[\pi_{t+1}]$$

The household chooses its intertemporal consumption allocation according to the Euler equation with rational expectations:

$$\frac{E_t[C_{t+1}]}{C_t} = \beta(1 + r_t)$$

1. Rewrite the left-hand side of the Euler equation in terms of consumption fluctuations $\tilde{c}_{t+1}$ and $\tilde{c}_t$.

2. Take the logs of your answer above and combine it with the Fisher equation to get the following:

$$E_t[\tilde{c}_{t+1}] - \tilde{c}_t = i_t - E_t[\pi_{t+1}] - \rho \tag{47.6}$$

where $\rho = -\log\beta$ is the rate of time preference.
[Hint: Recall that $\log(E[1 + x]) = E[x]$ when $E[x]$ is small.]

3. In the previous section we derived the equilibrium relationship between output and consumption fluctuations. Show that we can instead rewrite consumption fluctuations as a function of the fiscal shock: $\tilde{c}_t = (-\mu\gamma/\varepsilon)\tilde{g}_t$.

We now turn to the central bank. The central bank conducts monetary policy according to the following rule:

$$i_t = \rho + \phi\pi_t \tag{47.7}$$

4. If the central bank conducts monetary policy according to the Taylor principle, what is the lower bound on ϕ?

5. Combine the central bank's monetary policy rule with equation (47.6) to get the following equilibrium expression for inflation:

$$\pi_t = \frac{1}{\phi} E_t[\pi_{t+1}] + \left(\frac{\mu\gamma}{\phi\varepsilon}\right)(\tilde{g}_t - E_t[\tilde{g}_{t+1}]) \tag{47.8}$$

6. Write down the average value of $\tilde{g}_{t+1}$.
[Hint: Use the definition of $\tilde{g}$ and the fact that the average value of G_t is $\bar{G}$.]

7. Assume $E_t[\tilde{g}_{t+1}] = 0$. What is the economic meaning of this assumption?
[Hint: Recall that the expectation is taken with the information available at time t.]

8. Substitute the assumption above into equation (47.8). Apply the result from "A Not-So-Simple Model of Inflation" to show that the rational expectations solution to this equation is:

$$E_t[\pi_{t+1}] = 0 \tag{47.9}$$

9. What happens to inflation in the case of an unexpected increase in government purchases?

10. Appropriations bills—the laws that determine $\tilde{g}_t$—are often, though not always, separate from tax bills. If taxes remain constant what happens to the primary deficit in the case of a positive fiscal shock?

11. Some economists argue the large fiscal deficits during, and after, the Covid-19 pandemic contributed to the spike in inflation that followed. Explain whether this model is consistent with that view.

Suppose that the current fiscal shock is zero, $\tilde{g}_t = 0$, but an appropriations bill passed *today* has provisions for an increase in government spending in the future, $E_t[\tilde{g}_{t+1}] > 0$. Further, suppose that this will be a one-time increase so that going forward, we expect once again to be at the steady state, $E_t[\tilde{g}_{t+2}] = 0$.

12. Explain why $E_t[\pi_{t+2}] = 0$.
[Hint: Iterate equation (47.8) one period forward and solve it from the standpoint of $t + 1$.]

13. Given your answer above, show that:

$$E_t[\pi_{t+1}] = \frac{\mu\gamma}{\phi\varepsilon}\tilde{g}_{t+1} \tag{47.10}$$

14. Substitute your answer above into (47.8) to derive the following expression of inflation:

$$\pi_t = \frac{1}{\phi}\left(\frac{1}{\phi} - 1\right)\left(\frac{\mu\gamma}{\varepsilon}\right)\tilde{g}_{t+1} \tag{47.11}$$

15. What happens to the inflation rate today if agents expect government purchases in the future to increase? Give a brief economic explanation for this result.

16. We have interpreted $\tilde{g}$ as a shock, unrelated to any other economic variables. What type of government spending best fits this description?

Reference

Woodford, M. (2011). Simple analytics of the government expenditure multiplier. *American Economic Journal: Macroeconomics, 3*(1), 1–35.

48 Currency Pegs

When a country sets a fixed exchange rate between its own and a foreign currency we call it a *currency peg*. Pegs can be "soft" or "hard." Under a soft peg the exchange rate can fluctuate freely within a fixed range, but always remains within it. China, for example, maintains a soft peg against the US dollar. Under a hard peg, there is no range; the exchange rate is fixed at a single value. In the 1990s, as a precursor to the creation of the Euro, members of the European Union set up the European Exchange Rate Mechanism (EERM). All currencies in the EERM maintained a hard peg against the now-defunct Deutschmark, Germany's currency at the time. The most extreme form of peg happens when countries adopt a foreign currency altogether. The US dollar is the official currency in both Panama and Ecuador.

Why do countries peg their currencies? What are the consequences of doing so? And how can pegs fail? To answer these questions, we will take the point of view of a small open economy in relation to the international currency, the US dollar.

48.1   Interest and Exchange Rates

Consider two open economies, one foreign and one domestic. We will conduct our analysis from the perspective of the domestic economy, and use the superscript ^{f} to denote the foreign economy. Both economies have access to international financial markets and share the same net real interest rate, r. They also trade freely so that the law of one price holds:

$$P_t = X_t P_t^f \tag{48.1}$$

where P_t denotes domestic prices (in domestic currency), X_t is the exchange rate, and P_t^f denotes foreign prices.

1. Suppose that the domestic country's currency is the peso and the foreign country's currency is the US dollar, what are the units of X_t?

2. Define $\pi_{t+1} \equiv \log(P_{t+1}/P_t)$. What is π_{t+1}?

3. Let $x_t \equiv \log(X_t)$. Show that the law of one price, equation (48.1), implies

$$E_t[\pi_{t+1}] - E_t[\pi_{t+1}^f] = E_t[x_{t+1}] - x_t \qquad (48.2)$$

where $E_t[\pi_{t+1}]$ denotes the current expected value of future inflation and $E_t[x_{t+1}]$ is the current expected future log exchange rate.

[Hint: The law of one price holds in all time periods. Another hint: Recall that when fluctuations are small, $\log(E[\cdot]) = E[\log(\cdot)]$.]

4. Recall the Fisher equation

$$i_t = r_t + E_t[\pi_{t+1}].$$

Explain why the Fisher equation must hold in both countries. Which variables are the same in both, which are different?

5. Use your answer above to show that:

$$i_t - E_t[\pi_{t+1}] = i_t^f - E_t[\pi_{t+1}^f] \qquad (48.3)$$

6. Combine your results above to derive the following relationship between nominal interest rates and exchange rates:

$$i_t - i_t^f = E_t[x_{t+1}] - x_t$$

We now consider what happens if the domestic country decides to peg its currency. The country announces at time t that it will fix the exchange rate at $\bar{X}$ for all future periods.

7. Show that this requires the following monetary policy rule:

$$i_t = i_t^f \qquad (48.4)$$

8. If the domestic country adopts the US dollar, who ultimately conducts monetary policy for the domestic economy if the peg is implemented?

9. Given your answer above, explain why common currency areas like the Eurozone are equivalent to a strict currency peg. What is the fixed exchange rate in the Eurozone between each country?

[Hint: They all use the same currency.]

10. Offer a few reasons why countries might prefer to adopt a common currency rather than peg their currency.

11. Show that by adopting the peg, the expected inflation rate of the domestic economy will match that of the foreign economy:

$$E_t[\pi_{t+1}] = E_t[\pi_{t+1}^f] \qquad (48.5)$$

12. Given your answer above, why might countries with high inflation on average choose to peg their currency to currencies from countries with low average inflation?

13. Notice that our result that the domestic country must give up control over monetary policy, equation (48.4), arises from the fact that the real interest rate is the same in both countries, equation (48.3). This is, yet again, a no-arbitrage condition. If the domestic real interest rate was higher than the world real interest rate, what would international investors do?

14. *Capital controls* are restrictions that limit the movement of capital between domestic and international markets. Are investors able to arbitrage differences in the real interest rate if a government imposes capital controls?

15. Given your answers above, if a government wanted to peg its currency but retain monetary policy independence, what would it have to impose?

This is known as the *Mundell-Fleming trilemma*. It says that a government can pursue only two of the following three policies simultaneously: open capital markets, a currency peg, or an independent monetary policy.

48.2   Don't Cry for Me Argentina

Argentina first pegged its currency to the US dollar in 1991 after hyperinflation in 1989 led to a 3,000 percent increase in prices. Figure 48.1 tells the story of the Argentine peg. As panel (a) shows, inflation quickly came down and began tracking US inflation until the peg was abandoned in 2001. The fallout from the failure of the peg was severe. Between December 21, 2001—the day the peg was abandoned—and January 2, 2002, Argentina went through five different presidents. In the previous section we analyzed the first half of figure 48.1: the reasons for and consequences of adopting a peg. In this section we consider the second half: the reasons for and consequences of abandoning it.

1. Given the inflation rate of Argentina before 1991, use the analysis from the previous section to explain why Argentina might have decided to peg its currency to the US dollar.

2. What happened to the average inflation rate of Argentina after adopting the peg? Explain whether the evolution of inflation after adopting the peg is consistent with the analysis from the previous section.

3. After implementing the peg Argentina ran large current account deficits and its foreign debt rose from 62.4 billion dollars in 1990 to 152.2 billion dollars in 2000. Use figure 48.1 to explain why this increase in foreign debt is both real and nominal.
[Hint: Think about the exchange and inflation rates during this period.]

By the start of 2001, Argentina's fiscal position was precarious. With tax revenues unable to pay its foreign debt, Argentina turned to the International Monetary Fund as a lender of last resort. In 2001, the IMF extended a credit line of $14.4 billion, more than twice the $5.5 billion credit line it had offered in 2000. Argentina was desperate for funds, and it became clear to Argentines and foreigners alike that the government would be forced to rely on *seigniorage*—the inflation tax—as an additional source of revenue.

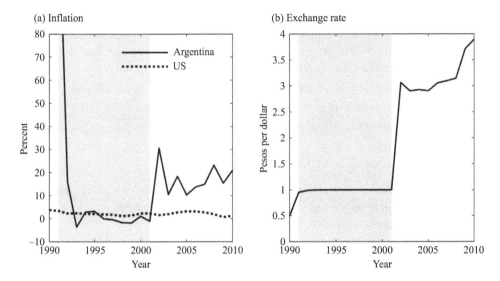

Figure 48.1
(a) Inflation rates in Argentina and the United States, according to the GDP deflator. (b) Peso to dollar exchange rate. Shaded region denotes the years the peg was in effect. *Source*: World Bank.

In what follows, we will analyze the unraveling of the Argentine peg from the perspective of investors at the *start* of 2001, before the peg was abandoned. We will assume that the peg remained in force throughout 2001 and was abandoned in 2002. Let t denote 2001 and $t + 1$, 2002. To minimize the algebraic clutter we will assume that the expected inflation rate in the US at the time was zero: $E_t[\pi_{t+1}^f] = 0$. As before, US variables are denoted with a superscript ^{f} while Argentine variables have no superscript.

4. Argentina set the exchange rate at 1. Show that $x_t = 0$ and $i_t = i_t^f$.
[Hint: Panel (b) of figure 48.1]

5. Explain why the expectation of seigniorage implies $E_t[\pi_{t+1}] > 0$.

6. Substitute your answers above into equation (48.2) to show:

$$E_t[\pi_{t+1}] = E_t[x_{t+1}] > 0 \tag{48.6}$$

Explain in words the economic implication of the above inequality.

7. Suppose you are an investor in 2001 and you decide to buy dollars and invest in US bonds. Show that your rate of return is:

$$R^f = \frac{1 + i_t}{X_t}$$

8. Alternatively, you can invest in Argentine bonds and then buy dollars after they pay out in 2002. Show that in that case your rate of return is:

$$R = E_t \left[\frac{1 + i_t}{X_{t+1}} \right]$$

9. Explain why $R^f > R$. Even though both investment strategies give a dollar return, which investment strategy will you pursue?

[Hint: Recall that $X_t = 1$ by law. Another hint: Do you expect X_{t+1} to remain at one?]

10. Explain why maintaining the peg in 2001 creates an arbitrage opportunity and how investors can exploit it. If the currency wasn't pegged, what would happen to X_t as investors tried to arbitrage the two rates of return?

11. The demand for dollars in Argentina went up in 2001. Yet the peg kept the price fixed at $X_t = 1$. Given the increase in the demand for dollars, would private investors be willing to sell dollars at the official exchange rate or would they demand a higher "black market" price?

12. Who would have to to step in and sell dollars at the official exchange rate?

13. In order to satisfy demand for dollars at the official exchange rate the Argentine government began selling its own dollar reserves to investors. Explain why this strategy to keep the exchange rate at one could not be sustained indefinitely.

[Hint: Over the course of 2001, the Argentine government lost over \$10 billion in dollar reserves.]

14. Consider figure 48.1(a) once more. Did inflation jump before or after the peg was abandoned? Is our model consistent with the timing of inflation?

15. Many Argentines today blame the abandonment of the peg for the ensuing inflation. Explain whether this view is consistent with our model.

References

Fleming, J. (1962). Domestic financial policies under fixed and under floating exchange rates. *IMF Staff Papers*, *9*(3), 369–380.

Krugman, P. (1979). A model of balance-of-payments crises. *Journal of Money, Credit and Banking, 11*(3), 311–325.

Mundell, R. (1963). Capital mobility and stabilization policy under fixed and flexible exchange rates. *Canadian Journal Journal of Economics and Political Science, 29*(4), 475–485.

Obstfeld, M., & K. Rogoff (1995). Exchange rate dynamics redux. *Journal of Political Economy, 103*(3), 624–660.

Obstfeld, R., J. Shambaugh, & A. Taylor (2005). The trilemma in history: Tradeoffs among exchange rates, monetary policies and capital mobility. *Review of Economics and Statistics, 87*, 423–438.

49 The Great Capitol Hill Babysitting Co-op Crisis

Recall the babysitting co-op of Capitol Hill from chapter 39. Young couples working as congressional staffers on Capitol Hill organized to babysit for each other. The novel feature of the co-op was that, rather than trade hours of babysitting for hours of babysitting directly, the couples traded hours of babysitting for vouchers. Any couple holding vouchers could use them to pay another couple to babysit their children. When we first analyzed it, however, I was not entirely forthcoming in my description of the co-op. I left out one additional rule: *each voucher was redeemable for one and only one hour of babysitting*. To determine the significance of this rule, we will compare the co-op as we analyzed it in chapter 39 and the co-op as it actually operated. As shorthand, we will refer to the former as the *classical co-op* and the latter as the *Keynesian co-op*.

49.1 Money and Prices

1. What does the rule imply about P_t in the Keynesian co-op?

2. We derived the following equilibrium relationship between prices and vouchers in the Classical co-op:

$$P_t = \lambda M_t \tag{49.1}$$

where $\lambda > 0$. Graph this relationship.
[Hint: Prices should be on the y axis, vouchers on the x axis.]

3. What is the equilibrium relationship between prices and vouchers in the Keynesian co-op? Graph this relationship.

4. Explain how the behavior of *prices* in the Keynesian co-op differs from that in the classical co-op.

5. What is the equilibrium relationship between real cash balances, M_t/P_t, and vouchers in the classical co-op? Graph this relationship.
[Hint: What does equation (49.1) imply?]

6. What is the relationship between real cash balances and vouchers in the Keynesian co-op? Graph this relationship.

7. Comment on how the behavior of *real cash balances* in the Keynesian co-op differs from that in the classical co-op.

49.2   The Keynesian Co-op

Let's reconsider the Sweeneys, now in the Keynesian co-op. Once again, for simplicity, we model the Sweeneys as living for two periods and maximizing the following utility function:

$$u(C_t, H_t) + \beta u(C_{t+1}, H_{t+1})$$

where $\{C_t, C_{t+1}\}$ denotes the allocation of hours of babysitting the Sweeneys *demand* in each period and $\{H_t, H_{t+1}\}$ denotes the allocation of hours of babysitting the Sweeneys *supply* in each period. The per-period utility function, $u(\cdot)$, is given by:

$$u(C_t, H_t) = \log(C_t) - \frac{H_t^{1+\phi}}{1+\phi}$$

1. Show that the budget constraint for the Sweeneys in period $t+1$ is given by:

$$C_{t+1} = M_t + H_{t+1} \tag{49.2}$$

2. Write down the marginal rate of substitution between C_{t+1} and H_{t+1}.

3. Write down the marginal rate of transformation between C_{t+1} and H_{t+1}.

4. Write down the optimality condition between C_{t+1} and H_{t+1}.

5. The optimality condition in the classical co-op is given by:

$$C_{t+1} H_{t+1}^{\phi} = 1$$

How does the condition above compare to the optimality condition in the Keynesian co-op?

6. Show that we can substitute the the optimality condition you derived above into the budget constraint to get the following relationship between M_t and C_{t+1}:

$$C_{t+1} = M_t + C_{t+1}^{-1/\phi} \tag{49.3}$$

Explain why C_{t+1} is an increasing function of M_t.

7. Write down the marginal rate of substitution between C_t and C_{t+1}.

8. Write down the marginal rate of transformation between C_t and C_{t+1}.

9. Write down the optimality condition between C_t and C_{t+1}. The optimality condition in the Classical co-op is given by:

$$\frac{C_{t+1}}{C_t} = \beta \frac{P_t}{P_{t+1}^e}$$

How does the above condition compare to the optimality condition in the Keynesian co-op?

We now have two equations—the Euler equation and condition (49.3)—and two unknowns, C_t and C_{t+1}. This system of equations, however, cannot be manipulated until we can write C_t as a function of C_{t+1} in a single equation. We will once again solve it graphically.

10. Set up the coordinate plane with C_{t+1} on the x axis and C_t on the y axis. Carefully graph the following two functions on the coordinate plane:

$$C_t = \frac{C_{t+1}}{\beta} \qquad\qquad C_t = \frac{M_t + C_{t+1}^{-1/\phi}}{\beta}$$

11. Explain why both relationships must hold in equilibrium. What does the intersection of the two functions denote?

12. Suppose that the number of vouchers in circulation, M_t, goes up. What happens to consumption, C_t? Is this result consistent with the classical dichotomy?

13. In reality, the Grants maintained only a very, very small number of vouchers in circulation. Given your answers above, describe the type of crisis that would arise from such a policy.

References

Sweeny, J., & R.J. Sweeny (1977). Monetary theory and the great Capitol Hill baby sitting co-op crisis: Comment. *Journal of Money, Credit and Banking, 9*(1), 86–89.

Krugman, P. (1999). *The return of depression economics*. New York: Norton.

50 The Phillips Curve

In a world where the classical dichotomy holds, prices are free to adjust to changes in either the money supply or the nominal interest rate. This free adjustment shields *relative prices*, which remain insensitive to changes in nominal variables. Since supply and demand are functions of relative prices, the allocations of output, consumption, and labor are also insensitive to changes in nominal variables.

Yet the assumption that *all* prices adjust freely seems counterfactual to daily experience. Jo (2019), for example, estimates that in 2010 over 20 percent of hourly nominal wages in the United States remained constant. In this chapter we will work out the implications of inflexible, what economists often call "sticky," wages.

50.1 Flexible Wages

Before we model sticky wages we will consider a baseline economy with flexible wages and prices. This equilibrium can then serve as a benchmark against which we can compare the sticky-wage equilibrium allocations.

Utility-maximizing households will set the the marginal rate of substitution between hours worked, H_t, and consumption, C_t, equal to the relative price of labor. The household has the following per-period utility function:

$$u(C_t, H_t) = \log(C_t) - \frac{1}{1+\phi} H_t^{1+\phi}$$

where $\phi > 0$.

1. Write down the relative price of labor.

2. Write down the marginal rate of substitution between hours worked and consumption.

3. Show that the household's optimality condition is given by:

$$C_t H_t^\phi = \frac{W_t}{P_t} \tag{50.1}$$

4. Use your answer above to sketch a graph the real wage, W_t/P_t, as a function of hours supplied by the household, H_t. What is the name of the function you have just graphed?

[Hint: Since we do not have values for ϕ, this is simply a rough sketch, it nonetheless needs to display certain properties that are independent of the precise value of ϕ.]

Profit-maximizing firms set the marginal product of labor equal to its relative price. The firm hires labor, L_t, to produce output, Y_t, subject to the following production function:

$$Y_t = L_t^{1-\alpha}$$

where $1 > \alpha > 0$.

4. Write down the profit function of the firm.

5. Write down the marginal rate of substitution between labor and output.

6. Write down the marginal rate of transformation between labor and output.

7. Show that the optimality condition for the firm is given by:

$$(1-\alpha)\frac{Y_t}{L_t} = \frac{W_t}{P_t} \tag{50.2}$$

8. On the same diagram as question 4, sketch graph the real wage, W_t/P_t, as a function of the total labor demanded by the firm, L_t. What is the name of the function you have just graphed?
[Hint: Both L_t and H_t are on the x axis.]

9. What does the intersection of the graph above indicate?

We will now solve for the equilibrium real wage, as well as the equilibrium allocations of output and labor.

10. Write down the market clearing conditions in the labor and goods markets.

11. Combine the market clearing conditions with the supply and demand schedules for labor—equations (50.1) and (50.2), respectively—to derive the following equilibrium allocation of labor:

$$\bar{L}_t = (1-\alpha)^{1/(1+\phi)} \tag{50.3}$$

12. Combine the equilibrium allocation of labor with the production function to show that the equilibrium allocation of log output, $\log(\bar{Y}_t)$, is given by:

$$\log \bar{Y}_t = \left(\frac{1-\alpha}{1+\phi}\right)\log(1-\alpha) \tag{50.4}$$

We call the log output that would have arisen in the flexible-wage economy the *natural rate of output*. To distinguish it from the equilibrium output in the sticky-wage economy, we denote it with a bar: $\bar{Y}_t$.

13. Show that the equilibrium real wage is given by:

$$\frac{W_t}{P_t} = (1-\alpha)\bar{Y}^{-\alpha/(1-\alpha)} \tag{50.5}$$

50.2   Sticky Wages

Both the households and the firms in the sticky-wage economy are identical to those in its flexible-wage counterpart. In particular, households have the same utility function and firms face the same production function.

To model sticky wages, we will relax the assumption that the nominal wage can adjust freely in the labor market. In its place, we will assume that households must choose the *nominal* wage, W_t, one period in advance, in $t - 1$. To operationalize this assumption we will say that households set the nominal wage so that the *expected* ratio of the marginal rate of substitution to the marginal rate of transformation is one:

$$E_{t-1}\left[\frac{\text{MRS}(C_t, H_t)}{\text{MRT}(C_t, H_t)}\right] = 1 \tag{50.6}$$

where $E_{t-1}[\cdot]$ denotes the expectation taken in period $t - 1$.

Having set the nominal wage in the previous period, households then fulfill the firms' demand for labor given the equilibrium real wage in the current period. Importantly, we will continue to assume that the price of consumption, P_t, can adjust freely.

1. Substitute the marginal rate of substitution and the marginal rate of transformation terms into the expectation above from the optimality condition, equation (50.1).
[Hint: Rearrange equation (50.1) into a ratio and take the expected value at $t - 1$.]

2. Show that if the nominal wage was set at time t, as in the previous section, the household would set the ratio of the marginal rate of substitution to the real wage equal to one.
[Hint: What is the household's optimality condition?]

Although the household does not know in period $t - 1$ what the equilibrium *allocations* will be in period t, it nonetheless understand the equilibrium *conditions* that will determine those allocations. It can therefore use those conditions to form expectations about allocations and, in turn, use those expectations to set the nominal wage in period $t - 1$. We now proceed as the household would in forming rational expectations.

3. Substitute the labor demand schedule, equation (50.2), and the market-clearing conditions in the goods and labor markets in (50.6).

4. At this point the left-hand side of equation (50.6) is written in terms of labor, L_t. Use the production function to rewrite it in terms of output:

$$E_{t-1}\left[\frac{Y_t^{(1+\phi)/(1-\alpha)}}{1 - \alpha}\right] = 1$$

5. The equation above looks very similar to the expression that defines output in the flexible-price economy, $\bar{Y}$. Show that it can be rewritten as:

$$E_{t-1} \left[\frac{Y_t^{(1+\phi)/(1-\alpha)}}{\bar{Y}^{(1+\phi)/(1-\alpha)}} \right] = 1 \qquad (50.7)$$

6. Explain why $\bar{Y}$ is not a random variable.

7. Although Y_t is random variable, we will assume that its value never deviates too far from the flexible-price level of output, $\bar{Y}$. What does this imply about the ratio, $Y_t/\bar{Y}$?

8. Recall from chapter 45 that when a random variable is close to one, as we have assumed is true for $(Y_t/\bar{Y})^{(1+\phi)/(1-\alpha)}$, then $\log(E[\cdot]) = E[\log(\cdot)]$. Use this fact to rewrite equation (50.7) as:

$$E_{t-1} [\log Y_t] = \log \bar{Y} \qquad (50.8)$$

[Hint: Begin by taking the log.]

9. Explain in words what the equation above says.

10. Take the log of the labor demand schedule, equation (50.2), and the production function, to write log output as a function of the log real wage:

$$\log Y_t = \left(\frac{\alpha - 1}{\alpha} \right) (\log W_t - \log P_t - \log(1 - \alpha)) \qquad (50.9)$$

We are now ready to write the log of the nominal wage set at $t - 1$, $\log W_t$, as a function of expected log price, $E_{t-1}[\log P_t]$.

11. Explain why $E_{t-1}[\log W_t] = \log W_t$.

12. Use equation (50.9) to rewrite the left-hand side of equation (50.8) in terms of the log real wage and show that the log nominal wage is a function of the log expected price and the natural rate of output:

$$\log W_t = \log(1 - \alpha) + E_{t-1}[\log P_t] - \left(\frac{\alpha}{1 - \alpha} \right) \log \bar{Y} \qquad (50.10)$$

In what follows, we are going to analyze the labor market when nominal wages are sticky. To simplify the algebraic and graphical analysis, let lowercase variables denote logs, $x_t \equiv \log X_t$, for any variable X_t.

13. Explain why all the variables on the right-hand side of equation (50.10) are *constant* at time t.

14. Show that the log real wage under flexible wages is:

$$\psi = \log(1 - \alpha) - \left(\frac{\alpha}{1 - \alpha} \right) \bar{y}$$

15. Show that the equilibrium log real wage is given by:

$$w_t - p_t = \psi + E_{t-1}[p_t] - p_t \qquad (50.11)$$

16. Rewrite the labor demand schedule, equation (50.2), in terms of logs:

$$w_t - p_t = \log(1 - \alpha) + y_t - \ell_t \tag{50.12}$$

17. Equations (50.11) and (50.12) describe the supply and demand schedules, respectively, in the sticky-wage economy. Show that if $p_t = E_{t-1}[p_t]$ then the equilibrium real wage and equilibrium allocation of labor will be the same as in the flexible-wage economy.

18. Set up a large coordinate plane with the log real wage on the y axis and log labor, ℓ_t, on the x axis, and graph the line given by equation (50.12).
[Hint: Treat the log real wage $w_t - p_t$ as a single variable that you are plotting on the y axis.

19. In the same diagram as above, graph (50.11) when $p_t = E_{t-1}[p_t]$.
[Hint: Does (50.11) depend on ℓ_t?]

20. In the same diagram as above, graph (50.11) when $p_t > E_{t-1}[p_t]$.

21. What happens to the equilibrium allocation of labor and the real wage as p_t increases? How does this compare to the flexible-wage economy?

22. What happens to the real wage if prices end up being higher than households anticipated when setting the nominal wage?

23. Given your answer above, what happens to the amount of labor demanded by firms?

50.3   The Inflation-Output Tradeoff

1. Solve for the log wage in equation (50.9), set it equal to equation (50.10), and solve for p_t.
[Hint: Recall that $p_t = \log P_t$.]

2. Let $\pi_t \equiv p_t - p_{t-1}$. What is π_t?

3. Subtract p_{t-1} from both sides of your equation above to get the following relationship:

$$\pi_t = \kappa \tilde{y}_t + E_{t-1}[\pi_t] \tag{50.13}$$

where $\kappa \equiv \alpha/(1 - \alpha)$ and $\tilde{y}_t \equiv \log Y_t - \log \bar{Y}_t$ is called the *output gap*.

4. What does the output gap measure?

The relationship between inflation and output, equation (50.13), is called the *Phillips curve*. Every model where the classical dichotomy fails has a Phillips curve, although the exact equation will depend on the specific assumptions of each model. *All* Phillips curves, however, have three terms in common: a nominal term (inflation), a real term (sometimes output, sometimes unemployment), and an expectations term.

50.4   You Can't Fool Everyone All the Time

At first glance, the Phillips curve we have derived seems to suggest that a central bank can achieve higher output if it is prepared to accept higher inflation. To test this proposition, consider a central bank that does just that and announces that it will maintain a constant rate of inflation, $\bar{\pi}$. Will the choice of $\bar{\pi}$ allow it to achieve different levels of output?

1. Explain why $E_{t-1}[\pi_t] = \bar{\pi}$ and substitute it into the Phillips curve, equation (50.13).

2. Take the expectations of both sides and show that, regardless of the level of inflation announced by the central bank, the output gap will be zero, $\tilde{y}_t = 0$.

3. Given your answers above, explain why the central bank cannot *systematically* exploit the Phillips curve to achieve higher output by stoking inflation.

4. Rearrange the Phillips curve to get the output gap as a function of inflation and expectations:

$$\tilde{y}_t = \frac{1}{\kappa}(\pi_t - E_{t-1}[\pi_t]) \qquad (50.14)$$

5. What is the economic interpretation of the term in parentheses on the right hand side of the equation above?

6. Suppose that when period t arrives, inflation is higher than the household had expected. What happens to the output gap?

7. Graph the output gap $\tilde{y}_t$ as a function of surprise inflation, $\pi_t - E_{t-1}[\pi_t]$, for different values of κ: $\kappa \to 0$, $\kappa = 1$ and $\kappa \to \infty$. How does the sensitivity of the output gap to inflation change as κ increases?

8. κ is called the *slope* of the Phillips Curve. What does the slope of the Phillips Curve tell us?

References

Christiano, L., M. Eichenbaum, & C. Evans (2005). Nominal rigidities and the dynamic effects of a shock to monetary policy. *Journal of Political Economy, 113*(1), 1–45.

Fischer, S. (1977). Long-term contracts, rational expectations, and the optimal money supply rule. *Journal of Political Economy, 85*(1), 191–205.

Jo, Y. (2019). *Downward nominal wage rigidity in the United States.* Mimeo, Columbia University.

Sargent, T., & N. Wallace (1981). Some unpleasant monetary arithmetic. *Federal Reserve Bank of Minneapolis Quarterly Review, 5*(3), 1–17.

51 Testing for the Real Effects of Monetary Policy

In an economy that exhibits the classical dichotomy, monetary policy can affect only inflation. In an economy where the classical dichotomy fails, however, monetary policy is able to affect real variables like output. Identifying whether monetary policy has real effects is therefore an important empirical question. How can we do so?

51.1 A Tale of Two Economies

We will take the point of view of an economist who is interested in testing whether monetary policy has real effects. She can observe the equilibrium outcomes of the economy, such as inflation and interest rates, but does not know the exact equilibrium relationships that give rise to these outcomes. If she knew the relationships she wouldn't need to run any tests; those relationships would tell her whether the nominal interest rate affects real variables. She has a straightforward test in mind: measure the effect of the nominal interest rate, i_t, on the real interest rate, r_t.

We will consider two counterfactual economies, one where monetary policy has no real effects and one where it does. In both economies the central bank sets the nominal interest rate according to the following Taylor rule:

$$i_t = \rho + \phi \pi_t + u_t \tag{51.1}$$

where ρ is the rate of time preference, π_t is inflation, and u_t is a *random variable* with mean zero, $E[u_t] = 0$. We call u_t a *monetary policy shock* because it is both unexpected (i.e., its expected value is zero) and unrelated to economic conditions.

In addition to the monetary policy rule, the Fisher equation also holds in both economies:

$$r_t = i_t - E_t[\pi_{t+1}] \tag{51.2}$$

Finally, in both economies the household chooses consumption across time to satisfy the Euler equation, leading to the following aggregate demand condition:

$$\tilde{y}_t = E_t[\tilde{y}_{t+1}] - (r_t - \rho) \tag{51.3}$$

where $\tilde{y}$ is the output gap.

We will begin with the classical dichotomy.

1. If the central bank is following the Taylor principle, what inequality must the coefficient on inflation, ϕ, satisfy in the central bank's monetary policy rule?

2. Recall that the output gap is defined as $\tilde{y}_t \equiv y_t - \bar{y}_t$, where y_t is the log output and $\bar{y}_t$ is the log output under the classical dichotomy. Explain why this implies that the output gap is always zero.

3. Given your answer above, show that $r_t = \rho$.

4. Show that the rate of inflation in equilibrium is a function of expectations and the monetary policy shock:

$$\pi_t = \frac{1}{\phi} E_t[\pi_{t+1}] - \frac{1}{\phi} u_t \tag{51.4}$$

5. Guess that, in equilibrium, inflation expectations are constant and equal to zero: $E_t[\pi_{t+1}] = 0$. Verify that if this is the case, then the expected value of inflation, $E[\pi_t]$, is, in fact, zero.
[Hint: Equation (51.4) describes the equilibrium inflation process.]

6. Show that, in equilibrium, $i_t = r_t$.

7. Now suppose that our economist plots the real interest rate, r_t, as a function of the nominal interest rate, i_t. Plot this relationship on a graph.

8. Is the real interest rate in this economy a function of the nominal interest rate? Explain.

9. Suppose that, instead, the economist decides to plot the real interest rate as a function of the monetary policy shock, u_t. Plot this relationship on a graph.

We now turn to the alternative case where the classical dichotomy doesn't hold. In addition to equations (51.1)–(51.3) this economy also has a Phillips curve:

$$\pi_t = \kappa \tilde{y}_t + E_t[\pi_{t+1}]. \tag{51.5}$$

10. Show that, in equilibrium, aggregate demand is a function of expectations, inflation and the monetary policy shock:

$$\tilde{y}_t = E_t[\tilde{y}_{t+1}] + E_t[\pi_{t+1}] - (\phi \pi_t + u_t) \tag{51.6}$$

11. Show that the rate of inflation in equilibrium is a function of expectations and the monetary policy shock:

$$\pi_t = \left(\frac{\kappa}{1+\phi\kappa}\right) E_t[\tilde{y}_{t+1}] + \left(\frac{1+\kappa}{1+\phi\kappa}\right) E_t[\pi_{t+1}] - \left(\frac{\kappa}{1+\phi\kappa}\right) u_t \tag{51.7}$$

12. Guess that, in equilibrium, expectations of the output gap and inflation are both zero: $E_t[\pi_{t+1}] = 0$ and $E_t[\tilde{y}_{t+1}] = 0$. Verify that if this is the case, then the expected value of inflation inflation, $E[\pi_t]$, is, in fact, zero. Then, given this fact, verify that the expected value of the output gap, $E[\tilde{y}_t]$, is also zero.

13. Given your results above, what does equation (51.7), reduce to?

14. Combine the Fisher equation and the Taylor rule with equilibrium inflation to derive the following equilibrium expression of the real interest rate:

$$r_t = \rho + \left(\frac{1}{1 + \phi\kappa} \right) u_t \qquad (51.8)$$

15. Plot the real interest rate, r_t , as a function of the nominal interest rate, i_t.
[Hint: The Fisher equation still holds.]

16. How does the diagram above compare to the one from question 7? Does the relationship between the nominal interest rate and the real interest rate tell us anything about the real effects of monetary policy?

17. Now graph the real interest rate, r_t, as a function of the monetary policy shock, u_t.

18. How does the diagram above compare to the one from question 9? What does your result suggest about how economists can differentiate between an economy where the classical dichotomy holds and one where it doesn't?

51.2   How to Recover a Shock

Since the test of the real effects of monetary policy relies on the monetary policy shock, and not on the nominal interest rate, we now turn to how we can measure u_t.

1. Explain why the economist cannot observe the monetary policy shock directly.
[Hint: Recall that she can observe equilibrium outcomes, but not equilibrium relationships.]

So far, we have thought of time as atomistic, with the economy existing at a *point in time*, t, and then proceeding to $t + 1$. Alternatively, we can interpret each t as a *period of time*. This interpretation allows us to think about the timing of events *within* each period; specifically, we are going to narrow our focus to the day that the central bank announces its nominal interest rate target, i_t.

2. Consider the morning of the announcement, only a few hours before the central bank sets the nominal interest rate. Explain why, within this narrow window, the financial markets and the Fed all agree on the rate of inflation, π_t.

3. Our economist does not know exactly how the central bank conducts monetary policy—she does not know either ρ or ϕ. Suppose, however, that agents in the economy do know ρ and ϕ. Let i_t^f denote agents' forecast of the upcoming monetary policy announcement. Write down an expression of their forecast.
[Hint: What do agents know the morning of the announcement? What do they now know?]

4. Given your previous answers, show that $u_t = i_t - i_t^f$

Table 51.1
Effects of monetary policy shocks on nominal and real interest rates.

Forward Rates	2-Year	5-Year	10-Year
Real	0.99	0.47	0.12
	[0.41, 1.47]	[0.14, 0.80]	[−0.12, 0.36]
Nominal	1.14	0.26	−0.08
	[0.23, 2.04]	[−0.12, 0.64]	[−0.43, 0.28]

Source: Nakamura & Steinsson (2018a).

5. Let r_t^f denote agents' forecast of the real interest rate the morning before the announcement. Show that $r_t^f = \rho$ regardless of whether the economy displays the classical dichotomy or not.

6. Let $\Delta r_t \equiv r_t - r_t^f$. What does Δr_t equal in the case where the classical dichotomy holds? What does Δr_t equal in the case where the classical dichotomy doesn't?

Financial markets trade contracts on the future value of the federal funds rate. Gürkaynak, Sack, and Swanson (2005) developed a method for using these contracts to infer i_t^f and recover the monetary policy shock, u_t. Nakamura and Steinsson (2018a) then applied this method to test the effect of monetary policy shocks on real and nominal interest rates at different horizons. They considered a narrow window looking at only the half hour before and after the monetary policy announcement by the Fed.

Table 51.1 displays their results. The table reports their estimates of the change in real and nominal interest rates at different time horizons from a 1 percent monetary policy shock. In brackets below each estimate is the margin of error of that estimate. If the margin of error straddles zero, we conclude that, regardless of the estimate, the effect of the monetary policy shock is zero.

7. Consider the entries in the top row of table 51.1. To what variable in our model do those entries correspond?

8. If monetary policy did not affect real variables, what would be true about the margins of error below the estimates of the real interest rate?

9. If monetary policy did not affect real variables, what would be true about the margins of error below the estimates of the nominal interest rate?

10. Given the evidence from table 51.1, do we live in a world where the classical dichotomy holds? Or does monetary policy have real effects?

References

Gürkaynak, R., B. Sack, & E. Swanson (2005a). Do actions speak louder than words? The response of asset prices to monetary policy actions and statements. *International Journal of Central Banking, 1*(1), 55–94.

Nakamura, E., & J. Steinsson (2018a). High frequency identification of monetary non-neutrality: The information effect. *Quarterly Journal of Economics, 133*(3), 1283–1330.

Nakamura, E., & J. Steinsson (2018b). Identification in macroeconomics. *Journal of Economic Perspectives, 32*(3), 59–86.

52 Optimal Monetary Policy

The Federal Reserve Act gives the Fed a *dual mandate* to both keep prices stable and achieve full employment. Since labor is one of the factors of production, the full-employment mandate translates into maintaining a desired level of output. The Fed is, of course, constrained by the Phillips curve. Given a level of expectations by market participants, the Phillips curve constrains the Fed's ability to achieve both low inflation and the desired level of output.

Here we will solve the problem that the Fed faces: what are the optimal monetary policy outcomes—inflation and output—that the Fed can achieve in response to economic shocks? We will consider this question under two different regimes. Under *discretion*, the Fed reacts optimally every period to economic shocks. Under *commitment*, the Fed chooses an optimal policy *before* any shocks materialize.

52.1 The Efficiency Gap

While market economies with flexible prices can be efficient, they need not be. We thus want to distinguish between two counterfactual targets for the central bank. The *natural* rate of output, $\bar{y}_t$, is the log output that would prevail under flexible prices. The *efficient* rate of output, y_t^*, is the log output that would maximize the utility of the representative household.

1. If the central bank is acting on behalf of the representative household's interests, should it aim to close the gap between output and its natural rate or its efficient rate?

Suppose the economy behaves according to the following Phillips curve:

$$\pi_t = \kappa \tilde{y}_t + \beta \, E_t[\pi_{t+1}] \tag{52.1}$$

where $\tilde{y}_t \equiv y_t - \bar{y}_t$ is the output gap, $\beta < 1$ is the household's discount factor, and κ is the slope of the Phillips curve.

2. What is the economic interpretation of κ?

3. Consider the difference between output and its efficient level $\hat{y}_t \equiv y_t - y_t^*$. We will call $\hat{y}_t$ the *efficiency gap*. Show that the Phillips curve can be rewritten in terms of the efficiency gap:

$$\pi_t = \kappa \hat{y}_t + \beta \, E_t[\pi_{t+1}] + \kappa (y_t^* - \bar{y}_t) \tag{52.2}$$

[Hint: Add zero to the left-hand side of (52.1)]

We now suppose that the gap between the efficient and natural rate of output is the sum of a constant and a random variable:

$$y_t^* - \bar{y}_t = \Delta + \varepsilon_t \tag{52.3}$$

where $E_t[\varepsilon_t] = 0$. We call the mean zero random variable, ε_t, a *cost-push shock*.

4. Combine equations (52.2) and (52.3) to rewrite the Phillips curve in terms of the cost-push shock:

$$\pi_t = \kappa \hat{y}_t + \beta \, E_t[\pi_{t+1}] + \kappa (\Delta + \varepsilon_t) \tag{52.4}$$

5. Offer an economic interpretation of Δ.

6. What happens to the rate of inflation required to achieve an efficient level of output, $\hat{y}_t = 0$, if $\varepsilon_t > 0$?

7. Given your answer above, offer an educated guess about why ε_t is called a cost-push shock.

52.2   Discretion

Consider a central bank that is trying to *minimize* both inflation, π_t, and the deviations of the log of output, y_t, from its efficient level, y^*. We can think of the bank as trying to minimize two distances: the distance between the inflation rate and zero inflation, and the distance between the log output and its efficient level. The following objective loss function formalizes the central bank's dual mandate:

$$\frac{1}{2} \left(\pi_t^2 + \lambda \hat{y}_t^2 \right) \tag{52.5}$$

where $\lambda \geq 0$.

A *discretionary* central bank optimizes period by period. It will adjust both inflation, π_t and the efficiency gap, $\hat{y}_t$, optimally in response to economic shocks.

1. What is the economic interpretation of λ?

2. The bank is trying to minimize (52.5). If it could operate without any constraints, what inflation/efficiency gap pair, $\{\pi_t, \hat{y}_t\}$, would the central bank choose?
[Hint: The minimum value that (52.5) can attain is zero.]

3. Explain why the Phillips curve, equation (52.4), constrains the central bank's ability to choose the inflation/efficiency gap pair you identified above.

4. Write down the central bank's constrained optimization problem, where the Phillips curve is given by equation (52.4).

5. Write down the marginal rate of substitution between inflation, π_t, and the efficiency gap, $\hat{y}_t$.

6. Write down the marginal rate of transformation between inflation, π_t, and the efficiency gap, $\hat{y}_t$.

7. Show that the optimality condition can be written as:

$$\hat{y}_t = \frac{-\kappa}{\lambda}\pi_t \tag{52.6}$$

8. Explain why equations (52.4) and (52.6) must both hold in equilibrium. Then combine them to derive the following equilibrium expression for inflation:

$$\pi_t = \left(\frac{\lambda\kappa}{\lambda+\kappa^2}\right)\Delta + \left(\frac{\lambda\beta}{\lambda+\kappa^2}\right)E[\pi_{t+1}] + \left(\frac{\lambda\kappa}{\lambda+\kappa^2}\right)\varepsilon_t \tag{52.7}$$

According to equation (52.7), in equilibrium, inflation is a linear function of expected inflation, $E[\pi_{t+1}]$, and the cost-push shock, ε_t. In other words, equation (52.7) is of the form:

$$\pi_t = \alpha + \theta\, E[\pi_{t+1}] + \sigma\varepsilon_t$$

We have already solved this equation under the rational expectations hypothesis in chapter 44: "A Not-So-Simple Model of Inflation." We showed that, under the rational expectations hypothesis, equilibrium expectations are given by:

$$E[\pi_{t+1}] = \frac{\alpha}{1-\theta}$$

Which requires that the coefficient on expectations, θ, is less than one.

9. Explain why the coefficient on expectations in equation (52.7) is, in fact, less than one. [Hint: Recall that β is less than one.]

10. Show that, in equilibrium, expected inflation is given by:

$$E[\pi_{t+1}] = \left(\frac{\lambda\kappa}{\lambda(1-\beta)+\kappa^2}\right)\Delta \tag{52.8}$$

11. Show that, in equilibrium, inflation is given by:

$$\pi_t = \left(\frac{\lambda\kappa}{\lambda(1-\beta)+\kappa^2}\right)\Delta + \left(\frac{\lambda\kappa}{\lambda+\kappa^2}\right)\varepsilon_t \tag{52.9}$$

12. Consider the equilibrium expressions for inflation and expected inflation derived above. Show that $E[\pi_{t+1}] = E[\pi_t]$.

13. Show that, in equilibrium, the efficiency gap is given by:

$$\hat{y}_t = \left(\frac{\lambda(1-\beta)}{\lambda(1-\beta)+\kappa^2} \right) \Delta - \left(\frac{\kappa^2}{\lambda+\kappa^2} \right) \varepsilon_t \tag{52.10}$$

14. Suppose that $\lambda = 0$. What does this imply about how important the efficiency gap is to the central bank relative to inflation?

15. What are the equilibrium expressions of inflation, inflation expectations, and the efficiency gap when $\lambda = 0$? Give a brief economic interpretation of your results.

16. Suppose that $\lambda \to \infty$. What does this imply about how important the efficiency gap is to the central bank relative to inflation?

17. What are the equilibrium expressions of inflation, inflation expectations, and the efficiency gap when $\lambda \to \infty$? Give a brief economic interpretation of your results.

52.3   Commitment

A discretionary central banker reacts optimally every period to economic conditions. Yet there is another way for her to proceed. Instead of reserving for herself the right to respond to economic conditions optimally period by period, she could instead *commit* herself to a monetary policy once and for all. Under commitment, she would implement that policy every period without re-optimizing in response to economic conditions.

1. Explain why under commitment the central bank can always achieve the same outcomes as under discretion.
[Hint: How could the central bank commit to act?]

2. Given that the central bank can always commit to its discretionary policy, what must be true of the bank's optimal commitment policy if it is not the same as the optimal policy under discretion?

3. Suppose that the central bank's optimal policy under commitment is not the same as the optimal policy under discretion. If the central bank implements its commitment policy, will its policy choices necessarily be optimal at any given period, t?

4. Explain why under commitment the central bank cannot minimize (52.5) and must instead minimize

$$\frac{1}{2} E\left[\pi_t^2 + \lambda \hat{y}_t^2 \right] \tag{52.11}$$

5. Explain why under commitment the central bank's constraint is similarly not (52.4) but is instead

$$E[\pi_t] = E\left[\kappa \hat{y}_t + \beta\, E_t[\pi_{t+1}] + \kappa \Delta\right] \tag{52.12}$$

[Hint: Recall that $E[\varepsilon_t] = 0$.]

6. Under the rational expectations hypothesis, how are $E[\pi_t]$ and $E[E_t[\pi_{t+1}]]$ related? [Hint: The answer to this question is an equation. Another hint: Recall that under the law of iterated expectations, $E[E_t[\pi_{t+1}]] = E[\pi_{t+1}]$.]

7. Substitute your answer above into (52.12) to write the central bank's constraint only in terms of $E[\pi_t]$ and not $E[\pi_{t+1}]$.

8. Write down the central bank's constrained optimization problem.

9. Show that the central bank's marginal rate of substitution between expected inflation and the expected efficiency gap is given by:

$$\frac{E[\pi_t]}{\lambda(E[\hat{y}_t])}$$

How does the marginal rate of substitution between *expected* inflation and the *expected* efficiency gap under commitment compare to the marginal rate of substitution between inflation and the efficiency gap under discretion?

10. Show that the central bank's marginal rate of transformation between expected inflation and the expected efficiency gap is given by:

$$\frac{\beta - 1}{\kappa}$$

How does the marginal rate of transformation under commitment compare to the marginal rate of transformation under discretion?

11. Write down the bank's optimality condition.

12. Combine the optimality condition above with the Phillips curve, equation (52.12), to derive the following equilibrium expression for expected inflation:

$$E[\pi_t] = \left(\frac{\lambda \kappa (1 - \beta)}{\lambda(1 - \beta)^2 + \kappa^2}\right)\Delta \tag{52.13}$$

13. We have now derived expressions for the expected rate of inflation under discretion and commitment, equations (52.8) and (52.13), respectively. In the same diagram, graph the expected inflation rate on the y axis as a function the household's time preference parameter, β, on the x axis for each case. For ease of graphing, assume that $\lambda = \kappa = \Delta = 1$.

14. Is expected inflation higher under discretion or under commitment?

15. How does commitment expand central bank's scope to influence equilibrium outcomes?

References

Barro, R., & R. Gordon (1983). A positive theory of monetary policy in a natural rate model. *Journal of Political Economy, 91*(4), 589–610.

Benigno, P., & M. Woodford (2003). Optimal monetary and fiscal policy: A linear-quadratic approach. *NBER Macroeconomics Annual, 18*, 271–333.

Gali, J. (2008). *Monetary policy, inflation and the business cycle: An introduction to the new Keynesian framework.* Princeton: Princeton University Press.

Kydland, F., & E. Prescott (1980). Rules rather than discretion: The inconsistency of optimal plans. *Journal of Political Economy, 85*(3), 473–492.

Woodford, M. (2003). *Interest and prices*. Princeton: Princeton University Press.

53 Utility and Uncertainty

So far we have studied how agents might form expectations about market conditions in the future. To analyze the impact of those expectations, we have, in a somewhat ad hoc manner, replaced future values with the expectations of those values in our equilibrium conditions. But how might agents evaluate their objectives when outcomes that directly affect their utility are uncertain?

Consider the cake-eating problem: How much of the cake will an agent eat today when they are unsure about how much cake will be around tomorrow? The standard model of choice under uncertainty used in economics postulates that agents evaluate their *expected* utility.

53.1 Cake and Certainty

An agent has one cake and is deciding what fraction to eat today, C_1, and what fraction to leave for tomorrow, C_2. For simplicity, assume that the agent cares about the future just as much as the present, so that the discount factor β is also one. The intertemporal utility function of eating cake is therefore given by:

$$U(C_1, C_2) = \log C_1 + \log C_2 \tag{53.1}$$

1. Write down the budget constraint of the cake eater.
[Hint: Recall that there is one cake and C_1 and C_2 are fractions of that cake.]

2. Write down the constrained optimization problem of the cake eater.

3. Write down the marginal rate of substitution between C_1 and C_2.

4. Write down the marginal rate of transformation between C_1 and C_2.

5. Write down the optimality condition of the cake eater.

6. Combine the optimality condition and the budget constraint to solve for the chosen allocation $\{C_1^*, C_2^*\}$.

53.2   Cake and Uncertainty

We now introduce uncertainty into the problem. Not unreasonably, we assume that there is
a positive probability that part of the cake might go bad by tomorrow. Alternatively, you
might get more cake. For simplicity, we assume that the amount of cake that spoils is the
same as the amount of cake that someone might give you, and that either the cake will spoil
or someone will give you more cake. Specifically, we assume that the amount of cake you
have tomorrow is equal to what is left over from the slice you eat today *plus* the following
random variable, which can take two values:

$$x = \begin{cases} \sigma & \text{with probability } 0.5 \\ -\sigma & \text{with probability } 0.5 \end{cases} \tag{53.2}$$

1. What is the expected value of x?

2. On average, will the cake eater have more, less, or the same amount of cake as in the
case with certainty?

3. Write down the two budget constraints for the two possible outcomes of x.

4. Show that the *expected* budget constraint is the same as the budget constraint under
certainty.

5. Explain why the marginal rate of transformation is still equal to one.
[Hint: Has the rate at which you can turn one slice of cake in the present into a slice of cake
in the future changed?]

Under uncertainty there are *two* possible utility functions, one for each of the possible outcomes of the random variable x. Notice that, ex ante, the cake eater does not know what her
actual utility will end up being—she has to choose how much cake to eat *today* before the
realization of the random variable x.

6. Is the marginal utility of today's consumption, C_1, uncertain?

7. Explain why the following expression is the marginal utility of consuming today:

$$\frac{1}{C_1} \tag{53.3}$$

8. Is the marginal utility of tomorrow's consumption, C_2, uncertain?

9. Explain why the *expected marginal utility* of consuming tomorrow can be written as a
function of C_1:

$$\mathrm{E}\left[\frac{1}{C_2}\right] = \mathrm{E}\left[\frac{1}{1 - C_1 + x}\right]$$

10. Solve for C_2 in the budget constraints you wrote in question 3.

11. Use your answers above to show that the expected marginal utility of consuming tomorrow, $E\left[\frac{1}{C_2}\right]$, can be written as:

$$\frac{1}{2}\left(\frac{1}{1-C_1+\sigma}+\frac{1}{1-C_1-\sigma}\right) \tag{53.4}$$

[Hint: What is the probability that each outcome occurs?]

12. Write down the *expected* marginal rate of substitution between consuming today and consuming tomorrow.
[Hint: You have an *expected* marginal utility and a marginal utility.]

13. Show that the optimality condition implies that the marginal utility of consuming today, expression (53.3), is equal to the *expected* marginal utility of consuming tomorrow, expression (53.4).

We are going to graph the two marginal utilities—expressions (53.3) and (53.4) above—as a function of C_1 for different values of σ. C_1 will be on the x axis while the [expected] marginal utility is on the y axis. We will put them all on the same graph so make sure you draw a large enough diagram. Also, recall that C_1 and C_2 are fractions of the cake, so the values of the x axis should only go from 0 to 1.

10. Plot expression (53.3).

11. In the same graph, plot (53.4) for each of the following values of σ: 0, 0.1, 0.15, and 0.2.

12. Explain why the intersection of the two graphs is the amount of cake eaten today, C_1.

13. What happens to this amount as σ increases?

14. What happens to the expected amount of cake available tomorrow as σ increases?

15. Loosely speaking, would you say that the amount of cake available for consumption tomorrow is more or less uncertain as σ increases?

16. Given your answers to the previous two questions, what happens to *savings* today as the world becomes more uncertain? Savings arising from uncertainty are called *precautionary savings*.

54 The Risk Premium

No-arbitrage conditions are ubiquitous in economics. So far we have considered investors who are interested only in the expected returns of two assets. In that case, the no-arbitrage condition requires that the expected returns of the assets are equal.

We now consider the case where the investor is interested in the expected return of the asset in terms of the *utility* derived from consuming those returns rather than the returns themselves.

Consider an arbitrary asset that has a possibly random, gross return, Q_{t+1}. The household must decide whether to give up one unit of consumption at time t, for the random return of Q_{t+1} in period $t+1$. The household's marginal rate of substitution is given by:

$$M_{t+1} \equiv \frac{u'(C_{t+1})}{u'(C_t)} \beta$$

where $u'(C)$, the marginal utility of consumption, is a decreasing function of C. M_{t+1} is called the *Stochastic discount factor*.

1. Explain why $1/Q_{t+1}$ is the marginal rate of transformation.

2. Explain why the marginal rate of substitution is also a random variable.

3. Suppose that neither C_{t+1} nor Q_{t+1} were random variables. Show that the household's optimality condition would be:

$$\frac{u'(C_{t+1})}{u'(C_t)} \beta Q_{t+1} = 1$$

4. Given that they are random variables, explain why the household's optimality condition becomes:

$$E_t[M_{t+1}Q_{t+1}] = 1 \tag{54.1}$$

where $E_t[\cdot]$ denotes the expected value taken at time t.

5. Explain why (54.1) must hold for *any* asset.

6. Consider another asset that pays a rate of return R_t. This is the real interest rate, which has a rate of return known at time t. Show that the no-arbitrage condition between the real

interest rate and any asset is:

$$E_t[M_{t+1}Q_{t+1}] = R_t E_t[M_{t+1}] \tag{54.2}$$

[Hint: Is the real rate of return, R_t, a random variable at time t?]

The expected value of the product of two random variables, in this case, M_{t+1} and Q_{t+1}, is not equal to the product of the expected values of each. The formula is:

$$E_t[M_{t+1}Q_{t+1}] = E_t[M_{t+1}] E_t[Q_{t+1}] + \text{Cov}_t(Q_{t+1}, M_{t+1}) \tag{54.3}$$

where $\text{Cov}(M_{t+1}, Q_{t+1})$ is the covariance between the two random variables. The covariance tells us about how two random variables move together. If the covariance is positive, the variables tend to increase and decrease together. If the covariance is zero, the variables are unrelated. If the covariance is negative, when one variables tends to increase, the other one tends to decrease—they move in opposite directions.

7. Combine the formula for the expectation of the product, equation (54.3), with the no-arbitrage condition to get the following relationship between the real interest rate and the expected return of any other asset:

$$R_t = E_t[Q_{t+1}] + \left(\frac{\text{Cov}_t(M_{t+1}, Q_{t+1})}{E_t[M_{t+1}]} \right) \tag{54.4}$$

8. What must be the correlation between the asset and the stochastic discount factor in order for the no-arbitrage condition to reduce to equating the real interest rate with the expected rate of return?

9. Suppose that the covariance between the asset and the stochastic discount factor is negative, will the expected rate of return on the asset be higher or lower than the real interest rate?

10. If an asset positively covaries with the stochastic discount factor, how does it covary with future consumption?
[Hint: Recall that $u'(C_{t+1})$ is a decreasing function of consumption.]

11. We define the risk premium, ρ, as the difference between the expected return on a risky asset and the real interest rate:

$$\rho \equiv E_t[Q_{t+1}] - R_t \tag{54.5}$$

Show that the no-arbitrage condition, equation (54.4), implies that the risk premium can be equivalently written as:

$$\rho = -R_t \text{Cov}_t(M_{t+1}, Q_{t+1}) \tag{54.6}$$

12. What must be the sign of the covariance between the return on an asset and the stochastic discount factor in order for the asset to pay a premium?

13. Suppose that $u(C) = \log(C)$. Show that $M_{t+1} = \beta \frac{C_t}{C_{t+1}}$.

(a) Net returns

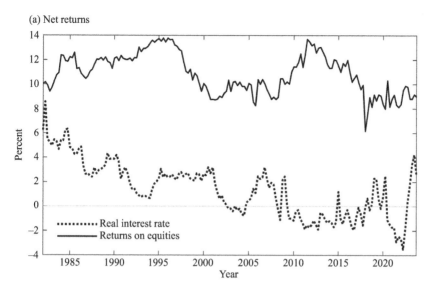

(b) Return on equities and consumption growth

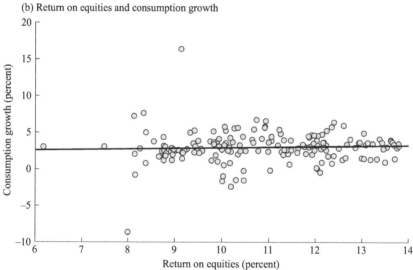

Figure 54.1
Equity premium. Consumption growth is calculated using personal consumption expenditures of nondurable goods. Returns on equity are deflated using the PCEPI for nondurable goods. *Sources*: Federal Reserve Bank of Cleveland, Board of Governors of the Federal Reserve, and Bureau of Economic Analysis.

14. Figure 54.1(b) plots the growth rate of consumption and the return on nonfinancial equities. Is their correlation positive, negative, or zero?

15. Assume logarithmic utility, as in question 13. Is the correlation between the stochastic discount factor and the return on equities positive, negative, or zero?

16. Figure 54.1(a) plots the return on equities and the real interest rate. Is the average return on equities higher or lower than the real interest rate? Is this consistent with the correlations in figure 54.1(b)?

17. The covariance between equities and the stochastic discount factor from figure 54.1(b) is 0.00003, statistically indistinguishable from zero. From figure 54.1(a) we get the average net real interest rate is 1.42 percent and the average net return on equities is 10.33 percent. Calculate the risk premium according to its *definition*. Now calculate the risk premium as *predicted* by our model. How do they compare?

[Hint: Which equation *defines* the risk premium? Which equation yields a *theoretically equivalent* method of calculating it?]

18. The failure of equation (54.6) to account for the difference between the returns on equities, stocks, and riskless returns, bonds, is called the *equity premium puzzle*. Replace the equal sign between the two sides of equation (54.6) with the inequality that is consistent with your empirical results from the previous question.

19. Consider the assumptions we made in our model; pick one assumption and explain how it might be responsible for the equity premium puzzle.

Reference

Mehra, R., & E. Prescott (1985). The equity premium: A puzzle. *Journal of Monetary Economics, 15*(2), 145–161.

55 Uncertainty Shocks

Consider a two-period economy with two agents—households and firms—where labor is the only factor of production. Households supply labor and demand goods, while firms demand labor and supply goods. The future in this economy is uncertain; specifically future income, Y_{t+1}, is a random variable that takes two values:

$$Y_{t+1} = \begin{cases} 1 + \sigma_t & \text{with probability } 0.5 \\ 1 - \sigma_t & \text{with probability } 0.5 \end{cases}$$

Note that σ_t is not fixed. It is itself a random variable that can take different values in period t.

Given the presence of uncertainty, the household maximizes its *expected* utility:

$$E[U(C_t, C_{t+1})] = \log C_t + \beta\, E[\log C_{t+1}]$$

where C_t denotes present consumption, C_{t+1} denotes future consumption and β is the discount factor. The household's real *expected* intertemporal budget constraint is given by:

$$C_t + \frac{1}{1+r_t} E_t[C_{t+1}] = Y_t + \frac{1}{1+r_t} E_t[Y_{t+1}]$$

where Y_t and $E[Y_{t+1}]$ denote present real income and *expected* future real income, respectively, and r_t is the present real interest rate.

1. Suppose that $\sigma_t = 0$. How uncertain is the household about its future income? Now, suppose that σ_t increases, what happens to the variability of future output?

2. Based on your answer above, give brief economic interpretation of σ_t.

3. Write down the *expected* marginal rate of substitution between present consumption, C_t and future consumption C_{t+1}.
[Hint: Find the marginal utility for C_{t+1} and then take its expectation.]

4. Write down the marginal rate of transformation between present consumption, C_t, and *expected* future consumption, $E[C_{t+1}]$. Is the marginal rate of transformation known in period t?

5. Show that the Euler equation can be written as:

$$\frac{1}{C_t} = \beta(1+r_t)\,E\left[\frac{1}{C_{t+1}}\right] \tag{55.1}$$

6. How many components does aggregate demand have in this economy?
[Hint: Is there a government? Is there capital? Are there foreign economies?]

7. Given your answer above, show that, in equilibrium, the expected marginal utility of future consumption can be written as follows:

$$E\left[\frac{1}{C_{t+1}}\right] = \frac{1}{2}\left(\frac{1}{1+\sigma_t}\right) + \frac{1}{2}\left(\frac{1}{1-\sigma_t}\right)$$

$$= \frac{1}{1-\sigma_t^2}$$

8. Combine your answers above with the Euler equation to show that equilibrium output can be written as the following function of σ_t, β, and r_t:

$$Y_t = \frac{1-\sigma_t^2}{\beta(1+r_t)} \tag{55.2}$$

Rather than model the labor market, we will simplify our analysis by assuming that equilibrium output under flexible prices is one in period t, so that the natural rate of output is zero. We assume sticky prices, however, and so the output gap need not be zero. In what follows, we denote logs using lowercase variables, as in $y_t \equiv \log Y_t$.

9. Explain why the output gap, $\tilde{y}_t$, is equal to the log of output y_t.
[Hint: Recall that the output gap is the difference between the log of output and the natural rate of output.]

10. Is output an increasing or decreasing function of uncertainty?

11. The *natural rate of interest*, $\bar{r}_t$, is the real interest rate that would prevail in equilibrium under flexible prices. Show that the natural interest rate is given by:

$$\bar{r}_t = \rho - \sigma_t^2 \tag{55.3}$$

where $\rho \equiv -\log\beta$ is the rate of time preference.

12. Combine your answers above with the aggregate demand function, equation (55.2), to show that the aggregate demand gap is equal to the difference between the natural interest rate and the real interest rate:

$$\tilde{y}_t = \bar{r}_t - r_t \tag{55.4}$$

13. Graph the natural interest as a function of uncertainty. Can the natural interest rate become negative?

14. Recall the Fisher equation, $r_t = i_t - E_t[\pi_{t+1}]$. Suppose that inflation expectations remain constant, will the real interest rate always be able to match the natural interest rate if uncertainty becomes too large?

[Hint: what is the minimum value that that the nominal interest rate can take?]

56 The Zero Lower Bound

Central banks that set monetary policy according to the Taylor principle adjust the nominal interest rate by more than the change in inflation. At the same time, the nominal interest rate cannot be negative. So what happens when the Taylor Principle calls for a nominal interest rate below zero? In this chapter, we will analyze equilibrium outcomes when monetary policy hits the zero lower bound.

We will analyze an economy where the central bank sets the nominal interest rate, i_t, in response to the inflation rate, π_t, and the natural rate of interest, $\bar{r}_t$, according to the Taylor rule:

$$i_t = \bar{r}_t + \phi \pi_t \tag{56.1}$$

as long as $\bar{r}_t + \phi \pi_t \geq 0$. Otherwise, the central bank is stuck at the zero lower bound and $i_t = 0$. Importantly, the natural rate of interest is a random variable that can take positive and negative values. On average, however, the natural rate is positive. This implies that at any given time, agents have expectations: $E[\bar{r}_t] > 0$.

The economy can be summarized by the following aggregate supply and aggregate demand schedules:

$$\pi_t = \kappa \tilde{y}_t + E_t[\pi_{t+1}] \tag{56.2}$$

$$\tilde{c}_t = E_t[\tilde{c}_{t+1}] + (\bar{r}_t - r_t) \tag{56.3}$$

where $\tilde{y}_t$ and $\tilde{c}_t$ are the output and consumption gaps, respectively. The nominal and real interest rates must, as usual, satisfy the Fisher equation:

$$r_t = i_t - E_t[\pi_{t+1}] \tag{56.4}$$

56.1 Positive Nominal Interest Rates

We begin by analyzing the case where the central bank is not constrained by the zero lower bound.

1. What is another name for equation (56.2)?

2. If consumption is the only component of aggregate demand, explain why $\tilde{y}_t = \tilde{c}_t$.

3. We will proceed by first reducing the number of equations. Substitute the Fisher equation and then the Taylor rule into the aggregate demand schedule to get the following relationship:

$$\tilde{y}_t = E_t[\tilde{y}_{t+1}] + E_t[\pi_{t+1}] - \phi\pi_t \tag{56.5}$$

4. We will guess that, in equilibrium, agents expect inflation and the output gap to be zero. Plug in our guess into the Phillips curve and your answer above to show that the only values of inflation and the output gap consistent with this guess are $\pi_t = 0$ and $\tilde{y}_t = 0$, respectively.

5. Explain why our answers above mean our initial guess—that agents rationally expect inflation and the output gap to be zero—is correct.
[Hint: What are the equilibrium values of π_{t+1} and $\tilde{y}_{t+1}$?]

6. Show that, in equilibrium, the nominal interest rate will be equal to the natural interest rate.

56.2   Hitting the Zero Lower Bound

When the bank is able to follow its monetary policy rule, the equilibrium nominal interest rate is equal to the natural rate of interest. This is possible only if the natural rate of interest is positive. What happens when it turns negative?

1. Recall that $E_t[\bar{r}_{t+1}] > 0$. Explain why, even if the natural interest rate becomes negative, $\bar{r}_t < 0$, expected inflation and the expected output gap will remain at zero.

2. Use the Fisher equation to show that this implies that the equilibrium real interest rate is also subject to the zero lower bound in this economy.

3. Show that aggregate demand is given by:

$$\tilde{c}_t = \bar{r}_t - r_t \tag{56.6}$$

4. If $\bar{r}_t$ is negative, what values would the real interest rate have to take in order for the output gap to remain at zero? Can the real interest rate achieve those values?

5. The Euler equation tells us that the real interest rate is the relative price of consumption. Given your answers above, explain why this price is artificially high when the nominal interest rate is stuck at the zero lower bound.

6. If the equilibrium relative price of consumption is so high that the household chooses to consume less than the natural rate of consumption, what happens to aggregate demand? What happens to output?

7. Verify that your intuition is correct by showing that at the zero lower bound, $\tilde{y}_t = \bar{r}_t$. Is the output gap positive or negative? Has the economy entered a boom or a recession?

Reference

Eggertsson, G., & M. Woodford (2003). The zero bound on interest rates and optimal monetary policy. *Brookings Papers on Economic Activity, 1*, 139–233.

57 Forward Guidance

The Federal Open Market Committee, FOMC, sets monetary policy in the United States by targeting the nominal interest rate that banks charge one another for overnight loans: the *federal funds rate*. After every meeting, the committee puts out a press release announcing its target. In its last meeting of 2008, the press release said:

The Federal Open Market Committee decided today to establish a target range for the federal funds rate of 0 to 1/4 percent.

In the midst of the worst financial crisis since the Great Depression, the Fed had hit the zero lower bound.

While the target stayed the same after the first meeting of the FOMC in 2009, the press release did not. The January 2009 press release read:

The Federal Open Market Committee decided today to keep its target range for the federal funds rate at 0 to 1/4 percent. The Committee continues to anticipate that economic conditions are likely to warrant exceptionally low levels of the federal funds rate for some time.

The committee eventually replaced "for some time" with "for an extended period," but otherwise kept that second sentence in its press releases for years to come. By 2011, the committee had become even more specific; in its last meeting that year, "for an extended period" was replaced with "at least through mid-2013."

In chapter 56, "The Zero Lower Bound," we analyzed the economic implications of the first sentence of the press release. In this problem we will analyze the economic implications of the second sentence.

57.1 Speaking

1. What information does the first sentence of the press release contain?

2. What information does the second sentence add to the press release?

3. The second sentence is an example of *forward guidance*. Offer an educated guess about what we mean by "forward guidance."

4. What economic variable might the Fed have been trying to *directly* influence by revealing future nominal interest rates?

5. What economic variable might the Fed have been trying to *indirectly* influence through equilibrium by revealing future nominal interest rates?

57.2   A Three-Period Economy

The Fed's statements suggest a tripartite policy time frame. There's the present, when the nominal interest rate is at zero; the near future, when the nominal interest rate will remain at zero; and the far future, when the nominal interest rate will lift off. Therefore, to analyze what the Fed had in mind in 2009 we will build a three-period economy with the following aggregate supply and aggregate demand schedules, respectively:

$$\pi_t = \kappa \tilde{y}_t + E_t[\pi_{t+1}] \tag{57.1}$$

$$\tilde{c}_t = E_t[\tilde{c}_{t+1}] - i_t + E_t[\pi_{t+1}] + \bar{r}_t \tag{57.2}$$

where $\tilde{y}_t$ is the output gap, $\tilde{c}_t$ is the consumption gap, and $\bar{r}_t$ is the natural rate of interest. Note that consumption is the only component of aggregate demand in this economy.

The central bank sets monetary policy according to the following Taylor rule as long as the nominal interest rate is above the zero lower bound:

$$i_t = \bar{r}_t + \phi \pi_t \tag{57.3}$$

and follows the Taylor principle, setting $\phi > 1$.

1. Combine the central bank's monetary policy rule with the market-clearing condition in the goods market and equation (57.2) to derive the following relationship:

$$\tilde{y}_t = E_t[\tilde{y}_{t+1}] - \phi \pi_t + E_t[\pi_{t+1}] \tag{57.4}$$

Equations (57.1) and (57.4) describe the equilibrium relationship between inflation and the output gap in this economy, given expectations of future inflation and the future output gap. We will once again rely on the guess and check method to solve for the equilibrium. We will guess that inflation expectations in this economy are constant and we will denote them by λ:

$$E_t[\pi_{t+j}] = \lambda$$

for any future horizon, j. We will now proceed by verifying our guess.

2. Consider the Phillips curve in period $t + 1$, and show that expected inflation in period t is given by:

$$E_t[\pi_{t+1}] = \kappa \, E_t[\tilde{y}_{t+1}] + E_t[\pi_{t+2}]$$

3. Combine your answer above with our guess that inflation expectations are constant to show that the expected output gap is zero: $E_t[\tilde{y}_{t+1}] = 0$.

4. Apply this result to the aggregate demand schedule in period $t + 1$ and show that inflation expectations at different horizons must satisfy:

$$0 = E_t[\pi_{t+2}] - \phi E_t[\pi_{t+1}]$$

5. Combine your answer above with our guess that inflation expectations are constant to show that inflation expectations must be zero: $\lambda = 0$.
[Hint: Recall that $\phi > 1$.]

6. We have now shown our guess implies that all expectations are zero:

$$E_t[\pi_{t+1}] = E_t[\tilde{y}_{t+1}] = 0$$

Substitute these values into equations (57.1) and (57.4) and show that both the output gap and inflation are also zero in equilibrium: $\tilde{y}_t = 0$ and $\pi_t = 0$.

7. Now, to verify our guess, we need to show that the equilibrium we have solved implies constant expected inflation. If the equilibrium inflation rate in any period is zero, what is the rational expectation of future inflation?

8. What is the equilibrium nominal interest rate?

57.3   A Tale of Two Policies: No Forward Guidance

In the previous section we showed that when the equilibrium relationships between output and inflation are given by equations (57.1)–(57.2), if $\bar{r}_t > 0$ then $\tilde{y}_t = 0$, $\pi_t = 0$, and $i_t = \bar{r}_t$ in every period, t.

Now suppose that in period one the natural rate of interest suddenly becomes negative, $\bar{r}_1 < 0$, but is expected to be positive and constant in periods two and three, $\bar{r}_2 = \bar{r}_3 \equiv \rho > 0$. What happens to inflation and the output gap now?

Let's begin with the case of no forward guidance. Under this policy the central bank does not speak about the future path of the nominal interest rate—there is no second sentence in the FOMC press release. It simply sets the nominal interest rate each period either at zero or according to the Taylor rule, equation (57.3), if possible. To solve our model we will use backward induction, starting in period three and using the outcomes of the latter periods to derive the expected values in the earlier periods.

1. Given that the natural rate is positive in periods two and three, will the nominal interest rate be positive or at the zero lower bound?

2. Given your answer above, explain why $\pi_t = 0$ and $\tilde{y}_t = 0$ when $t = 2, 3$.

3. What is the real interest rate, r_t in periods two and three? How does it compare to the natural rate of interest?
[Hint: Think of the Fisher equation.]

4. We now turn to period one. Given your answers above, what are the expected inflation and expected output gap in period one? Substitute your answers into equation (57.2).

5. Combine your answer above with the fact that the central bank has hit the zero lower bound, $\bar{r}_1 < 0$ and $i_1 = 0$, to show that:

$$\tilde{y}_1 = \bar{r}_1$$

Is the output gap positive or negative? Is the economy in recession or in a boom?

6. Now substitute your answers above into the Phillips Curve, equation (57.1) to show that:

$$\pi_1 = \kappa \bar{r}_1$$

Is inflation positive or negative?

7. What is the real interest rate in period one? How does it compare to the natural rate of interest?

8. Assume $\rho = 0.02$, $\kappa = 1$, and $\bar{r}_1 = -0.06$. Substitute these values into the solutions for the equilibrium output gap, inflation, and interest rates (both nominal and real) to come up with numerical values for each of these variables in each of the three periods.
[Hint: For each variable x_t, you need to have a numerical value for $t = 1, 2, 3$.]

We have solved for the equilibrium sequences of the output gap, inflation, and the interest rates (both nominal and real). We will now proceed to graph them. In all the following graphs, time should be on the x axis. Each graph should contain only three points, one per period.

9. Graph the natural rate of interest, $\bar{r}_t$, as a function of time.

10. Graph the nominal interest rate, i_t, as a function of time.

11. Graph the real interest rate, r_t, as a function of time.

12. Graph the output gap, $\tilde{y}_t$, as a function of time.

13. Graph inflation, π_t, as a function of time.

57.4   A Tale of Two Policies: Forward Guidance

Let's now turn to the case with forward guidance. Under this policy, the central bank still hits the zero lower bound in period one: $\bar{r}_1 < 0$ and $i_1 = 0$. However, it now also announces that in period two it will keep the nominal interest rate at zero. As the name suggests, the central bank offers *guidance* about its *forward*, or future, policy. This announcement is the analogue to the second sentence of the FOMC press releases we discussed at the beginning of this problem. In period three, it will once again set monetary policy according to the Taylor rule, equation (57.3). We will proceed as before, solving the model backward starting from period three and using our solutions in the latter periods to come up with expectations in the earlier periods.

1. Given that the natural rate is positive in period three, will the nominal interest rate be positive or at the zero lower bound?

2. Given your answer above, explain why the the output gap and inflation will both be zero in period three: $\tilde{y}_3 = 0$ and $\pi_3 = 0$.

3. What is the real interest rate in period three?

4. Given your answers above explain why $E_2[\tilde{y}_3] = 0$ and $E_2[\pi_3] = 0$.

5. What is the nominal interest rate in period two?

6. Substitute your answers to the two previous questions into equation (57.2) to show that

$$\tilde{y}_2 = \rho$$

Is the output gap in period two positive or negative?
[Hint: Recall that $\bar{r}_2 = \rho > 0$.]

7. Use the Phillips curve, equation (57.1), to show that:

$$\pi_2 = \kappa \rho$$

Will the public characterize inflation in period two as higher than usual or lower than usual?

8. What is the real interest rate in period two?

9. Given your answers above, what are the expected inflation and expected output gap in period one?
[Hint: Are inflation or the output gap in period two random?]

10. Use equation (57.2) to derive the equilibrium output gap in period one:

$$\tilde{y}_1 = (1 + \kappa)\rho + \bar{r}_1$$

11. Use the Phillips curve, equation (57.1), to derive equilibrium inflation in period one:

$$\pi_1 = \kappa((1 + \kappa)\rho + \bar{r}_1) + \rho$$

12. What is the real interest rate in period one?

13. Assume $\rho = 0.02$, $\kappa = 1$, and $\bar{r}_1 = -0.06$. Substitute these values into the solutions for the equilibrium output gap, inflation, and interest rates (both nominal and real) to come up with numerical values for each of these variables in each of the three periods.
[Hint: For each variable x_t, you need to have a numerical value for $t = 1, 2, 3$.]

We have solved for the equilibrium sequences of the output gap, inflation, and the interest rates (both nominal and real) under forward guidance. We will now proceed to graph them. In all the following graphs, time should be on the x axis. Each graph should contain only three points, one per period.

14. Graph the natural rate of interest, $\bar{r}_t$, as a function of time. How does this graph compare to the case without forward guidance?

15. Graph the nominal interest rate, i_t, as a function of time. How does this graph compare to the case without forward guidance?

16. Graph the real interest rate, r_t, as a function of time. How does this graph compare to the case without forward guidance?

17. Graph the output gap, $\tilde{y}_t$, as a function of time. How does this graph compare to the case without forward guidance?

18. Graph inflation, π_t, as a function of time. How does this graph compare to the case without forward guidance?

19. Does inflation have to fall below its average level in order for the central bank to hit the zero lower bound?

20. By announcing that it would keep the nominal interest rate low in period two, what period one economic variable did the central bank *directly* change? As a result of this direct change, what other economic variables changed in equilibrium?

References

Eggertsson, G., & M. Woodford (2003). The zero bound on interest rates and optimal monetary policy. *Brookings Papers on Economic Activity, 1*, 139–233.

Gürkaynak, R., B. Sack, & E. Swanson (2005a). Do actions speak louder than words? The response of asset prices to monetary policy actions and statements. *International Journal of Central Banking, 1*(1), 55–94.

Federal Reserve Board (2008). *FOMC statement* [press release], December 16, 2008. https://www.federalreserve .gov/newsevents/pressreleases/monetary20081216b.htm

Federal Reserve Board (2009). *FOMC statement* [press release], January 28, 2009. https://www.federalreserve .gov/newsevents/pressreleases/monetary20090128a.htm

Federal Reserve Board (2011). *FOMC statement* [press release], December 13, 2011. https://www.federalreserve .gov/newsevents/pressreleases/monetary20111213a.htm

58 The Government Expenditure Multiplier Revisited

In a closed economy with flexible prices, the government expenditure multiplier, m, is less than one and greater than zero. An expansion in government purchases crowds out private expenditure and increases labor supply: output increases by less than the expansion in government purchases. In this chapter, we will analyze the relationship between the multiplier and the real interest rate. We will then see how the same real interest rate can lead to diametrically different multipliers in two contrasting examples.

58.1 The Multiplier and the Real Interest Rate

We have a two-period economy with households, firms, and the government.

Firms hire labor, L, from households to produce output, Y, according to the production function:

$$Y_t = AL_t \tag{58.1}$$

They sell their output to either households, C, or the government, G.

Households choose consumption across time to satisfy the Euler equation:

$$\frac{C_{t+1}}{C_t} = \beta(1+r) \tag{58.2}$$

where r is the real interest rate.

Finally, the market-clearing condition in the labor market is given by:

$$C_t L_t^\phi = \frac{Y_t}{L_t} \tag{58.3}$$

where the left-hand side is the household's marginal rate of substitution and the right-hand side is the marginal product of labor.

1. Write down the market-clearing condition in the goods market. Label the side of your equation that corresponds to output and the side of the equation that corresponds to aggregate demand.

2. Combine the production function with the market-clearing condition in the goods market to derive the following linear relationship between consumption, labor, and government purchases:

$$C_t = AL_t - G_t \tag{58.4}$$

3. Combine the production function with the market-clearing condition in the labor market to derive the following nonlinear relationship between consumption and labor:

$$C_t = \frac{A}{L_t^\phi} \tag{58.5}$$

Let $\bar{G}$ denote the baseline level of government purchases. Given this level of purchases, the goods and labor market must both clear simultaneously in general equilibrium. We now turn to the equilibrium allocations of consumption, labor, and output. And the equilibrium real interest rate.

4. Set up a large coordinate plane with C on the y axis and L on the x axis. Graph the market-clearing condition in the goods market and the labor market, equations (58.4) and (58.5), respectively.
[Hint: We will graph additional equations on this diagram later; make it large and clear.]

5. Let $(\bar{L}, \bar{C})$ denote their intersection. Explain why this point denotes the equilibrium allocations of consumption and labor in this economy.

6. Suppose that the government purchases remain constant across time at $\bar{G}$. Will consumption and labor also remain constant?

7. Given your answer above, show that the equilibrium real interest rate in this economy is:

$$\bar{r} = -\log(\beta) \tag{58.6}$$

Does the real interest rate depend on the level of government purchases, $\bar{G}$?

Now suppose that the government approves a fiscal stimulus in period one, so that $G_1 > \bar{G}$, but plans to return to its benchmark level, $\bar{G}$, in period two.

9. Let $\Delta G \equiv G_1 - \bar{G}$ denote the stimulus and $\Delta Y \equiv Y_1 - \bar{Y}$ denote the change in output that results from the stimulus. Recall the mathematical definition of the multiplier:

$$m \equiv \frac{\Delta Y}{\Delta G}$$

Write down the definition in words.

10. What effect, if any, does the increase in government purchases have on the market-clearing condition in the labor market? What effect, if any, does the increase in government purchases have on the market-clearing condition in the goods market?

11. In the same diagram as question 4, graph the goods market-clearing condition in period one, with the higher level of government purchases.

12. Let (L_1, C_1) denote the intersection of the two market-clearing conditions in period one. Is consumption in period one higher or lower than consumption in period two?

13. Given your answer above, show that the real interest rate increases, $r > \bar{r}$, as a result of the government stimulus.

58.2 A Small Open Economy

A small open economy has access to capital and goods markets abroad but is subject to world prices, including the real interest rate, r. We saw that in a closed economy an increase in government purchases leads to an increase in the real interest rate. In a small open economy this is no longer the case; the real interest rate is set in world markets and remains constant when government purchases increase. What happens to the multiplier now?

The two-period economy behaves exactly like the one developed in the previous section, with only two differences. First, the market clearing condition in the goods market reflects its ability to trade with the rest of the world; aggregate demand now includes the trade balance, denoted by TB. Second, the world real interest rate is fixed and unresponsive to local economic conditions. We can assume for simplicity that $\beta(1 + r) = 1$.

1. Show that consumption in the small open economy is constant:

$$\bar{C} \equiv C_t = C_{t+1}$$

2. Given your answer above, will changes to government purchases crowd out household consumption?

3. Offer an educated guess about the size of the multiplier in this economy. If Government purchases increase by one dollar, by how much do you expect output to increase?

4. Now consider the market-clearing condition in the labor market. If consumption is constant across time, show that labor is also constant across time:

$$\bar{L} = \left(\frac{A}{\bar{C}}\right)^{1/\phi}$$

5. If government purchases increase, what happens to labor supply in this economy?

6. Explain why the government expenditure multiplier in this economy is zero: $m = 0$. [Hint: Labor is the only factor of production.]

7. Write down the market-clearing condition in the goods market.

8. Let $\Delta G \equiv G_1 - \bar{G}$ denote the fiscal stimulus. Let ΔY, ΔC, and ΔTB denote the changes in output, consumption and the trade balance, respectively, that result from the stimulus.

Show that, in equilibrium:

$$- \Delta TB = \Delta G \tag{58.7}$$

9. The household earns income, which it then allocates among consumption, C_t, savings, S_t, and taxes, T_t. Write down the household's budget constraint.

10. Suppose the government runs a balanced budget. Any increase in government purchases is paid for by an increase in taxes: $\Delta G = \Delta T$. Show that, in equilibrium:

$$\Delta S = - \Delta G \tag{58.8}$$

What happens to national savings as a result of the increase in government purchases?

11. Suppose that, instead, the government keeps taxes constant. By how much does the deficit increase due to its increase in government purchases? Is the change to national savings different if the government runs a deficit or if it runs a balanced budget?

58.3   Monetary and Fiscal Policies

If the classical dichotomy holds, an increase in government purchases leads to a decrease in consumption and an increase in the real interest rate. What happens when monetary policy can have an effect on the real interest rate?

Consider once again a two-period, closed economy. The government has a benchmark level of government purchases, $\bar{G}$, and in period one approves a temporary stimulus so that $G_1 > \bar{G} = G_2$.

1. Suppose that the central bank conducts monetary policy to keep the real interest rate constant at $\bar{r} = - \log(\beta)$. Show that, in equilibrium, $C_1 = C_2 = \bar{C}$.

2. Let $\Delta G \equiv G_1 - \bar{G}$ denote the stimulus and $\Delta Y \equiv Y_1 - \bar{Y}$ denote that change in output that results from the stimulus. Combine your answer above with the market-clearing condition in the goods market to show that under the central bank's monetary policy:

$$\Delta Y = \Delta G \tag{58.9}$$

3. Show that under the monetary policy of constant real interest rates, the government expenditure multiplier is one: $m = 1$.

4. Does in increase in government purchases crowd out private expenditures under this type of monetary policy?

5. What can we conclude about the differences in the size of the government expenditure multiplier in an economy where the classical dichotomy holds versus one where it doesn't?

6. Suppose the central bank has hit the zero lower bound and that inflation expectations are constant. What happens to the real interest rate if government purchases increase? What is the size of the multiplier in this case?

Reference

Woodford, M. (2011). Simple analytics of the government expenditure multiplier. *American Economic Journal: Macroeconomics, 3*(1), 1–35.

59 Maturity Transformation

Households can save by lending to the government. Government bonds, however, have a fixed maturity; the government will not repay the household until the date specified on the bond. Households that value flexibility can instead save by lending to a commercial bank. Unlike government bonds, savings accounts allow the household to ask the bank to repay the loan at *any* time. In this chapter we will ask—and answer—why banks would make such an offer, why households would accept it, and what might happen when they do.

59.1 Flexibility and Maturity

Intuitively, the reason we value the flexibility—as *lenders*—of a savings account is that we are not certain when we will need to withdraw our assets. Yet the desire for flexibility is asymmetric: as *borrowers* we do not want flexibility. Would you be willing to sign a lease for a car if the bank could demand repayment at any time it wished? In fact, if the bank demanded such a repayment at an arbitrary time you might not be able to make it, forcing the bank to face a loss.

To capture these two competing desires, we will consider a household in period $t = 0$ that lives for *two* more periods, $t = 1$ and $t = 2$. The household has one unit of wealth to save for future consumption, and must choose *how* to allocate it among different savings vehicles. However, there's a catch: the household doesn't know *when* it will need to consume. It has the following utility function:

$$U(C_1, C_2) = (1 - \beta)u(C_1) + \beta u(C_2) \tag{59.1}$$

where β is a *random variable* that is unknown in period $t = 0$, when the household must decide how to allocate its savings.

$$\beta = \begin{cases} 1 & \text{with probability } \lambda \\ 0 & \text{with probability } 1 - \lambda \end{cases}$$

1. What is the economic interpretation of β?

[Hint: What feature of the world does β capture?]

2. Explain why the household will consume in either period one or two, but never both.

3. Does the household know its utility function, $U(C_1, C_2)$, in period $t = 0$?

4. Write down the two possible utility functions that the household may face in the future. Write down the respective probabilities of each possible future utility function.

5. Show that the household's *expected* utility in period $t = 0$ is:

$$E_{t=0}[U(C_1, C_2)] = (1 - \lambda)u(C_1) + \lambda u(C_2) \tag{59.2}$$

We call each of the two possible values that β can take a *state of the world*. An *allocation* in this context is a bundle $\{C_1, C_2\}$ that denotes the amount of consumption that is possible in either state of the world as a result of the saving decisions the household makes in period $t = 0$.

6. Given that the household makes its decision in period $t = 0$, explain why it cannot maximize (59.1) and must instead maximize (59.2).

7. If the household knew in period $t = 0$ the value that β would take, would the household choose an allocation where both C_1 and C_2 are positive?

8. Explain why this setup creates a *preference for flexibility* when it comes to savings.

The household has two options available to it as a saver. The first option is to store its unit of wealth; to put it under the mattress, so to speak. If it stores a fraction, s, it can consume s in either period one or two. Alternatively, the household can lend out its unit of wealth; it can become an investor. When the household recalls its loan, we say that the household *liquidates* its investment. The return on the investment depends on the period of liquidation. If the household liquidates in period one, it will face a loss: it will receive only a fraction, $L < 1$, of its initial investment. However, if it waits and liquidates in period two, it receives a positive return, $R > 1$, on its initial investment.

9. Write down the *expected* return for the household if it chooses to invest its unit of wealth.

10. Briefly describe the trade-off that the household faces.

11. Show that if the household decides to store s and invest the remaining $1 - s$, then if $\beta = 0$ it will consume:

$$C_1 = (1 - s)L + s \tag{59.3}$$

12. Show that if the household decides to store a fraction s and invest the remaining $1 - s$, then if $\beta = 1$ it will consume:

$$C_2 = (1 - s)R + s \tag{59.4}$$

In what follows, we will use expressions (59.3) and (59.4) to graph the household's budget constraint.

13. Set up a large coordinate plane with C_2 on the y axis and C_1 on the x axis. Plot the allocation, $\{C_1, C_2\}$, that arises if the household chooses $s = 0$.
[Hint: Equations (59.3)–(59.4) define the allocation $\{C_1, C_2\}$ as a function of s.]

14. In your same diagram plot the allocation, $\{C_1, C_2\}$, that arises if the household chooses $s = 1$.

15. Graph the line *segment* that connects the two allocations you have plotted on the graph. Explain why *any* point on this line segment is a feasible allocation.
[Hint: What are the values that s can take?]

16. Explain why the allocation $\{0, R\}$ is feasible.

17. Explain why every allocation on the line segment connecting $\{0, R\}$ and $\{L, R\}$ is also feasible. Plot the two allocations on your graph and draw the line segment connecting them.

18. Explain why the allocation $\{1, 0\}$ is feasible.

19. Explain why every allocation on the line segment connecting $\{1, 0\}$ and $\{1, 1\}$ is also feasible. Graph the line segment.

20. You now have a budget constraint that consists of a region bounded by three line segments and the coordinate plane. Assuming only that $u(\cdot)$ is an increasing function, identify the boundary in the budget constraint that is the set of allocations that the household will consider choosing.

59.2 Banks

So far, households can either store their assets under the mattress or find investment opportunities directly and assume the risk of having to liquidate those investments early. An agent with an entrepreneurial bent might look at this situation and ask: Why don't I offer my services as an intermediary between the households and the investments? This agent is the bank.

In period $t = 0$, the bank accepts deposits, D, from a very large number of households. In exchange, it offers depositors a *contract*, (r_1, r_2). The contract specifies the gross return, r_t, that depositors get when they withdraw in each time period. Crucially, the bank has access to the same savings technologies as the household—it can either invest or store its deposits. We are interested in describing the contracts that the bank *can* offer, assuming that households withdraw their deposits in the period that they need to use them.

1. What fraction of depositors will withdraw their savings in period one?

2. Given that the bank will pay r_1 on all deposits withdrawn in period one, explain why the bank will need to have a total of $D(1 - \lambda)r_1$ funds available in that period. We will say the bank is *liquid* if in period one it has the necessary funds needed to cover all withdrawals.

3. Will the bank invest or store the funds it needs to have available for withdrawal in period one?

[Hint: Compare the gross returns to each of these alternatives.]

4. After securing the funds it needs for period one, what amount remains? Will the bank invest or store the leftover funds?

5. Under the investments strategy just outlined, will the bank ever have to liquidate its investments early and face a loss?

6. The investment strategy just outlined is called *maturity transformation*. Given your answers above, write down an educated guess as to what this phrase means.

7. Write down the expression for the total amount of assets available to the bank in period two.

[Hint: What amount does the bank invest? What return does the bank earn on that investment, R or L?].

8. Write down an expression for the total amount of withdrawals the bank will face in period two.

9. Given your answers above, explain why any deposit contract, (r_1, r_2), that the bank offers must satisfy the following inequality:

$$R - R(1 - \lambda)r_1 \geq \lambda r_2 \qquad (59.5)$$

10. We will call inequality (59.5) the bank's *solvency* condition. Explain why, if the contracts the bank offers don't satisfy (59.5), the bank will be *insolvent* and have to file for bankruptcy.

[Hint: What kind of constraint is (59.5)?]

11. Explain why, in addition to (59.5), the deposit contract must also satisfy

$$r_2 \geq r_1 \qquad (59.6)$$

or else all households will withdraw in period one.

12. Given your answers above, explain why inequality (59.6) is necessary for the bank to remain *liquid*.

With the two constraints above, we are now in a position to compare the allocations available to the household without the bank with those available in the presence of a bank.

13. Isolate r_2 on the right-hand side of inequality (59.5).

14. In a large coordinate plane with r_2 on the y axis and r_1 on the x axis graph inequalities (59.5) and (59.6). Make sure you label the critical points on the graph, including the axis intercepts and the intersection of the two boundaries.

[Hint: Use the answer to the previous question to help you graph (59.5).]

15. Explain why the resulting triangular region is the set of all feasible contracts.

16. Suppose the household deposits its unit of wealth in the bank. Explain why $r_t = C_t$ for both $t = 1$ and $t = 2$.

17. Given that we can use C_t and r_t interchangeably, graph the set of feasible allocations that the household can achieve without the bank. This is the set you graphed in the previous section.

18. Explain why maturity transformation expands the allocations available to the household.

19. Suppose banks operate in a competitive market and hence make zero profits. In your graph depict the set of contracts that will be offered to households in equilibrium.
[Hint: With zero profits, will (59.5) hold as a strict inequality or with equality?]

20. If utility is increasing in consumption and the banking sector is competitive, will households deposit their savings in a bank, store them, invest them directly, or choose a mixture of the three?

Reference

Diamond, D., & P. Dybvig (1983). Bank runs, deposit insurance, and liquidity. *Journal of Political Economy, 91*(5), 401–419.

60 Diamond and Dybvig Run to the Bank

Maturity transformation is welfare-enhancing because it matches lenders' desire for flexibility with borrowers' desire for a fixed, long-term maturities. By pooling deposits, banks can eliminate the risk of liquidating investments early, while maintaining the liquidity necessary to fulfill withdrawals... Or can they?

When banks allocate their portfolio, they must guess what fraction of their lenders will liquidate their accounts early. In chapter 59, "Maturity Transformation," the banks guessed that only the households in need of liquidity would withdraw their funds early. In this problem we will revisit that model and reconsider that assumption.

As in chapter 59, there are three periods. Households deposit their savings in the bank in period zero. The bank must then decide what fraction of those deposits to invest, and what fraction to store. If liquidated in period two, investments have a positive rate of return, $R > 1$; if liquidated in period one, investments have a negative rate of return, $L < 1$. If instead of investing the bank stores the deposits, then their gross return is simply one. The bank offers depositors a gross rate of return, r_t, depending on the time period, t, when they withdraw their funds. Depositors who wait until period two get a weakly higher return: $r_2 \geq r_1 \geq 1$. A fraction, $1 - \lambda$, of households will need to withdraw their deposits in period one, while λ will need to withdraw their deposits in period two. The crucial question is: What fraction will actually end up withdrawing their funds in each period?

60.1 Liquidity

1. In what time period does the bank choose how to allocate deposits between storing and investing?

2. Given your answer above, explain why this investment strategy is based on the *assumption* by the bank that households withdraw their deposits in the time period they need to use them.

3. Will this assumption ever be violated by households who need to use their deposits in period one? How about households who need to use their deposits in period two?

Are there equilibria where households violate the bank's original—and seemingly reasonable—assumption? To characterize the equilibria that are possible, we will ask a related question: Is it ever optimal for an *individual* household, acting *independently*, to withdraw its funds early? We will call households that need to consume in period two the Diamonds, while households who need to consume in period one the Dybvigs.

4. Suppose you are one of the Diamonds in period one. As you look around you see that only the Dybvigs are withdrawing funds. Nonetheless you decide to withdraw your funds early and store them. How much will you be able to consume in period two?

5. Consider the same scenario as above, but instead you decide to wait, just like the bank assumed you would. How much will you be able to consume in period two?

6. Under which of the two behaviors will you be able to consume more? Which action will you take?

7. Explain why it is an equilibrium for the Dybvigs to withdraw their funds in period one and for the Diamonds to wait and withdraw their funds in period two.
[Hint: Can any agent change their behavior unilaterally to increase their payoffs?]

Now consider an alternative scenario. Suppose that this time around both the Diamonds and the Dybvigs withdraw their funds in period one. Can this be an equilibrium? And if so, what are its properties?

8. Explain why the bank has $(1 - \lambda)r_1$ on hand in period one.

9. Explain why if all households—both Diamonds and Dybvigs—withdraw their funds in the first period, the bank will need a total of r_1, per household. We will conduct our analysis on a per-household basis going forward. Is this more or less than what the bank has available?

10. You have shown that under this scenario, the bank will be forced to liquidate some of its investment portfolio early. Show that the maximum amount of funds that the bank can raise by liquidating its investments is:

$$(1 - (1 - \lambda)r_1)L \tag{60.1}$$

11. Show that the difference between the liquidity available to the bank—the funds on hand plus the value of the investments liquidated in period one at a loss—and the liquidity that the bank needs to honor its contract with depositors is:

$$\lambda(L - 1)r_1 + L(1 - r_1) \tag{60.2}$$

12. Given the expression above, will the bank have enough liquidity to fulfill its deposit contracts in period one?
[Hint: Recall that $L < 1$ and $r_1 \geq 1$.]

Suppose the bank defaults on the deposit contract by liquidating all of its investments early and then dividing all of its liquid assets equally among depositors in period one.

13. Explain why (60.2) is the loss that each depositor will be forced to take if all depositors decide to withdraw their funds in period one.

14. Now put yourself in the shoes of one of the Diamonds. You see all of the other Diamonds and all of the Dybvigs withdrawing their funds in period one. What is the total amount you will be able to withdraw in period two if you decide to wait? What is the total amount you will be able to withdraw in period one?

15. If you are a Diamond, will you wait until period two or withdraw in period one?

16. Given that all of the other Diamonds must independently reach the same conclusion as you have, explain why it is an equilibrium for *all households* to withdraw their funds in period one. What is such a scenario usually called?

60.2 Solvency

We have shown that in the bank-run equilibrium, the bank finds itself in a *liquidity* crisis, which justifies the run on the bank. There still remains the question of *solvency*: Does a liquidity crisis necessarily imply the bank must go bankrupt? We will consider the worst-case contract, $\{r_1, r_2\}$, for the bank. If the bank can avoid bankruptcy under the worst contract, then it can avoid bankruptcy for all contracts. Conversely, if the bank cannot avoid bankruptcy under the worst contract, we can ask what set of contracts are bankruptcy-proof.

1. Show that the liquidity gap, expression (60.2), becomes worse, i.e., more negative, as r_1 increases.

2. Show that the maximum feasible contract the bank can offer is such that $r_1 = r_2$ and:

$$r_1 = \frac{R}{\lambda + R(1 - \lambda)}$$

This is the worst-case contract.

3. The liquidity crisis arises because the bank's balance sheet loses value when the bank is forced to liquidate its investments in period one. Show that under the worst-case contract, the value of the investments if the bank does *not* liquidate early is:

$$\frac{\lambda R}{\lambda + R(1 - \lambda)} \tag{60.3}$$

4. Show that if all depositors withdraw in period one, the bank will need an additional λr_1 in funds to fulfill its contract without defaulting.

5. Show that under the worst-case contract, the value of the bank's investments is exactly equal to its outstanding liabilities in the bank-run equilibrium.

6. If the bank did not liquidate its investments to meet its funding needs and instead borrowed the necessary amount against the value of its investments, would it be able to pay

back the loan in period two? Does your answer depend on the type of contract the bank offers?

7. What is the most liquid asset in the economy? Who supplies this asset?

8. Suppose the bank finds itself facing a run on its deposits in period one. If the central bank has the authority to act as *lender of last resort* and the bank appealed to it for a loan against its investments, would the central bank be able to recoup its loan?

9. Given your answers above, does a liquidity crisis necessarily imply a solvency crisis?

Now suppose that in period $t = 0$ the Central Bank announces that all deposits are insured. That means that the Central Bank guarantees any *solvent* contract (r_1, r_2).

10. If you are one of the Diamonds and all the other Diamonds and the Dybvigs withdraw their funds in period one, what amount will you be able to withdraw if you wait until period two? What amount will you be able to withdraw if you do so in period one?

11. Will you wait until period two, or will you also run to the bank and withdraw your deposits in period one?

12. Given that all of the other Diamonds must independently reach the same conclusion as you have, explain why deposit insurance *eliminates* the bank-run equilibrium altogether.

13. By credibly promising to insure the deposits, will the central bank ever be forced to actually step in and pay out the insurance?

Reference

Diamond, D., & P. Dybvig (1983). Bank runs, deposit insurance, and liquidity. *Journal of Political Economy, 91*(5), 401–419.

61 A Contribution to the Theory of Orchards

Consider an apple orchard. The farmer—we'll call him Solow—uses labor to harvest the apples in the orchard. We will denote his total stock of trees at any given point by K_t, the amount of labor that he needs to pick the apples by L_t, and the total harvest by Y_t. Solow can do two things with the apples: he can either eat them, C_t, or plant them, I_t, so that they can become trees in the future. These are GMO apples and we assume that once planted they become fruit-bearing trees the following period. Like all living things, apple trees die from time to time. In each period, an apple tree has a probability of dying, δ.

61.1 The Trees

1. Solow begins each period, t, with a total of K_t trees. What fraction of the trees die in period t?

2. Write an expression for the total number of trees that die in period t.

3. How many trees are planted in period t?

4. Given your answers above, explain why the following equation describes the number of trees in period $t + 1$:

$$K_{t+1} = K_t + I_t - \delta K_t \tag{61.1}$$

We will call equation (61.1) the *law of motion* of trees in the orchard.

5. Explain why the number of new trees planted, I_t, must ultimately depend on the total number of trees in the orchard, K_t.

6. In what time period does Solow choose how many trees he wants to have in period $t + 1$?

7. The law of motion above is in *levels*; the left-hand side of the equation is the number of trees in period $t + 1$. Rearrange equation (61.1) so that the left hand side is the *gross* growth rate of the trees in period $t + 1$.
[Hint: Recall that gross growth rates are ratios.]

8. Show that the *net* growth rate of trees is given by:

$$\frac{I_t}{K_t} - \delta \tag{61.2}$$

[Hint: There are two ways to show this. If you use logs, consider the fact that both I_t/K_t and δ are close to zero.]

9. We will call I_t/K_t the *replacement rate* of trees. We will call δ the *depreciation rate* of trees. Given these definitions, what does the net growth rate equal?

61.2   The Harvest

Suppose that Solow always plants a fixed fraction, s, of the harvest, and that the harvest, Y_t, is produced according to the Cobb-Douglas production function:

$$Y_t = A_t K_t^\alpha L_t^{1-\alpha} \tag{61.3}$$

where $0 < \alpha < 1$.

1. What factor of production are the trees?

2. What factor of production is the farmer?

3. What is the interpretation of A_t?

4. What is the range of values that s can take?

5. Write down the total number of trees Solow plants, I_t, as a function of s, A_t, K_t, L_t, and α.
[Hint: Recall s is the fraction of the harvest that Solow plants.]

6. Show that the net growth rate of trees can be written as:

$$\log(K_{t+1}) - \log(K_t) = sA_t K_t^{\alpha-1} L_t^{1-\alpha} - \delta \tag{61.4}$$

where the first term on the right-hand side is the replacement rate and the second term is the depreciation rate.

7. Is the replacement rate an increasing or decreasing function of the number of trees, K_t?

8. In a large diagram, graph the the replacement rate as a function of the number of trees, K_t.
[Hint: The rate of replacement should be on the y axis, and K_t should be on the x axis.]

9. In the same diagram graph the depreciation rate as a function of K_t.
[Hint: Note that the rate of depreciation is constant and thus independent of the number of trees.]

10. Explain why the vertical distance between the two curves on your diagram is the growth rate of trees in the orchard.

11. Suppose that Solow starts the orchard with a single tree. Is the growth rate of trees in the orchard positive or negative? What about the growth rate of the harvest?

12. As the number of trees increases, what happens to the growth rate of trees? What happens to the growth rate of the harvest?

13. In a diagram with time on the x axis and the number of trees on the y axis, graph the evolution of the number of trees, K as a function of time.

14. Suppose that Solow starts the orchard with a very, very large number of trees. Is the growth rate of trees in the orchard positive or negative? What about the growth rate of the harvest?

15. As the number of trees decreases, what happens to the growth rate of trees? What happens to the growth rate of the harvest?

16. Consider the following thought experiment. If Solow's orchard sat on an infinite plane, would the orchard increase forever?

The value of K_t at which the depreciation and replacement rates intersect is called the *steady state* and we denote it by $\bar{K}$.

17. What is the net growth rate of trees at the steady state, $\bar{K}$?

18. Show that the steady state is given by:

$$\bar{K} = \left(\frac{sA_t}{\delta} \right)^{\frac{1}{1-\alpha}} L_t$$

19. Write down an expression for the steady-state level of output.

References

Barro, R., & X. Sala-i-Martin (2004). *Economic growth, second edition.* Cambridge, MA: MIT Press.

Solow, R. (1956). A contribution to the theory of economic growth. *Quarterly Journal of Economics, 70*(1), 65–94.

Swan, T. (1956). Economic growth and capital accumulation. *Economic Record, 32*, 334–361.

62 Income per Capita

In "A Contribution to the Theory of Orchards" we analyzed the dynamic properties of an economy with capital and labor. Our main result was that, for a given labor input, the economy moves to a steady-state level of capital and output. Prosperity, however, is not about how much value an economy can produce. After all, very large orchards with many workers will produce a lot of apples. The relevant question is: how many apples can the orchard produce *per worker*? India's population is 250 times larger than Ireland's so it's no surprise that India's GDP is larger. Yet India's output is only a mere six times higher that of Ireland. Ireland is more prosperous because each Irish worker produces more than her Indian counterpart. In this chapter, we will relax the assumption of fixed labor inputs from chapter 61, recast it in *per capita* terms, and reexamine its conclusions about growth.

62.1 Rescaling

Our economy produces output, Y_t, using both capital, K_t, and labor, L_t, as factors of production according to the following production function:

$$Y_t = A_t F(K_t, L_t)$$

where A_t denotes productivity. Output is either consumed by households or invested.

1. Write down the two components of aggregate demand in this economy.

2. Suppose households in this economy save a fixed fraction of their income. We call this the *savings rate* and denote it by s. Write down total investment, I_t, as a function of output and the savings rate.

3. Write down total investment as a function of the factors of production.

4. The net growth rate of capital is equal to the replacement rate, I_t/K_t, minus the depreciation rate. Show that if the depreciation rate is constant, δ, then the net growth rate of capital

can be written as:

$$\log K_{t+1} - \log K_t = sA_t \frac{F(K_t, L_t)}{K_t} - \delta \tag{62.1}$$

Equation (62.1) describes the growth rate of capital as a function of the total capital stock. Since our interest is in capital *per capita*, our goal is to transform equation (62.1) to derive the growth rate of capital per capita as a function of the capital stock per capita.

5. Define $k_t \equiv K_t/L_t$. Explain what k_t means.

6. Suppose that the production function, $F(K, L)$, exhibits constant returns to scale. Show that we can rewrite the replacement rate as:

$$sA_t F\left(1, \frac{L_t}{K_t}\right) \tag{62.2}$$

[Hint: Recall that if a function exhibits constant returns to scale, if you scale all the inputs by some factor, $1/x$, you also scale the output by the same factor, $1/x$: $(1/x)F(K, L) = F(K/x, L/x)$.]

7. Define the function $g(k_t) \equiv F(1, 1/k_t)$. Is $g(k_t)$ an increasing or decreasing function of k_t?

[Hint: The production function is increasing in its second input, $1/k_t$.]

8. Given your answer above, is the replacement rate expression (62.2), an increasing or decreasing function of capital per capita?

9. Translate the expression $\log(L_{t+1}) - \log(L_t)$ into words.

10. Subtract $\log(L_{t+1}) - \log(L_t)$ from both sides of equation (62.1) and show that the left-hand side can be written as:

$$\log\left(\frac{K_{t+1}}{L_{t+1}}\right) - \log\left(\frac{K_t}{L_t}\right)$$

Translate the above expression into words.

11. Show that if the rate of population growth is constant, λ, then the net growth rate of capital per capita can be written as:

$$\log(k_{t+1}) - \log(k_t) = sA_t g(k_t) - (\delta + \lambda) \tag{62.3}$$

12. Explain why the depreciation rate of capital per capita depends on λ.

13. Define $y_t \equiv Y_t/L_t$. Show that if the production function exhibits constant returns to scale we can write income per capita as a function of capital per capita:

$$y_t = A_t f(k_t) \tag{62.4}$$

where $f(k_t) \equiv F(k_t, 1)$.
[Hint: Same as in question 6.]

14. Is $f(k_t)$ and increasing or decreasing function of k_t?

62.2   The Dynamics of Capital and Income

Equation (62.3) describes the law of motion of capital per capita while equation (62.4) describes income per capita as a function of capital per capita. With these two equations, we can explore the dynamics of income per capita and capital per capita, as well as income and capital. In what follows, we will assume that the production function is Cobb-Douglas:

$$F(K_t, L_t) = K_t^{\alpha} L_t^{1-\alpha}$$

1. Show that the Cobb-Douglas production function exhibits constant returns to scale.

2. Show that if the production function is Cobb-Douglas,

$$g(k_t) = k_t^{\alpha-1} \qquad (62.5)$$

Is $g(k_t)$ an increasing or decreasing function of k_t?

3. In a coordinate plane with k_t on the x axis, graph the replacement rate, $sA_t k_t^{\alpha-1}$, and the depreciation rate $\delta + \lambda$.
[Hint: Does the depreciation rate depend on k_t?]

4. Show that the steady-state level of capital per capita, where the depreciation rate equals the replacement rate is given by:

$$\bar{k} = \left(\frac{sA_t}{\delta + \lambda} \right)^{\frac{1}{1-\alpha}} \qquad (62.6)$$

5. Label the steady state, $\bar{k}$, on your diagram above.

6. Suppose you start with a positive but small amount of capital per capita, $k_t < \bar{k}$. In a diagram with time on the x axis and capital per capita on the y axis, graph the the evolution of capital per capita, k_t, as a function of time.

7. Suppose you start with a very large amount of capital per capita, $k_t > \bar{k}$. In a diagram with time on the x axis and capital per capita on the y axis, graph the the evolution of capital per capita, k_t, as a function of time.

8. Show that if the production function is Cobb-Douglas, then $f(k_t) = k_t^{\alpha}$. Is $f(k_t)$ an increasing or decreasing function of k_t?

9. Write down the steady state level of income per capita, $\bar{y}$.

10. At what rate does capital per capita grow at the steady state? At what rate does income per capita grow at the steady state?

11. At what rate does capital grow at the steady state?
[Hint: Recall that that the steady state $\bar{k} = K_t/L_t = K_{t+1}/L_{t+1}$.]

12. At what rate does output grow at the steady state?
[Hint: Same as above.]

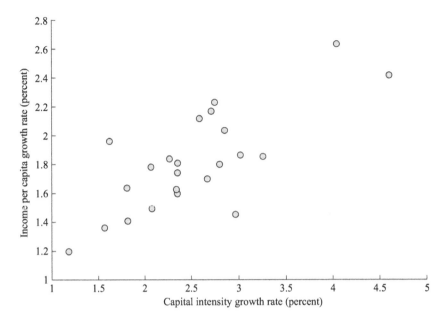

Figure 62.1
Average yearly growth rates of income per capita and capital intensity between 1890 and 2022. *Source*: Bergeaud, Cette & Lecat (2016).

13. Given your answers above, can capital per capita accumulation sustain the growth of income per capita over a long horizon?

14. Figure 62.1 plots the average yearly growth rate of income per capita, y, and capital intensity, k, over a very long horizon. Given your findings in question 4, explain whether the positive correlation implies that the long run growth rate of income per capita is caused by the sustained accumulation of capital per capita.

15. Given your answer above, is figure 62.1 at odds with our conclusions in this section?

16. Consider the steady-state level of capital per capita. What clues does equation (62.6) offer about the source of long-run growth?

62.3   The End of Growth?

We have shown that increases in the capital stock cannot sustain increases in income per capita indefinitely. Regardless of the initial stock of capital per capita, both capital per capita and output per capita eventually reach a steady state, where they remain. Now that we know *what* happens, we will answer *why*.

1. Let mpk(k_t) denote the marginal product per capita of k_t, and set $A_t = 1$. Show that if the production function is Cobb-Douglas, then:

$$\text{mpk}(k_t) = \alpha g(k_t) \tag{62.7}$$

[Hint: The marginal product is a derivative.]

We will now create two sets of diagrams. In the first set we will graph the per capita marginal product of capital per capita. In the second set, we will graph the replacement and depreciation rates of capital per capita.

2. Set up four large coordinate planes with k_t on the x axis. On each diagram you will graph the per capita marginal product of capital per capita, $\alpha k_t^{\alpha-1}$, as a function of k_t for a different value of α: 0.2, 0.6, 0.9, and 1.

3. In the first three cases, where α is less than one, what two characteristics does the marginal product of capital exhibit?

4. In the case where $\alpha = 1$, what characteristics does the marginal product of capital exhibit?

5. Set up four large coordinate planes with k_t on the x axis. On each diagram you will graph both the replacement rate of capital per capita, $sk_t^{\alpha-1}$, and the depreciation rate of capital per capita, $\delta + \lambda$, as a function of k_t for a different value of α: 0.2, 0.6, 0.9, and 1.

6. In the first three cases, where α is less than one, what happens to the steady-state level of capital per capita as α increases? Given the diagrams of the marginal product of capital per capita, offer an economic reason why this is the case.

7. In the case where $\alpha = 1$, what happens to the steady state? What is the long-run growth rate of this economy?

8. In light of your answers above, what feature of the production function gives rise to the steady-state level of capital per capita? Offer a brief economic explanation to justify your answer.

References

Barro, R., & X. Sala-i-Martin (2004). *Economic growth, second edition.* Cambridge, MA: MIT Press.

Bergeaud, A., G. Cette, & R. Lecat (2016). Productivity trends in advanced countries between 1890 and 2012. *Review of Income and Wealth, 62*(3), 420–444.

Solow, R. (1956). A contribution to the theory of economic growth. *Quarterly Journal of Economics, 70*(1), 65–94.

Swan, T. (1956). Economic growth and capital accumulation. *Economic Record, 32*, 334–361.

63 Diminishing Marginal Returns

Consider a two-tiered production economy with two goods, Z and X, where capital, K, is the only factor of production. Good Z is both an intermediate and a final good, while good X is only an intermediate good. Our economy has three agents, one firm for each good and the representative household.

63.1 The Market for X

In this section we solve the problem of the firm producing good X. Firms that produce good X use good Z as their only input using a linear production function, $F(Z_t)$:

$$X_t = Z_t \tag{63.1}$$

Firms take the price of X and Z, P_x and P_z, respectively, as given. Since only relative prices matter, we will reduce our algebraic clutter by normalizing the price of Z to one: $P_z = 1$.

1. Show that $F(Z_t)$ has constant returns to scale.
2. Show that $F(Z_t)$ has constant marginal returns.
3. Write down the profit function of the firm.
4. Write down the optimization problem of the firm.
5. Write down the marginal rate of substitution between goods X and Z.
6. Write down the marginal rate of transformation between goods X and Z.
7. Show that the optimality condition of the firm implies that the price of good X, P_x, is equal to one.

63.2 The Market for Z

In this section we solve the problem of the firm producing good Z. Firms that produce good Z use both capital, K, and the intermediate good, X, as inputs in a Cobb-Douglas production function:

$$Z_t = K_t^\alpha X_t^{1-\alpha}. \tag{63.2}$$

They hire capital at the rental rate R, and buy the intermediate good, X, at its equilibrium price, $P_X = 1$.

1. Write down the profit function of the firm.

2. Write down the constrained optimization problem of the firm.

3. Write down the marginal rate of substitution between goods Z and X.

4. Write down the marginal rate of transformation between goods Z and X.

5. Write down the optimality condition of the firm.

6. Combine the optimality condition with the production function to show that, in equilibrium, Z is a *linear* function of capital:

$$Z_t = (1 - \alpha)^{(1-\alpha)/\alpha} K_t \tag{63.3}$$

7. Does the *equilibrium* production function exhibit diminishing marginal returns?

63.3   Growth

We have described the intermediate and final goods markets. To solve for the general equilibrium in this economy, we now describe the capital market. Our household can either consume or save the final good, Z, and it does so by saving a fixed fraction, s, of its income, Y.

1. Write down the two components of aggregate demand in this economy.

2. Explain why Z in this economy is not equal to output.

3. Show that output in this economy is only a fraction of the final good:

$$Y_t = \alpha Z_t \tag{63.4}$$

[Hint: You need to show what share of Z is purchased by the household and what share is purchased by the intermediate goods firm in equilibrium.]

4. Show that, in equilibrium, output is a *linear* function of capital:

$$Y_t = AK_t \tag{63.5}$$

where $A \equiv \alpha(1 - \alpha)^{(1-\alpha)/\alpha}$.

5. Show that the growth rate of output in this economy is equal to the growth rate of capital.

6. Show that the replacement rate in this economy, I_t/K_t, is equal to sA.

7. Show that under the assumption that capital depreciates at the constant rate δ, the growth rate of capital is given by:

$$\log(K_{t+1}) - \log(K_t) = sA - \delta \tag{63.6}$$

8. Graph the replacement rate, sA, and the deprecation rate, δ, of capital as a function of K_t.

9. How does the growth rate of this economy change as it accumulates more capital?

Now consider an alternate economy with both capital and labor as factors of production. Good Z is produced according to $K^\alpha (HL)^{1-\alpha}$, where L is constant and equal to one. In this economy, H is produced exactly as X, with Z as its only input: $H = Z$.

10. Offer an interpretation of H in this alternate economy.

11. Explain why this economy also grows at the rate $sA - \delta$.

12. Given your answers above, what intangible might a country try to accumulate in order to sustain growth in the long run?

13. Is it reasonable to expect that this intangible can grow indefinitely?

References

Aghion, P., & P. Howitt (2009). *The economics of growth*. Cambridge, MA: MIT Press.

Acemoglu, D., & J. Ventura (2002). The world income distribution. *Quarterly Journal of Economics, 117*(2), 659–694.

Jones, L., & R. Manuelli (1990). A convex model of equilibrium growth: Theory and policy implications. *Journal of Political Economy, 98*(5), 1008–1038.

64 Poverty Traps

One of the explanations offered for differences in income per capita across countries is that poorer nations are "trapped." The argument is that poverty itself creates barriers that make escaping it impossible. In this chapter, we will consider one such argument: population growth.

64.1 Steady States

Under the assumption of a constant savings rate, s, and Cobb-Douglas production we derived the following expression for the replacement rate of capital per capita, k_t:

$$sA_t k_t^{\alpha-1} \tag{64.1}$$

where A_t is a productivity constant and $0 < \alpha < 1$.

Under the assumption of constant depreciation rate of capital, δ, and constant population growth, λ, we derived the following expression for the depreciation rate of capital per capita, k_t:

$$\delta + \lambda \tag{64.2}$$

1. On a coordinate plane with k_t on the x axis, graph both the replacement rate, expression (64.1), and depreciation rate, expression (64.2). What does the vertical distance between the two curves measure?

2. What is true about the growth rate of capital per capita at the intersection of the replacement and depreciation rate curves in your graph above? The two curves intersect at the steady state-level of capital per capita, $\bar{k}$. Show that the steady-state level of capita per capita is:

$$\bar{k} = \left(\frac{sA_t}{\delta + \lambda}\right)^{\frac{1}{1-\alpha}}$$

3. Set up the coordinate plane with $\bar{k}$ on the y axis and s on the x axis. Graph the steady state level of capital per capita as a function of the savings rate. Is $\bar{k}$ and increasing or decreasing function of s? Can increasing s lead to sustained increases in capital per capita?

4. Set up the coordinate plane with $\bar{k}$ on the y axis and n on the x axis. Graph the steady-state level of capital per capita as a function of the population growth rate. Is $\bar{k}$ an increasing or decreasing function of λ? Can decreasing λ lead to sustained increases in capital per capita?

64.2   Birth Rates

The assumption that the population growth rate is constant is not consistent with empirical evidence. Income per capita is negatively correlated with population growth. As nations become richer, the growth rate of their populations declines. We also observe that countries with higher income per capita tend to have lower population growth rates than countries with lower income per capita.

   We will relax our assumption minimally by assuming that there exists a threshold level of capital per capita, k^*. At and below this threshold, the growth rate of population is constant and equal to λ. Above this threshold, the population growth rate drops to zero. More formally we have that the growth rate of population is the following piecewise function of capital per capita:

$$\log(L_{t+1}) - \log(L_t) = \begin{cases} \lambda \text{ if } k_t \leq k^* \\ 0 \text{ if } k_t > k^* \end{cases}$$

1. Does relaxing the assumption of constant population growth affect the replacement rate of capital per capita? How about the depreciation rate of capital per capita?

2. Graph the depreciation rate of capital per capita as a function of k_t when $k_t \leq k^*$ and when $k_t > k^*$. Is the depreciation rate still independent of the stock of capital per capita in the economy?
[Hint: The depreciation rate of capital per capita is equal to the depreciation rate of capital, δ, plus population growth, $\log L_{t+1} - \log L_t$.]

3. On the same graph as above, add the replacement rate of capital per capita as a function of k_t.
[Hint: The replacement rate is given by expression (64.1).]

4. How many steady states are in your graph? How does the number of steady states depend on k^*?

5. Suppose that $k^* < \left(\frac{sA_t}{\delta + \lambda}\right)^{\frac{1}{1-\alpha}}$. Show that there is only one steady state. Solve for this steady-state level of capital per capita.

6. Suppose that $k^* < \left(\frac{sA_t}{\delta + \lambda}\right)^{\frac{1}{1-\alpha}}$. What is true of the growth rate of capital per capita when it is below the steady state? What is true of the growth rate of capital per capita if it is above the steady state?

In what follows we will assume that there are two steady states. We will denote the first steady state by $\bar{k}^\ell$, and the second steady state by $\bar{k}^h$, where $\bar{k}^\ell < \bar{k}^h$.

7. In a new diagram, graph the replacement and depreciation rates of capital per capita as a function of k_t.

8. What is the growth rate of capital per capita when $\bar{k}^\ell < k_t < k^*$?

9. What is the growth rate of capital per capita when $\bar{k}^\ell > k_t > 0$?

10. If an economy starts off with a level of capital per capita *below* k^*, to which steady state will it converge? Explain.

11. What is the growth rate of capital per capita when $\bar{k}^h < k_t$?

12. What is the growth rate of capital per capita when $\bar{k}^h > k_t > k^*$?

13. If an economy starts off with a level of capital per capita *above* k^*, to which steady state will it converge? Explain.

14. Given your analysis above, explain why an economy at $\bar{k}^\ell$ might find itself "trapped."

15. Would a "large enough" infusion of outside capital release the economy from its trap? What does "large enough" mean?

16. How else might the economy be able to escape the trap?

References

Kray, A., & D. McKenzie (2014). Do poverty traps exist? Assessing evidence. *Journal of Economic Perspectives, 28*(3), 127–148.

Oded, G., & D. Weil (2000). Population, technology, and growth: From Malthusian stagnation to the demographic transition and beyond. *American Economic Review, 90*(4), 806–828.

65 Exogenous Technological Progress

The tyranny of diminishing marginal returns means that capital accumulation cannot be the key to long-run growth of income per capita. As more capital is accumulated, its marginal product decreases until it can no longer replace the capital that depreciates. To unlock long-run growth, we must counter diminishing marginal returns. How can we do we sustain such an effort? To answer this question we must first rescale the law of motion of capital per capita yet again and turn it into a law of motion of capital per *effective* worker.

Consider the Cobb-Douglas production function:

$$Y_t = A_t K_t^\alpha L_t^{1-\alpha} \tag{65.1}$$

where $0 < \alpha < 1$. To rescale our model we will first redefine technology. Let $A_t \equiv Z_t^{1-\alpha}$ and $E_t \equiv Z_t L_t$.

1. What does Z_t represent? Is this interpretation any different for A_t?

2. What is the interpretation of E_t?

3. Rewrite Y_t as a function of K_t and E_t.
[Hint: Equation (65.1) expresses Y_t as a function of Z_t, K_t and L_t.]

Now recall the law of motion of capital:

$$\log(K_{t+1}) - \log(K_t) = s\frac{Y_t}{K_t} - \delta \tag{65.2}$$

4. Rewrite the replacement rate, $s\frac{Y_t}{K_t}$, as a function of s, K_t, and E_t.

5. Suppose that technology, Z_t, grows at the constant rate γ and labor, L_t, grows at the constant rate λ. Show that E grows at the rate $\lambda + \gamma$.

6. Define $x_t \equiv K_t/E_t$. Subtract $\log(E_{t+1}) - \log(E_t)$ from both sides of equation (65.2) and show the resulting equation can be written as:

$$\log(x_{t+1}) - \log(x_t) = sx_t^{\alpha-1} - (\delta + \lambda + \gamma) \tag{65.3}$$

This is the *fundamental equation of Solow-Swan*.

7. What is the economic interpretation of x_t?

8. In the same diagram graph the replacement rate and the depreciation rate as a function of x_t.

9. Show that the steady state of x_t is given by

$$\bar{x} = \left(\frac{s}{\delta + \lambda + \gamma} \right)^{\frac{1}{1-\alpha}}$$

10. Show that output per capita, y_t, is a function of capital per capita, k_t, and A_t.

11. Show that in steady state, capital per worker, $k \equiv K/L$, grows at the rate γ.
[Hint: Recall that in steady state, the left-hand side of equation (65.3) is equal to zero.]

12. Draw a qualitative graph of the growth rate of capital per capita, k_t, as a function of time when $x_t < \bar{x}$ and when $x_t > \bar{x}$.
[Hint: Time should be on the x axis.]

13. Suppose that output per capita is not necessarily a Cobb-Douglas production function of k_t and A_t, only that the production function exhibits *constant returns to scale* in k_t and A_t. What will be the growth rate of output per capita in the steady state?

14. Suppose that output is not necessarily a Cobb-Douglas production function of K_t and E_t; only that the production production exhibits *constant returns to scale* in K_t and E_t. What will be the growth rate of output in the steady state?

References

Barro, R., & X. Sala-i-Martin (2004). *Economic growth, second edition.* Cambridge, MA: MIT Press.

Solow, R. (1956). A contribution to the theory of economic growth. *Quarterly Journal of Economics, 70*(1), 65–94.

Swan, T. (1956). Economic growth and capital accumulation. *Economic Record, 32*, 334–361.

66 The Solow Residual

Output is a function of the factors of production—capital and labor—and how efficient they are—productivity. An economy can grow by increasing the factors of production, or alternatively by using those factors more efficiently so that they become more productive.

Unlike capital and labor, however, productivity is not tangible and therefore not susceptible to direct measurement. So we measure it indirectly. In the same way that astrophysicists measure a black holes, we measure productivity by its effects. In this chapter we will take up two approaches of doing so.

66.1 Production and Competition

Because we cannot measure productivity growth directly, any indirect measure requires that we make some auxiliary assumptions about the structure of the economy. In this chapter we will make stronger assumptions than are strictly necessary, but this will buy us tractability.

First, we will assume that firms in the economy have a Cobb-Douglas production function:

$$Y_t = A_t K_t^\alpha L_t^{1-\alpha} \tag{66.1}$$

where Y_t is output, K_t is capital, L_t is labor, and A_t is *total factor productivity*, or TFP. Second, we will assume that α does not change with time. Third, we will assume that firms operate in a perfectly competitive market. Their objective is to maximize profits, while taking the price of output, P_t, capital, R_t, and labor, W_t, as given.

1. Why do economists use the qualifier *total factor* to refer to A_t?

2. Consider equation (66.1). Which of its variables can be measured directly? Which of its variables cannot?

3. Write down the profit function of the firm.

4. Write down the constraint of the firm.
[Hint: Recall that constraints equal zero.]

5. Write down the marginal rate of substitution between labor and output.

6. Write down the marginal rate of transformation between labor and output. What is the the name of this ratio?

7. Write down the optimality condition between labor and output.

8. Show that the optimality condition between labor and output can be written as:

$$1 - \alpha = \frac{W_t L_t}{P_t Y_t} \tag{66.2}$$

9. Can the variables on the left-hand side of equation (66.2) be measured directly? How about the variables on the right-hand side?

10. Explain why $1 - \alpha$ is labor's share of income.

11. Write down the marginal rate of substitution between capital and output.

12. Write down the marginal rate of transformation between capital and output.

13. Write down the optimality condition between capital and output.

14. Show that the optimality condition between capital and output can be written as:

$$\alpha = \frac{R_t K_t}{P_t Y_t} \tag{66.3}$$

15. Can the variables on the left-hand side of equation (66.2) be measured directly? How about the variables on the right-hand side?

16. Explain why α is capital's share of income.

17. What share of income is profits?

66.2 The Primal Approach

The *primal approach* measures total factor productivity by isolating its effect on quantities.

1. Let lowercase variables denote logs; for example, $y_t \equiv \log Y_t$, is log output. Rewrite equation (66.1) in logs.

2. Let Δ denote log the difference; for example $\Delta y_t \equiv y_t - y_{t-1}$ is the growth rate of output. Show that the growth rate of output is a function of the growth rate of capital, labor, and productivity:

$$\Delta y_t = \Delta a_t + \alpha \Delta k_t + (1 - \alpha) \Delta \ell_t \tag{66.4}$$

3. Solve for the growth rate of productivity, Δa_t. Are there any terms on the other side of the equation that cannot be measured directly?

4. Economists call the statistic from this method of measurement the *Solow residual*. Explain why we use the word, residual, to describe it.
[Hint: Begin by describing in words equation (66.4).]

66.3   The Dual Approach

The *dual approach* measures total factor productivity by isolating its effect on relative prices.

1. Let $w_t \equiv \log W_t - \log P_t$ denote the log of the real wage. As in the previous section, all lowercase variables denote logs. Take the log of equation (66.2).

2. As before, let Δ denote differences. Show that the growth rate of the real wage is a function of the growth rate of output and labor:

$$\Delta w_t = \Delta y_t - \Delta \ell_t \tag{66.5}$$

3. Let $r_t \equiv \log R_t - \log P_t$ denote the log of the rental rate of capital. Take the log of equation (66.3).

4. Show that the growth rate of the real rental rate of capital is a function of the growth rate of output and capital:

$$\Delta r_t = \Delta y_t - \Delta k_t \tag{66.6}$$

5. Multiply equation (66.5) by $1 - \alpha$ and equation (66.6) by α. Then add them together to derive the following relationship:

$$(1 - \alpha)\Delta w_t + \alpha \Delta r_t = \Delta y_t - \alpha \Delta k_t - (1 - \alpha)\Delta \ell_t \tag{66.7}$$

6. Simplify the right-hand side of equation (66.7).
[Hint: Use your results from the primal approach.]

7. Consider the two sides of equation (66.7). Where would you find data to estimate the right-hand side? How about the left hand-side? Might any of the data sources be problematic?

66.4   The East Asian Tigers

The countries of Hong Kong, South Korea, Singapore, and Taiwan have been dubbed the East Asian Tigers as a result of the high growth rates of both output and income per capita they experienced in the second half of the twentieth century. Table 66.1 shows the growth rates of output and factor prices for all four countries between 1966 and 1990, as well as labor's share of income. In what follows, we will exploit the theoretical structure we have built in the previous sections to estimate growth rates from the data in Table 66.1.

1. Relabel each of the data columns in table 66.1 with its corresponding variable or mathematical expression from the previous sections.

2. Relabel each of the data columns in table 66.2 with its corresponding variable or mathematical expression from the previous sections.

Table 66.1
Growth rates of output and factor prices of the East Asian Tigers between 1966 and 1990.

Country	Labor share	Percent annual growth rate (1966–1990)		
		Output	Rental rate	Real wage
Hong Kong	0.63	7.30	0.29	4.04
South Korea	0.70	8.50	−3.88	4.38
Singapore	0.51	8.70	1.21	2.69
Taiwan	0.74	8.50	−0.77	5.26

Sources: Hsieh (1999) and Young (1995).

Table 66.2
Growth rates of the factors of production and total factor productivity of the East Asian Tigers between 1966 and 1990.

Country	Capital share	Percent annual growth rate (1966–1990)		
		Capital	Labor	TFP
Hong Kong				
South Korea				
Singapore				
Taiwan				

3. Table 66.2 is conspicuously blank. Combine your theoretical results from the previous sections with the data in table 66.1 to fill out the entries in table 66.2.

[Hint: Work your way through each column, rather than each row, from left to right.]

References

Hsieh, C. (1999). Productivity growth and factor prices in East Asia. *American Economic Review, 89*(2), 133–138.

Solow, R. (1957). Technical change and the aggregate production function. *Review of Economics and Statistics, 39*, 312–320.

Young, A. (1995). The tyranny of numbers: Confronting the statistical realities of the East Asian growth experience. *Quarterly Journal of Economics, 110*(3), 641–680.

67 Convergence

Consider an economy with no technological progress, a constant savings rate, s, a constant capital depreciation rate, δ, and a constant population growth rate, λ. We have shown that when the production function in that economy is Cobb-Douglas, output per capita, y_t, is a function of capital per capita, k_t:

$$y_t = k_t^\alpha \tag{67.1}$$

and the law of motion of capital per capita is given by:

$$\log(k_{t+1}) - \log(k_t) = sk_t^{\alpha-1} - (\delta + \lambda) \tag{67.2}$$

where $0 < \alpha < 1$ and we have normalized the level of technology to one.

Suppose you have two different countries whose economies behave according to (67.1) and (67.2) but who might nonetheless differ in their savings rate, depreciation rate, or population growth.

1. If the two countries have similar levels of capital per capita, what can you conclude about their growth rates of output per capita?

2. If the two countries have similar growth rates of output per capita, what can you conclude about their respective levels of capital per capita?

3. Show that the steady-state income per capita, $\bar{y}$, is given by:

$$\bar{y} = \left(\frac{s}{\delta + \lambda}\right)^{\alpha/(1-\alpha)}$$

4. In the long run, do you expect two different countries to have the same income per capita?

5. In the long run, do you expect two different countries to have the same growth rate of income per capita?

6. What does your analysis suggest about the correlation between initial income per capita and a country's subsequent growth rate?

7. Figure 67.1 plots the income per capita in 1960 against the subsequent average yearly growth of income per capita. We can think of 1960 as the initial level of income per capita.

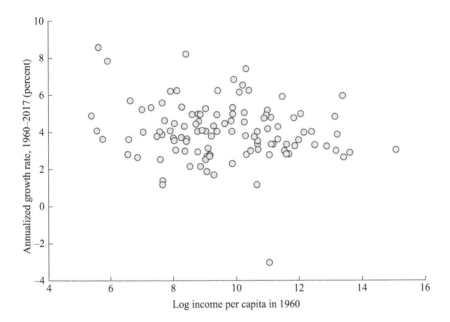

Figure 67.1
Average annual growth rate of income per capita between 1960 and 2017 versus income per capita in 1960. *Source*: Maddison Project Database.

Is the lack of correlation in figure 67.1 consistent with your analysis? If so, explain why. Otherwise explain what correlation in the data would be consistent.

8. Consider the following statement. "Regions with lower incomes per capita grow faster than regions with high incomes per capita *conditional on* ..." Write down the condition that would make it consistent with the Solow-Swan growth model developed in chapter 62. This result is known as *conditional convergence*.

9. What data might you look at in order to test the hypothesis of *conditional convergence*?

World War II offers us a way to test the convergence predictions of the Solow-Swan growth model. The major belligerents were likely already in their steady states at the time the war broke out. In a short period of time, most of their capital stock was destroyed. What happened after? Table 67.1 tells us. It has data on real income per capita of five major powers who fought in the war. Crucially, while four of them were devastated by the fighting, one was left relatively unscathed.

10. Calculate the average annual growth rate of income per capita between 1939 and 1946 in all five countries.
[Hint: Take the logs.]

11. Calculate the average annual growth rate of income per capita between 1946 and 1960 in all five countries.

Table 67.1
Income per capita in 2011 US dollars.

Year	France	Germany	Japan	USSR	US
1885	3,518	3,532	1,729	1,379	6,424
1939	7,640	8,617	4,804	3,566	11,171
1946	6,145	3,534	2,771	3,049	14,822
1960	11,792	12,282	6,354	6,288	18,057
2018	38,516	46,178	38,674	19,539	55,516

Source: Maddison Project Database.

12. Plot the average annual growth rate between 1946 and 1960 on the y axis against the average annual growth rate between 1939 and 1946 on the x axis.

13. How does your plot compare to figure 67.1? Use the Solow-Swan framework to explain the differences.

14. Calculate the average annual growth rate of income per capita between 1885 and 1939 for all five countries.

15. Calculate the average annual growth rate of income per capita between 1885 and 2018 for all five countries.

16. How do the 1885–1939 growth rates compare to the 1885–2018 growth rates?

17. Now consider the per capita incomes in 2018. Did any of the countries catch up to any other?

18. If the incomes per capita of France, Germany, Japan, and the former USSR were not converging to the income per capita of the US, to what alternative target were they converging during their postwar growth spurts between 1946 and 1960?
[Hint: Use the Solow-Swan model.]

References

Barro, R., & X. Sala-i-Martin (1992). Convergence. *Journal of Political Economy, 100*(2), 223–251.

Barro, R., & X. Sala-i-Martin (2004). *Economic growth, second edition.* Cambridge, MA: MIT Press.

Bolt, J., & J. Luiten van Zanden (2020). Maddison style estimates of the evolution of the world economy. A new 2020 update. *Maddison Project Database.* Accessed online at https://www.rug.nl/ggdc/historicaldevelopment /maddison/releases/maddison-project-database-2020

68 Perfect Competition, Constant Returns and Technology

Consider a profit-maximizing firm that produces output according to $Y = AF(K, L)$, where A is productivity, $F(\cdot)$ is a production function, K is capital, and L is labor. The firm operates in a competitive market and hires labor at wage W, rents capital at a rate R, and sells its output for a price P, which we normalize to one for simplicity (i.e., $P = 1$).

1. Write down the constrained optimization problem of the firm.
[Hint: What constrains the perfectly competitive firm?]

2. Write down the marginal rate of substitution between to labor and output.

3. Write down the marginal rate of transformation between to labor and output.

4. Write down the optimality condition with respect to labor and output.

5. Write down the marginal rate of substitution between capital and output.

6. Write down the marginal rate of transformation between capital and output.

7. Write down the optimality condition with respect to capital and output.

A production function displays *constant returns to scale* if multiplying the factors of production by a factor, λ, also leads to an increase in output by the same factor. Mathematically, a production function $F(K, L)$ has constant returns if $F(\lambda K, \lambda L) = \lambda F(K, L)$. *Euler's theorem* says that if $F(K, L)$ displays constant returns to scale, then the following must also be true:

$$F_L(K, L)L + F_K(K, L)K = F(K, L) \tag{68.1}$$

where $F_L(\cdot)$ denotes the partial derivative of $F(\cdot)$ with respect to L, and $F_K(\cdot)$ denotes the partial derivative of $F(\cdot)$ with respect to K. Assume that the firm has a production function that exhibits constant returns to scale.

8. Substitute the optimality conditions of the firm into equation (68.1).

9. Explain why WL is the total cost of labor.

10. Explain why RK is the total cost of capital.

Among other things, total factor productivity, A, embodies the stock of knowledge in the economy. As knowledge accumulates, the economy becomes more productive.

11. What part of output goes to pay for A?

12. If developing knowledge is *costly*, in equilibrium what will be the growth rate of A?

69 Endogenous Technological Change (or, Romer's Ideas)

The Solow-Swan growth model demonstrates that technological innovation—not capital accumulation—is the key to long-run growth. It does not, however, take up the question of how technological innovation arises in equilibrium. That is the question we take up here.

As long as the production function exhibits constant returns to scale, in competitive markets the factors of production will claim all income, and no resources will be left to devote to research and development. So the story of technological progress is one with market power; where firms who innovate will be able to hold a monopoly over their innovation and use the present discounted value of their profits to pay for the research costs of coming up with new ideas.

69.1 Production

We have a two-tiered production economy. There are N_t intermediate goods firms, indexed by i, a representative final goods firm, and a fixed supply of labor, L.

We begin with the final goods firm. The firm produces output, Y_t, using all N_t intermediate goods as inputs, according to the production function:

$$Y_t = \sum_{i=1}^{N_t} X_{i,t}^{1-\alpha} \tag{69.1}$$

where $0 < \alpha < 1$, and $X_{i,t}$ is the quantity of intermediate good i, which the firm buys at price $P_{i,t}$ in period t. We normalize the price of the final good to one in all periods.

1. Write down the profit function of the final goods firm.
2. Write down the constrained optimization problem of the final goods firm.
3. Write down the marginal rate of substitution between $X_{i,t}$ and Y_t.
4. Write down the marginal rate of transformation between $X_{i,t}$ and Y_t.

5. Show that the inverse demand of intermediate good i is:

$$(1 - \alpha)X_{i,t}^{-\alpha} = P_{i,t} \tag{69.2}$$

The intermediate goods producer is a monopolist with a linear production technology:

$$X_{i,t} = L_{i,t} \tag{69.3}$$

where $L_{i,t}$ denotes the total labor hired by firm i. Because the firm is a monopolist it chooses a price, quantity pair $(P_{i,t}, X_{i,t})$ to maximize its profits given the [inverse] demand function for its good, equation (69.2).

6. Show that the profit function of the firm, π_i, is

$$\pi_{i,t} = X_{i,t}(P_{i,t} - W_t) \tag{69.4}$$

where W is the wage.

7. Write down the constrained optimization problem of the intermediate goods firm.

8. Write down the marginal rate of substitution between price, $P_{i,t}$, and quantity, $X_{i,t}$.

9. Write down the marginal rate of transformation between price, $P_{i,t}$, and quantity, $X_{i,t}$.

10. Write down the optimality condition of the intermediate goods firm.

11. Combine the optimality condition with the demand function to show that firm will choose a price marked up over marginal cost:

$$P_{i,t} = \mu W_t \tag{69.5}$$

where $\mu \equiv 1/(1 - \alpha)$ is the markup.

12. What is the range of values that μ can take? How does the market power of the intermediate goods firm vary with μ?
[Hint: What are the values that α can take?]

We can now derive the economy-wide production function.

13. Combine the pricing condition of the intermediate goods firm, (69.5), with the inverse demand function of the final goods firm, (69.2), to show that the final goods firm will demand the same amount of all N_t intermediate goods.

14. Given your answer above, show that, in equilibrium:

$$X_{i,t} = \frac{L}{N_t} \tag{69.6}$$

for all intermediate goods firms.

15. Substitute your result into the production function of the final goods firm to get the following equilibrium economy-wide production function

$$Y_t = N_t^{\alpha} L^{1-\alpha} \tag{69.7}$$

16. Is output an increasing or decreasing function of N_t?

17. Recall that each intermediate goods firm produces a unique good over which it holds a patent. Offer a brief economic interpretation of N_t.

69.2   Innovation

In the previous section we showed that output is an increasing function of the total level of technology, which is indexed by the total number of ideas in the market, N_t. New ideas—and new products—however, are not free. New vaccines, new chips, new algorithms all require investment in research and development, R&D. We now turn to the entrepreneurs in the economy who pay the cost of R&D to produce technological innovations.

1. Physical goods like the dose of a vaccine are *rival* because the use of a single dose by one person precludes all others from using it. Is the vaccine itself, the recipe so to speak, also rival?

2. If there were no patents, would a firm who comes up with a new idea remain the only producer of the new good? What will happen to the firms' profits in equilibrium?

3. Suppose that a new invention requires a fixed research cost, κ. If there were no patents, would any firm pay the research costs?

4. Patents prevent those not holding the patents from profiting from a new invention. Although *nonrival*, a patent makes an idea *excludable*: it excludes everyone except the holder of the patent from profiting. Goods that are both nonrival and excludable are called *club goods*. Offer a few other examples of a club good.

In our particular economy, new ideas are implemented as intermediate goods. Each entrepreneur who brings a new idea to market retains a monopoly over that good and can therefore price above marginal cost and make profits. Since the entrepreneur must pay the costs of R&D upfront, they will do so only if those costs are lower than the present discounted value of the new intermediate good. We now turn to this decision.

5. Combine the pricing strategy of firm i, (69.5), and the inverse demand for good i, (69.2), and substitute them into the profit function to get profits only as a function of $X_{i,t}$:

$$\pi_{i,t} = X_{i,t}^{1-\alpha} \left(\frac{\mu - 1}{\mu} \right) (1 - \alpha)$$

6. Substitute equation (69.6) into the expression above to show that profits at time t are only a function of the total level of technology, N_t:

$$\pi_{i,t} = N_t^{\alpha - 1} \bar{\pi} \tag{69.8}$$

where $\bar{\pi} \equiv L^{1-\alpha}(1 - \alpha)(\mu - 1)/\mu$ is constant across time.

7. Are profits increasing or decreasing in the level of technology?

8. Let $V_{i,t}$ denote the value of firm i at time t. Households can invest either in the firm or in a bond that has a gross rate of return $(1+r)$. Show that, in equilibrium the following no-arbitrage condition must hold:

$$1+r = \frac{\pi_{i,t+1} + V_{t+1}}{V_t} \tag{69.9}$$

9. If profits are decreasing in N_t, explain why the value of the firm is also decreasing in N_t. [Hint: Solve the equation above for V_t.]

10. If entrepreneurs can enter freely into the R&D market, what happens if the cost of research, κ_t, is lower than the value of the firm?

11. As more entrepreneurs enter, what happens to N_t? What happens to the value of the firm?

12. Given your previous answers, explain why, in equilibrium, the cost of research must equal the value of the firm:

$$\kappa_t = V_{i,t} \tag{69.10}$$

This is called the *free entry condition*.

13. Now suppose that the cost of research is constant and technology is increasing, $N_{t+1} > N_t$. Explain why this fixed cost implies that technological innovation must eventually stop. [Hint: What is happening to the value of firm i as technology increases?]

14. Given that we do not see technological innovation coming to a stop, what must be true about the cost of research as a function of technology?

Paul Romer argued that the nature of ideas lowers the cost of research as the number of ideas increases. The reason, according to Romer, is the nonrivalry of ideas. Ideas are like recipes. Patents make innovations excludable—no one can use the recipe to make a profit—but they cannot make innovations rival. Just because no one can use the recipe doesn't mean that no one can see it and get new ideas from it. And furthermore, someone using the recipe to come up with a new one does not prevent anybody else from doing the same. Take, for example, the mRNA vaccines that were developed against Covid-19. The original mRNA vaccine technology took years to develop; yet in one year two different companies were able to simultaneously apply the initial idea to develop two new vaccines.

In this spirit we will assume that the cost of R&D, κ_t, is also a decreasing function of N_t:

$$\kappa_t = \theta N_t^{\alpha-1} \tag{69.11}$$

where κ_t is in units of the final good, Y_t.

15. Combine the free entry condition, equation (69.10), and the cost of research equation above to write the value of the firm as a function of N_t.

16. Substitute your answer above and the profit function of the firm, (69.8), into the no arbitrage condition, (69.9), to derive the following relationship between the gross real interest

rate and the gross growth rate of technology:

$$1 + r = \left(\frac{N_{t+1}}{N_t}\right)^{\alpha-1} \left(\frac{\bar{\pi} + \theta}{\theta}\right)$$ (69.12)

69.3 Growth

In the previous two sections we saw how equilibrium in the production markets and in the asset markets pinned down the real interest rate in this economy. We also know from the Euler equation that the real interest rate is the relative price of current consumption in future consumption units. With the equilibrium real interest rate in hand we can now characterize the growth rate of consumption and, by extension, the growth rate of output and technology in this economy.

1. Write down the two components of aggregate demand in this economy.

2. Write down expressions for the gross growth rates of consumption, C, investment, I, output, Y, and technology, N.
[Hint: Gross growth rates are ratios.]

3. Explain why $\kappa_t(N_{t+1} - N_t)$ is total investment in this economy.

4. Show that if the growth rate of technology is constant, the growth rate of investment is:

$$\frac{I_{t+1}}{I_t} = \left(\frac{N_{t+1}}{N_t}\right)^{\alpha}$$ (69.13)

5. Use the economy-wide production function (69.7) to show that the growth rate of output is also:

$$\frac{Y_{t+1}}{Y_t} = \left(\frac{N_{t+1}}{N_t}\right)^{\alpha}$$ (69.14)

6. Combine your previous answers to show that the investment-to-output ratio, I/Y, in this economy is constant.

7. Explain why the previous result implies that the consumption-to-output ratio, C/Y, in this economy is constant.
[Hint: Divide the market-clearing condition in the final goods market by output.]

8. Show that your answer above implies the growth rate of consumption is also constant and the same as the growth rate of output and investment.
[Hint: The consumption-to-output ratio must be the same in periods t and $t + 1$.]

We have shown that under the assumption that the growth rate of technology is constant, the growth rate of consumption is also constant. We now verify that our assumption is correct by showing that it is consistent with the household's intertemporal consumption choices, given by the Euler equation:

$$\frac{C_{t+1}}{C_t} = \beta(1+r) \tag{69.15}$$

where $\beta < 1$ is the household's discount factor.

9. Consider the expression for the real interest rate, equation (69.12). Explain why a constant growth rate of technology implies a constant real interest rate and, therefore, a constant growth rate of consumption.

10. Substitute the expression for the growth rate of consumption we derived in question 8 on the left-hand side of the Euler equation and the expression for the real interest rate, equation (69.12), into the right-hand side of the Euler equation to derive the equilibrium growth rate of technology:

$$\frac{N_{t+1}}{N_t} = \beta\left(1 + \frac{\bar{\pi}}{\theta}\right) \tag{69.16}$$

Is the growth rate of technology constant?

Now that we have an expression for the equilibrium growth rate of this economy we are interested in its determinants. Since we have assumed a constant labor supply, we will normalize it to $L = 1$. This leaves us with the following expression:

$$\frac{\bar{\pi}}{\theta} = \left(\frac{1}{\theta}\right)\left(\frac{\mu - 1}{\mu}\right)(1 - \alpha) \tag{69.17}$$

In what follows we will examine how each of the variables in equations (69.16) and (69.17) affect the growth rate, N_{t+1}/N_t, and graph the growth rate as a function of each. While your graphs will be sketches, they should nonetheless be the right shape.

11. Offer a brief economic interpretation of $1/\theta$.

12. Graph N_{t+1}/N_t as a function of $1/\theta$. Is the growth rate increasing or decreasing in $1/\theta$? Is this consistent with your economic interpretation?

13. Offer a brief economic interpretation of μ.

14. Graph N_{t+1}/N_t as a function of μ. Is the growth rate increasing or decreasing in μ? Is this consistent with your economic interpretation?

15. Offer a brief economic interpretation of $1 - \alpha$.

16. Graph N_{t+1}/N_t as a function of $1 - \alpha$. Is the growth rate increasing or decreasing in $1 - \alpha$? Is this consistent with your economic interpretation?

References

Jones, C. (1995). R&D-based models of economic growth. *Journal of Political Economy, 103*(4), 759–784.

Romer, P. (1986). Increasing returns and long-run growth. *Journal of Political Economy, 94*(5), 1002–1037.

Romer, P. (1990). Endogenous technological change. *Journal of Political Economy, 98*(5), Part 2: S71–S102.

A Mathematical Appendix

This appendix serves as a quick reference for the mathematical tools and notation we use in this book; a cheat sheet of sorts. It is meant neither to be exhaustive nor to teach you math. For that reason, it is direct, not too technical, and light on explanations.

A.1 Sums and Vectors

Vectors

A vector is a collection of variables $(x_1, x_2, \ldots, x_n)$. The *dimension* of the vector is given by the number of variables, n. Each of the entries of the vector is called an *element* of the vector. Consider a consumer choosing between apples and oranges. The vector of prices would be $(p_{\text{apples}}, p_{\text{oranges}})$ and have a dimension of two. Similarly, the vector of quantities would be $(q_{\text{apples}}, q_{\text{oranges}})$ and would also have a dimension of two.

Sums

Because vectors often have very high dimensions, writing down the sum of the elements can be quite cumbersome. To avoid having to write out each element of the sum, we have a special notation. We write the sum of the elements of vector $(x_1, x_2, \ldots, x_n)$ as

$$\sum_{i=1}^{n} x_i = x_1 + x_2 + \ldots + x_n$$

Suppose we want to add only up the kth element of the vector:

$$\sum_{i=1}^{k} x_i = x_1 + x_2 + \ldots + x_k$$

Similarly, if we wanted to add only starting at the kth element of the vector:

$$\sum_{i=k}^{n} x_i = x_k + x_{k+1} + \ldots + x_n$$

Dot Products

If two vectors, X and Y, have the same *dimension*, then you can evaluate their *dot product*. The *dot product* is the sum of the product of each corresponding element in X and Y. For $X = (x_1, x_2, \ldots, x_n)$ and $Y = (y_1, y_2, \ldots, y_n)$, the dot product is given by

$$XY = \sum_{i=1}^{n} x_i y_i$$

$$= x_1 y_1 + x_2 y_2 + \cdots + x_n y_n$$

Consider again the consumer choosing between apples and oranges. Let's denote apples as good one and oranges as good two. The *dot product* of the price vector, $P = (p_1, p_2)$, and the quantity vector, $Q = (q_1, q_2)$, is given by:

$$PQ = \sum_{i=1}^{2} p_i q_i$$

$$= p_1 q_1 + p_2 q_2$$

A.2   Exponents

An exponential function of x is a base, b, exponentiated by x:

$$f(x) = b^x$$

If b is less than one, the function is decreasing. If b is greater than one, the function is increasing. If $b = 1$ the function is always one.

The Natural Base

Although any real number can be a base, we call the transcendental number, e, the *natural base*. When we write exponential functions with base e we usually write them as:

$$\exp(x) \equiv e^x$$

Products of Exponential Functions

The product of two exponential functions with the *same* base is the sum of their exponents:

$$b^x b^y = b^{x+y}$$

Or with the natural base:

$$\exp(x) \exp(y) = \exp(x + y)$$

Powers of Exponential Functions

When an exponential function is raised to a power, the power is multiplied by the exponent.

$$\left(b^x\right)^y = b^{yx}$$

Or with the natural base:

$$(\exp(x))^y = \exp(yx)$$

Sums of Exponential Functions

Consider an exponential function where $b < 1$. Now let X be the vector of the exponential function evaluated for different values of $x = 0, 1, 2, \ldots, n$. For example, if $b = \frac{1}{2}$, then $X = \left(1, \frac{1}{2}, \frac{1}{4}, \frac{1}{8}, \ldots, (\frac{1}{2})^n\right)$. We write the sum of the elements of vector X as:

$$\sum_{x=0}^{n} b^x = b^0 + b^1 + b^2 + \ldots + b^n$$

The formula to evaluate this sum without having to add up every term is:

$$\sum_{x=0}^{n} b^x = \frac{1 - b^{n+1}}{1 - b}$$

Infinite Sums of Exponential Functions

Now, suppose we want to let n go to infinity. In other words, we want to consider the vector of b raised to *every* natural number. In the example above with $b = \frac{1}{2}$ we would now have $X = \left(1, \frac{1}{2}, \frac{1}{4}, \frac{1}{8}, \ldots\right)$ but now instead of one largest number n, we would simply keep going. As long as b is less than one, the sum of this *infinite* vector is finite. Or, as mathematicians will put it, "the sum converges:"

$$\sum_{x=0}^{\infty} b^x = b^0 + b^1 + b^2 + \ldots$$

$$= \frac{1}{1 - b}$$

If, instead of starting with $x = 0$, we start with $x = 1$ so that $X = (b^1, b^2, \ldots)$ the sum is now:

$$\sum_{x=1}^{\infty} b^x = b^1 + b^2 + \ldots$$

$$= \frac{b}{1 - b}$$

A.3   Logarithms

Logarithms are the inverse function of exponential functions. Since exponential functions have a base number that is exponentiated, so too, do logarithms. For example, the logarithm with base 10 of 1000, is 3. In economics we almost exclusively use the natural log, which is the logarithm with base e. Because we do not use other bases, unless otherwise stated, $\log(\cdot)$, stands for the natural logarithm.

Inverse of the Exponential Function

$$\log(\exp(x)) = x$$
$$\exp(\log(x)) = x$$

The log of the Product is the Sum of the logs

For any two variables, x and y:
$$\log(xy) = \log(x) + \log(y)$$

More generally, for any number of variables, $x_1, x_2, \ldots, x_n$:

$$\log(x_1 x_2 \cdots x_n) = \log(x_1) + \log(x_2) + \cdots + \log(x_n)$$
$$= \sum_{i=1}^{n} \log(x_i)$$

The log of the Exponent is the Coefficient of the log

For any two variables, x and y:
$$\log(x^y) = y \log(x)$$

A.4   Derivatives

The derivative of a function $f(x)$ *with respect to* x gives the slope of the line tangent to $f(x)$ at x. If a function has a derivative at x, then it must be continuous at x. Not all continuous functions, however, have a derivative. If a function has a derivative at x, we say it is *differentiable at x*. There are two main notations for derivatives:

$$\text{Leibniz notation: } \frac{d}{dx} f(x)$$

$$\text{Lagrange notation: } f'(x)$$

Lagrange notation is used only when dealing with functions of a *single* variable. When dealing with *multivariate* functions, the Lagrange notation becomes ambiguous and cannot be used.

Chain Rule

Consider the function $h(x) = f(g(x))$, where both $f(\cdot)$ and $g(\cdot)$ are also functions. The derivative of $h(x)$ with respect to x is given by:

Leibniz notation:

$$\frac{d}{dx}h(x) = \left(\frac{d}{dg(x)}f(g(x))\right)\left(\frac{d}{dx}g(x)\right)$$

Lagrange notation:

$$h'(x) = f'(g(x))g'(x)$$

Sums of Derivatives Are the Derivatives of the Sums

Consider the function $h(x) = f(x) + g(x)$, where both $f(\cdot)$ and $g(\cdot)$ are also functions. The derivative of $h(x)$ with respect to x is given by:

Leibniz notation:

$$\frac{d}{dx}h(x) = \frac{d}{dx}f(x) + \frac{d}{dx}g(x)$$

Lagrange notation:

$$h'(x) = f'(x) + g'(x)$$

Product Rule

Consider the function $h(x) = f(x)g(x)$, where both $f(\cdot)$ and $g(\cdot)$ are also functions. The derivative of $h(x)$ with respect to x is given by:

Leibniz notation:

$$\frac{d}{dx}h(x) = g(x)\left(\frac{d}{dx}f(x)\right) + f(x)\left(\frac{d}{dx}g(x)\right)$$

Lagrange notation:

$$h'(x) = g(x)f'(x) + f(x)g'(x)$$

Second Derivatives

The second derivative is the derivative of the derivative. Consider the function $h(x)$ and denote its derivative with respect to x by $f(x)$:

Leibniz notation:

$$f(x) \equiv \frac{d}{dx}h(x)$$

Lagrange notation:

$$f(x) \equiv h'(x)$$

The *second derivative* of $h(x)$ is the derivative of $f(x)$. The second derivative of $h(x)$ can also be written in two notations:

Leibniz notation:

$$\frac{d^2}{dx^2}h(x) = \frac{d}{dx}f(x)$$

Lagrange notation:

$$h''(x) = f'(x)$$

Derivatives of Polynomials

Consider a function $f(x) = x^p$, where p is any real number. Its derivative is given by:

$$f'(x) = px^{p-1}$$

Note that this applies to derivatives of fractions:

$$\frac{1}{x} = x^{-1} \text{ and } \left(\frac{1}{x}\right)^p = x^{-p}$$

which means that if $f(x) = \left(\frac{1}{x}\right)^p$:

$$f'(x) = -px^{-p-1}$$

Derivative of the Natural Base

The natural base for exponential functions is the number e. Consider the function $f(x) = \exp(x)$. Its derivative is given by:

$$f'(x) = f(x) = \exp(x)$$

The derivative of the natural exponential function is itself.

Derivative of an Arbitrary Base

Consider the function $f(x) = b^x$. To differentiate this function with respect to x, we first rewrite it as a function with the natural base:

$$b^x = (\exp(\log b))^x$$
$$= \exp(x \log b)$$

This function can be written as $g(h(x))$, where $g(\cdot) = \exp(\cdot)$ and $h(x) = x \log b$. We apply the chain rule and get

$$\frac{d}{dx}\exp(x \log b) = \exp(x \log b)\log(b)$$
$$= b^x \log b$$

Derivative of the Natural Log

Consider the function $f(x) = \log(x)$. Its derivative is given by:

$$f'(x) = \frac{1}{x}$$

Partial Derivatives

A function often has several variables. For example, a utility function for apples and bananas is a function of *two* variables: a and b. When taking the derivative of a function $f(x, y)$ with respect to x, while holding y constant, we are taking the *partial derivative* of $f(x, y)$ *with respect* to x. Similarly for y. This applies to functions of n variables: $f(x_1, \ldots, x_n)$.

To take the partial derivative of $f(x, y)$ with respect to x, you treat y as a constant and proceed as if $f(\cdot)$ were only a function of x. Once again, this argument holds for any $f(x_1, \ldots, x_n)$; if $f(\cdot)$ is a function of x and n other variables you treat all n variables as constants and proceed as if $f(\cdot)$ were only a function of x.

There are also two notations for partial derivatives:

Leibniz Notation:

$$\frac{\partial}{\partial x} f(x, y) \qquad\qquad \frac{\partial}{\partial y} f(x, y)$$

Subscript Notation:

$$f_x(x, y) \qquad\qquad f_y(x, y)$$

A.5   Linear Equations

Linear Equations in Two Dimensions

A linear function of only one variable $y = f(x)$ can be written in three equivalent forms:

Standard Form

$$Ax + By = C$$

The vector $[A, B]$ is orthogonal to the line.

Economists write linear budget constraints in standard form. In that case, x and y are goods, A and B are their respective prices, and C is the expenditure constraint.

Point Slope Form

$$y - \hat{y} = m(x - \hat{x})$$

The point $(\hat{x}, \hat{y})$ is on a line with slope m.

Slope Intercept Form

$$y = mx + b$$

b is the y intercept.

The slope intercept form is a special case of the point slope form when $(\hat{x}, \hat{y}) = (0, b)$. The slope m can be recovered from the normal vector $[A, B]$: $m = -A/B$. And similarly, the y intercept can be written as $b = C/B$.

Linear Equations in n Dimensions

Linear Equations in n dimensions are written as the dot product of two vectors. A vector of variables and vector of coefficients. Consider a budget constraint with more than two goods. The quantity vector $Q = (q_1, \ldots, q_n)$ is the vector of variables. The price vector $P = (p_1, \ldots, p_n)$ is the vector of coefficients. C once again denotes the expenditure constraint. This linear budget constraint with n dimensions would be written as:

$$C = PQ$$

$$C = \sum_{i=1}^{n} p_i q_i$$

$$C = p_1 q_1 + p_2 q_2 + \ldots + p_n q_n$$

Linear Approximations

A nonlinear, differentiable function, $f(x)$, can be approximated at a point, $\hat{x}$, by its tangent line. This linear approximation is called the *first order Taylor expansion* of $f(x)$ around $\hat{x}$. The equation for the line tangent at $f(\hat{x})$ in point slope form is:

$$y = f(\hat{x}) + f'(\hat{x})(x - \hat{x})$$

where $f(\hat{x})$ is the value of the function at $\hat{x}$ and $f'(\hat{x})$ is the value of the *derivative* of the function at $\hat{x}$.

A nonlinear, differentiable, multivariate function $f(x_1, \ldots, x_n)$ can by approximated at a point $(\hat{x}_1, \ldots, \hat{x}_n)$ by its tangent *hyperplane*. The hyperplane is the n-dimensional counterpart of a line. This is still a linear approximation and is also called the first order Taylor expansion of $f(x_1, \ldots, x_n)$ around $(\hat{x}_1, \ldots, \hat{x}_n)$. The equation for the hyperplane tangent at $f(\hat{x}_1, \ldots, \hat{x}_n)$ is:

$$y = f(\hat{x}_1, \ldots, \hat{x}_n) + \sum_{i=1}^{n} f_{x_i}(\hat{x}_1, \ldots, \hat{x}_n)(x_i - \hat{x}_i)$$

where $f(\hat{x}_1, \ldots, \hat{x}_n)$ is the value of the function at $(\hat{x}_1, \ldots, \hat{x}_n)$ and $f_{x_i}(\hat{x}_1, \ldots, \hat{x}_n)$ is the *partial derivative* of $f(\cdot)$ with respect to x_i, evaluated at $(\hat{x}_1, \ldots, \hat{x}_n)$.

A.6   Probability and Expectation

A *random variable*, X, is a variable that can take different values with different probabilities. A discrete random variable can be described by two vectors. The vector of values associated with each outcome, $(x_1, x_2, \ldots, x_n)$, and the vector of probabilities associated with each outcome, $(p_1, p_2, \ldots, p_n)$. The outcome of a fair coin toss, for example, can be described as a random variable that can take two values, $(0, 1)$, with probability $\left(\frac{1}{2}, \frac{1}{2}\right)$.

Expectation

The *average* value of random variable can be computed as the sum of the product of the probabilities and the values of each outcome. The average is also called the *mean* or the *expectation*. In economics, we almost always use the term *expectation* or *expected value*. The expected value of random variable X is written as $E(X)$, and is computed as:

$$E(X) = \sum_{i=1}^{n} p_i x_i$$

Notice that the expectation of a random variable is the *dot product* of the outcome vector and the probability vector.

Expectations Are Linear

Consider a random variable X and two constants, a and b.

$$E(a + bX) = a + b E(X)$$

Consider two random variables, X and Y

$$E(X + Y) = E(X) + E(Y)$$

Expectations Are Not Multiplicative

Consider two random variables, X and Y:

$$E(XY) \neq E(X) E(Y)$$

Consider a random variable, X, and a constant, $a \neq 1$.

$$E(X^a) \neq E(X)^a$$

Variance and Standard Deviation

The *variance* of a random variable X, denoted $\text{Var}(X)$, is defined as:

$$\text{Var}(X) = E(X^2) - E(X)^2$$

In English, it is the expected value of the random variable, X^2, minus the square of the expected value of the random variable, X. Note that X and X^2 are related, yet different, random variables.

The *standard deviation* of a random variable, X, is the square root of the variance: $(\text{Var}(X))^{1/2}$. The standard deviation has the same units as the expectation. The variance of a random variable, X, is sometimes denoted as σ_X^2; the standard deviation of a random variable, X, is sometimes denotes as σ_X.

Variance Is Not Linear

Consider two random variables, X and Y:

$$\text{Var}(X + Y) \neq \text{Var}(X) + \text{Var}(Y)$$

Consider a random variable, X, and two constants, a and b:

$$\text{Var}(a + bX) = b^2 \text{Var}(X)$$

Covariance

Consider two random variables, X and Y. Their *covariance*, $\text{Cov}(X, Y)$, is defined as:

$$\text{Cov}(X, Y) = \text{E}(XY) - \text{E}(X)\,\text{E}(Y)$$

The covariance of X and X is simply the variance of X.

Glossary

allocation A vector that specifies quantities of each alternative, usually, though not necessarily, goods. Also called a *bundle*. A rational agent chooses the allocation that maximizes her objective function given the constraint.

aggregate demand The value of all purchases of domestically produced final goods and services. In equilibrium, *aggregate demand* is equal to *output* and also equal to *income*.

arbitrage Selling goods or assets in one market for a different price than the same goods or assets can be sold in another market, to make a profit.

asset A technology that allows the transfer of resources from the present to the future.

Beveridge curve The inverse relationship between vacancies and unemployment.

bonds The generic term for debt. Bonds issued by the United States are considered *riskless assets*.

capital One of the two factors of production. The stock of all machines and physical equipment that, combined with labor, produces output.

capital controls restrictions on the free flow of capital across international markets.

central bank The bank that conducts monetary policy and serves as the lender of last resort to other banks in the economy.

classical dichotomy The result that in economies with fully flexible prices, nominal variables have no effect on real variables. Note that the converse is not true.

constant returns to scale A function exhibits constant returns to scale if scaling all inputs by a factor, λ, results in output being scaled by the same factor, λ.

consumer price index A *Laspeyres* index. It is used by the social security administration to calculate cost-of-living adjustments to benefits.

consumption The component of *aggregate demand* that is purchased by households. Also called *personal consumption expenditures*.

constrained optimization problem A mathematical problem that consists of finding the allocation that maximizes the *objective function* and also satisfies the *constraint*. The standing assumption in economics is that choices are the solutions to constrained optimization problems.

constraint function One of the two functions that constitute a *constrained optimization problem*. The other is the *objective function*. Its inputs are the choice variables, and it always equals zero. This requirement constitutes the constraint.

conditional convergence   The property that countries with different starting levels of income per capita converge to the same income per capita *conditional* on them sharing the same steady state.

cost-push shock   Shocks to the *Phillips curve* that increase the costs of production. A positive cost-push shock shifts the Phillips curve, adding to inflation without affecting the output gap.

crowding out   A drop in demand from the private sector that arises when an increase in government purchases leads to an increase in the real interest rate.

current account   The total net income from abroad. It is the sum of exports, income from assets held abroad, and remittances from abroad, minus imports, income paid to foreign-owned domestic assets, and remittances to foreigners.

currency peg   A system by which the value of a currency is tied, or *pegged*, to the value of another currency. A floating peg allows the exchange rate to fluctuate within a narrow band. A hard peg fixes the exchange rate at a single value.

debt   A technology that allows the transfer of resources from the future to the present.

demand schedule   The function that relates the quantity demanded of a good or service to its relative price. Also called *demand function*.

depreciation rate   The rate at which capital becomes obsolete.

diminishing marginal returns   A function exhibits diminishing marginal returns with respect to an input if the partial derivative with respect to that input is decreasing. This is equivalent to saying that its second partial derivative with respect to that input is negative.

dual mandate   The Federal Reserve Act requires that the Fed aim for both low inflation and stable employment.

efficient market hypothesis   The hypothesis that markets aggregate all relevant information required to evaluate the expected value of firms, so that asset prices reflect the expected present discounted value of all profits.

elasticity   The elasticity of a variable, Y, with respect to another variable, X, is the change in $\log Y$ over the change in $\log X$. It measures the percentage change in Y from a one percent change in X.

equity premium puzzle   The name for the difference between the risk premium of stocks predicted by the stand consumption-savings model with rational expectations and the empirical premium. The empirical premium is much higher than the premium predicted by the model.

Euler equation   The optimality condition between current and future consumption.

exchange rate   The price of one currency in terms of another currency.

excludability   A good is said to be excludable if it is possible to prevent agents from using it. Property rights make goods excludable.

expectation   The forecast of a random variable. Not necessarily its *expected value*. If the expectation is equal to the expected value we say that agents have *rational expectations*.

expected value   A mathematical operator on random variables. It is computed by adding up the product of the probabilities of each outcome of a random variable with the value of that outcome. Not to be confused with *expectation*.

exports   The value of all domestically produced goods and services sold abroad.

extensive margin   The margin concerning the binary choice of whether or not to enter a market. An adjustment along the extensive margin changes the number of participants in a market.

factor prices   The prices of the factors of production. The relative price of labor is the *real wage*. The relative price of hiring capital is the *real rental rate*.

federal funds rate   The nominal interest rate that commercial banks charge each other for overnight loans. This is the rate that the Federal Reserve targets when conducting monetary policy.

final goods and services   Goods and services that are not themselves used up as inputs in the production of other goods and services.

fiscal deficit   The difference between government expenditures and government revenue. The negative of the *fiscal surplus*.

fiscal surplus   The difference between government revenue and government expenditures. The negative of the *fiscal deficit*.

Fisher equation   A *no-arbitrage condition* that relates the *nominal interest rate*, the *real interest rate*, and inflation expectations. According to the Fisher equation, the nominal interest rate is equal to the real interest rate plus expected inflation.

forward guidance   An unconventional monetary policy tool where the central bank reveals the future path of nominal interest rates in order to influence current expectations of future inflation.

free entry condition   When there are no barriers to entry, participants will enter a market until the surplus benefits from entry are driven down to zero.

government expenditures   The sum of government purchases, interest payments on outstanding debt, and subsidies to private agents.

government expenditure multiplier   The marginal increase in output from a one unit increase in government purchases.

government purchases   The value of final goods and services purchased by the government.

gross domestic product (GDP)   The market value of all final goods and services produced in an economy over a fixed period of time.

GDP deflator   The ratio of nominal GDP to real GDP. A price index.

gross rate   The gross growth rate of a variable, X_t, is the ratio of its current value to its previous value, X_t/X_{t-1}.

imports   The value of all goods and services purchased from abroad.

income   The sum of pretax payments to the domestically employed factors of production, plus the pretax profits of domestic firms. In equilibrium, *income* is equal to *output* and *aggregate demand*.

inflation   The growth rate of a price index.

inflation tax   See *seigniorage*.

intensive margin   Once an agent is engaged in a market, the intensive margin relates to the choice of how much to trade in that market. An adjustment along the intensive margin affects the amount that each participant trades or how *intensely* each participant engages in the market.

intermediate goods and services   Goods and services that are themselves inputs in the production of other goods and services.

investment   The component of aggregate demand that goes to accumulating or replacing private capital.

job market tightness   The ratio of jobs, filled and unfilled, to workers, employed and unemployed. Sometimes also defined as the ratio of the vacancy rate to the unemployment rate.

labor   One of the two factors of production. Labor is the total amount of human hours devoted to work.

labor force participation rate   The sum of employed and unemployed workers divided by the working-age population. The share of the working-age population that participates in the labor market.

Laspeyres index   An index that measures the cost of a fixed basket using equilibrium prices in each time period.

law of one price   A *no-arbitrage* condition that says that a tradable good or service must have the same price wherever it is sold.

liquid assets   Assets that can be readily exchanged for goods. The most liquid asset is cash.

liquidity constraint   A constraint that requires a certain share of wealth to remain liquid, that is, held as cash.

lump-sum tax   A tax whose burden is independent of the size of the variable being taxed. A tax on the *extensive margin*.

marginal product   The amount by which output increases as a result of a one unit increase in one of its inputs, holding all other inputs fixed.

marginal propensity to consume   The fraction from a marginal increase in income that goes toward consumption.

marginal rate of substitution   The rate at which an agent is willing to trade between two alternatives. It is obtained by taking the ratio of the partial derivatives of the objective function with respect to each alternative.

marginal rate of transformation   The rate at which an agent is able to trade between two alternatives. It is obtained by taking the ratio of the partial derivatives of the constraint function with respect to each alternative.

marginal tax   A tax whose burden is proportional to the size of the variable being taxed. A tax on the *intensive margin*.

matching function   In markets where participants must search and match with one another, the matching function takes as inputs the number of participants by type and outputs the number of matches. A production function for matches.

maturity transformation   The process by which banks borrow (i.e., accept deposits) at short, flexible maturities, and lend those funds at long, fixed maturities.

monetary policy shock   The component of the central bank's adjustment of the nominal interest rate that was unforeseen by the private sector. The difference between what agents expected the nominal interest rate to be and the bank's actual target rate.

Mundell-Flemming trilemma   A constraint on the number of policies that can be pursued simultaneously. A government can only pursue two of the following three policies simultaneously: free capital markets, a currency peg, or an independent monetary policy.

natural debt limit   The maximum amount of debt an agent can incur while still being able to repay it. The amount of debt equal to the agent's present discounted value of all future income.

natural rate of output   The equilibrium log of output in an economy with flexible prices. Sometimes also refers to the equilibrium log of output in an economy with the natural rate of unemployment.

natural rate of unemployment   The rate of unemployment that is expected to prevail when output is on its long-run trend, that is, at the natural rate of output.

net exports   The market value of exports minus the market value of imports. One of the four components of aggregate demand. Also called the *trade balance*.

net rate   The net rate is the gross rate minus one. When the gross rate is close to one, the net rate can be defined as the log of the gross rate.

net remittances   The difference in the value of transfers to the rest of the world minus the value of transfers from the rest of the world.

no-arbitrage condition   A condition that requires that, in equilibrium, no arbitrage opportunities exist. See *law of one price*.

nominal GDP   The market value of all final goods and services produced in an economy over a fixed period of time, as measured by current prices.

nominal interest rate   Rate of return of a riskless nominal asset.

objective function   One of the two functions that constitute a *constrained optimization problem*. The other is the *constraint function*. The function whose value an agent is trying to either maximize or minimize.

Okun's law   The 1965 estimate by Arthur Okun that one percent increase in the output gap leads to a one percent drop in the unemployment rate. It is not a "law" since this empirical relationship is not stable and has changed considerably through time.

optimality condition   The solution to a *constrained optimization problem*. The optimality condition requires that the marginal rate of substitution between two goods is equal to the marginal rate of transformation between the same goods.

output   The value of production. In equilibrium, output is equal to aggregate demand, and also equal to income. See *real gross domestic product*.

output gap   The difference between the log of output and the natural rate of output.

Paasche index   An index that measures the cost of of purchasing the basket defined by current equilibrium quantities using past equilibrium prices.

patent   An intellectual property right. The holder of the patent has the right to exclude others from using the invention without permission. See *excludability*.

permanent income   Income whose changes are expected to prevail forever into the future.

personal consumption expenditures   See *consumption*.

personal consumption expenditure price index   The ratio of nominal personal consumption expenditures to real personal consumption expenditures. Its growth rate is the Federal Reserve's preferred measure of inflation.

Phillips curve   An aggregate supply relationship between inflation and production, given expectations. The Phillips curve arises in economies where the classical dichotomy does not hold.

positive marginal returns   A function exhibits positive marginal returns with respect to one of its inputs if its partial derivative with respect to that input is positive.

precautionary savings   Savings that arise from uncertainty about future consumption. The higher the uncertainty, the higher the precautionary savings.

present discounted value   The value, in the present time period, of a future outcome. Evaluated by dividing the future value of the outcome by the compounded gross real interest rate over the relevant time horizon.

price index   A one-dimensional statistic that summarizes the level of prices for a given basket of goods.

primary fiscal deficit   The difference government purchases and net tax revenue. The negative of the *primary fiscal surplus*.

primary fiscal surplus   The difference between net tax revenue and government purchases. The negative of the *primary fiscal deficit*.

production function   A mapping from inputs, usually the factors of production, into output. In perfectly competitive markets, the profit function constrains the firm.

profit function   Total revenue minus total costs. This is the *objective function* of the firm.

purchasing power parity (PPP) adjustment   A unit-conversion factor used to compare real GDP across countries. PPP adjustment measures GDP in units of a fixed basket of goods, usually measured in international US dollars.

purchasing power parity hypothesis   The hypothesis that the relative prices of tradable goods is the same wherever those goods are traded.

rational expectations hypothesis   A hypothesis about how agents form forecasts. According to the rational expectations hypothesis, agents compute the *expected value* of economic variables given the equilibrium relationships that determine them.

real cash balances   The total amount of consumption, or output, that the money in circulation can buy.

real interest rate   Rate of return of a riskless real asset in a competitive equilibrium.

real GDP   The market value of all final goods and services produced in an economy over a fixed period of time, as measured by the prices of a base year. The real value of production. Also called *output*.

real variable   Theoretically: variables that affect the objectives of agents. Empirically: variables measured using a common, standard unit of account.

real wage   The amount of consumption that the nominal wage can buy. A real variable.

relative price   The price of good *a*, relative to good *b*, is the amount of good *b* that you have to give up in order to purchase one unit of good *a*.

replacement rate   The rate at which the capital stock is accumulated through investment. It is the investment-to-capital ratio.

Ricardian equivalence   The result that the present discounted value, but not the timing, of lump-sum taxes affects consumption.

risk premium   The difference between the rate of return of a risky asset and a riskless asset.

riskless asset   An asset whose rate of return is known at the time of investment.

risky asset   An asset whose rate of return is unknown—a random variable—at the time of investment.

rivalry   A good is said to be rival if its use by one agent precludes its use by another agent.

seigniorage   The real revenue that the money-printing authority can extract by exchanging money for goods and services. Also called the inflation tax.

Solow residual   The component of output growth that cannot be accounted for by the growth rate of the factors of production. A method of measuring *total factor productivity*.

solvency   Solvency requires that the present discounted value of all net revenues, plus the value of net assets, be greater than the present discounted value of all expenses.

stochastic discount factor   The rate at which the household is willing to give up current consumption for future consumption. It discounts the gross rate of return on an asset by the, possibly random, growth rate of the marginal utility of consumption. See *marginal rate of substitution*.

supply schedule   The function that relates the quantity supplied of a good or service to its relative price. Also called supply function.

tax wedge   The wedge, generated by marginal taxes, between the relative price that the buyer pays and the relative price that the seller receives.

Taylor principle   The theoretical principle that puts a lower bound, usually one, on the sensitivity of the central bank's interest rate rule to the rate of inflation. In practice, it requires that central banks make large changes to the nominal interest rate in response to inflation.

T-bills Nominal bonds issued by the US Department of the Treasury.

temporary income Income whose changes are expected to die down over time.

terms of trade The ratio of the price index of exports to the price index of imports.

TIPS An acronym for Treasury Inflation Protected Securities. Real bonds issued by the US Department of the Treasury.

total factor productivity (TFP) A factor that scales the production function. When total factor productivity goes up, the same inputs generate more output.

trade balance See *net exports.*

trade deficit When the value of imports exceeds the value of exports. A negative trade balance.

trade surplus When the value of exports exceeds the value of imports. A positive trade balance.

transversality condition Terminal debt condition. It says that the present value of the terminal outstanding debt is zero. In finite horizons, it requires the debt to be zero. In infinite horizons, it requires that the debt grow at a slower rate than the compounded rate of discounting.

twin deficits A term that refers to the *fiscal deficit* and the *trade deficit*, which often occur together.

unemployment rate The number of workers without, but for, divided by the total number of workers in the labor market.

uncertainty shocks A type of demand shock that changes the variance of future output. A change in uncertainty induces households to adjust their precautionary savings and consumption, shifting the aggregate demand curve.

unconditional convergence The property that countries with different starting levels of income per capita converge to the the same income per capita.

utility function The *objective function* that the household maximizes. The utility function captures the household's preferences for its input variables, usually consumption and leisure. More preferred allocations achieve a higher value of the utility function.

value added Value generated by the factors of production at each stage of the production process.

vacancy rate The number of unfilled job openings divided by the total number of jobs, filled and unfilled, in the labor market.

zero lower bound The lower bound on the net nominal interest rate. The net nominal interest rate cannot be negative.

References

Acemoglu, D., & J. Ventura (2002). The world income distribution. *Quarterly Journal of Economics, 117*(2), 659–694.

Aghion, P., & R. Griffith (2005). *Competition and growth: Reconciling theory and evidence.* Cambridge, MA: MIT Press.

Aghion, P., & P. Howitt (2009). *The economics of growth.* Cambridge, MA: MIT Press.

Barro, R. (1974). Are government bonds net wealth? *Journal of Political Economy, 82*(6), 1095–1117.

Barro, R., & R. Gordon (1983). A positive theory of monetary policy in a natural rate model. *Journal of Political Economy, 91*(4), 589–610.

Barro, R., & X. Sala-i-Martin (1992). Convergence. *Journal of Political Economy, 100*(2), 223–251.

Barro, R., & X. Sala-i-Martin (2004). *Economic growth, second edition.* Cambridge, MA: MIT Press.

Basu, S., J. Fernald, & M. Kimball (2006). Are technology improvements contractionary? *American Economic Review, 96*(5), 1418–1448.

Benigno, P., & M. Woodford (2003). Optimal monetary and fiscal policy: A linear-quadratic approach. *NBER Macroeconomics Annual, 18*, 271–333.

Bergeaud, A., G. Cette, & R. Lecat (2016). Productivity trends in advanced countries between 1890 and 2012. *Review of Income and Wealth, 62*(3), 420–444.

Blanchard, O., & N. Kiyotaki (1987). Monopolistic competition and the effects of aggregate demand. *American Economic Review, 77*(4), 647–666.

Blanchard, O., & M. Watson (1982). Bubbles, rational expectations and financial markets. In P. Wachtel (ed.), *Crises in the economic and financial structure: Bubbles, bursts, and shocks.* Lexington, MA: Lexington.

Blinder, A. (1998). *Central banking in theory and practice.* Cambridge, MA: MIT Press.

Bolt, J., & J. Luiten van Zanden (2020). Maddison style estimates of the evolution of the world economy. A new 2020 update. *Maddison Project Database.* Accessed online at https://www.rug.nl/ggdc/historicaldevelopment/maddison/releases/maddison-project-database-2020

Bray, M. (1982). Learning, estimation and stability of rational expectations. *Journal of Economic Theory, 26*(2), 318–339.

Caselli, F., & J. Feyrer (2007). The marginal product of capital. *Quarterly Journal of Economics, 122*(2), 535–568.

Chetty, R. (2012). Bounds on elasticities with optimization frictions: A synthesis of micro and macro evidence on labor supply. *Econometrica, 80*(3), 969–1018.

Chetty, R., A. Guren, D. Manoli, & A. Weber (2011). Are micro and macro labor supply elasticities consistent? A review of evidence on the intensive and extensive margins. *American Economic Review, 101*(3), 471–475.

Christiano, L., M. Eichenbaum, & C. Evans (2005). Nominal rigidities and the dynamic effects of a shock to monetary policy. *Journal of Political Economy, 113*(1), 1–45.

Clarida, R., J. Gali, & M. Gertler (1999). The science of monetary policy: A new Keynesian perspective. *Journal of Economic Literature, 37*(4), 1661–1707.

Daly, M., B. Hobijn, A. Sahin, & R. Valletta (2012). A search and matching approach to labor markets: Did the natural rate of unemployment rise? *Journal of Economic Perspectives, 26*(3), 3–26.

Deaton, A. (1992). *Understanding consumption.* Oxford: Oxford University Press.

Diamond, P. (1982). Wage determination and efficiency in search equilibrium. *Review of Economics Studies, 49*(2), 217–227.

Diamond, D., & P. Dybvig (1983). Bank runs, deposit insurance, and liquidity. *Journal of Political Economy, 91*(5), 401–419.

Dixit, A., & J. Stiglitz (1977). Monopolistic competition and optimum product diversity. *American Economic Review, 67*(3), 297–308.

Economist, The (2013). *The Big Mac index.* Accessed online at https://economist.com/big-mac-index

Eggertsson, G., & M. Woodford (2003). The zero bound on interest rates and optimal monetary policy. *Brookings Papers on Economic Activity, 1*, 139–233.

Elsby, M., R. Michaels, & D. Ratner (2015). The Beveridge curve: A survey. *Journal of Economic Literature, 53*(3), 571–630.

Fama, E. (1970). Efficient capital markets: A review of theory and empirical work. *Journal of Finance, 25*(2), 383–417.

Federal Reserve Board (2008). *FOMC statement* [press release], December 16, 2008. https://www.federalreserve.gov/newsevents/pressreleases/monetary20081216b.htm

Federal Reserve Board (2009). *FOMC statement* [press release], January 28, 2009. https://www.federalreserve.gov/newsevents/pressreleases/monetary20090128a.htm

Federal Reserve Board (2011). *FOMC statement* [press release], December 13, 2011. https://www.federalreserve.gov/newsevents/pressreleases/monetary20111213a.htm

Feenstra, R. (1986). Functional equivalence between liquidity costs and the utility of money. *Journal of Monetary Economics, 17*, 271–291.

Feenstra, R., R. Inklaar, & M. Timmer (2015). The next generation of the Penn World Table. *American Economic Review, 105*(10), 3150–3182. Available at www.ggdc.net/pwt

Fischer, S. (1977). Long-term contracts, rational expectations, and the optimal money supply rule. *Journal of Political Economy, 85*(1), 191–205.

Fleming, J. (1962). Domestic financial policies under fixed and under floating exchange rates. *IMF Staff Papers, 9*(3), 369–380.

Gali, J. (2008). *Monetary policy, inflation and the business cycle: An introduction to the new Keynesian framework.* Princeton: Princeton University Press.

Giannoni, M., & M. Woodford (2003). Optimal inflation targeting rules. In B. Bernanke & M. Woodford (eds.), *The inflation targeting debate.* Chicago: Chicago University Press.

Gordon, R. (2010). Okun's law and productivity innovations. *American Economic Review: Papers & Proceedings, 100*(2), 11–15.

Gürkaynak, R., B. Sack, & E. Swanson (2005a). Do actions speak louder than words? The response of asset prices to monetary policy actions and statements. *International Journal of Central Banking, 1*(1), 55–94.

Gürkaynak, R., B. Sack, & E. Swanson (2005b). The sensitivity of long-term interest rates to economic news: Evidence and implications for macroeconomic models. *American Economic Review, 95*(1), 425–436.

Hall, R. (2009). By how much does GDP rise if the government buys more output? *Brookings Papers on Economic Activity,* 183–231.

Hansen, G. (1985). Indivisible labor and the business cycle. *Journal of Monetary Economics, 16*(3), 309–327.

Hayashi, F. (1982). Tobin's marginal q and average q: A neoclassical interpretation. *Econometrica, 50*(1), 213–224.

Hsieh, C. (1999). Productivity growth and factor prices in East Asia. *American Economic Review, 89*(2), 133–138.

Jo, Y. (2019). *Downward nominal wage rigidity in the United States.* Mimeo, Columbia University.

Jones, C. (1995). R&D-based models of economic growth. *Journal of Political Economy, 103*(4), 759–784.

Jones, L., & R. Manuelli (1990). A convex model of equilibrium growth: Theory and policy implications. *Journal of Political Economy, 98*(5), 1008–1038.

Katz, L., & A. Krueger (1999). The high-pressure US labor market of the 1990s. *Brookings Papers on Economic Activity, 30*(1), 1–88.

King, R., C. Plosser, & S. Rebelo (1988a). Production growth and business cycles: I. The basic neoclassical model. *Journal of Monetary Economics, 21*(2), 195–232.

King, R., C. Plosser, & S. Rebelo (1988b). Production growth and business cycles: II. New directions. *Journal of Monetary Economics, 21*(3), 309–341.

Kray, A., & D. McKenzie (2014). Do poverty traps exist? Assessing evidence. *Journal of Economic Perspectives, 28*(3), 127–148.

Krugman, P. (1979). A model of balance-of-payments crises. *Journal of Money, Credit and Banking, 11*(3), 311–325.

Krugman, P. (1999). *The return of depression economics*. New York: Norton.

Kydland, F., & E. Prescott (1980). Rules rather than discretion: The inconsistency of optimal plans. *Journal of Political Economy, 85*(3), 473–492.

Langfeld, J., E. Seskin, & B. Fraumeni (2008). Taking the pulse of the economy: Measuring GDP. *Journal of Economic Perspectives, 22*(2), 193–216.

Levin, A., & D. Dean (2012). *Generation on a tightrope: A portrait of today's college student*. San Francisco: Wiley.

Lucas, R. (1982). Interest rates and currency prices in a two-country world. *Journal of Monetary Economics, 10*(3), 335–359.

Lucas, R. (1987). *Models of of business cycles*. Oxford: Blackwell.

Lucas, R. (1990). Why doesn't capital flow from rich to poor countries? *American Economic Review. Papers and Proceedings of the Hundred and Second Annual Meeting of the AEA, 80*(2), 92–96.

Mankiw, G., & R. Reis (2001). Sticky information versus sticky prices: A proposal to replace the new Keynesian Phillips curve. *Quarterly Journal of Economics, 117*(4), 1295–1328.

Mankiw, G., D. Romer, & D. Weil (1992). A contribution to the empirics of economic growth. *Quarterly Journal of Economics, 107*(2), 407–437.

Mehra, R., & E. Prescott (1985). The equity premium: A puzzle. *Journal of Monetary Economics, 15*(2), 145–161.

Mundell, R. (1963). Capital mobility and stabilization policy under fixed and flexible exchange rates. *Canadian Journal Journal of Economics and Political Science, 29*(4), 475–485.

Nakamura, E., & J. Steinsson (2008). Five facts about prices: A reevaluation of menu cost models. *Quarterly Journal of Economics, 123*(4), 1415–1464.

Nakamura, E., & J. Steinsson (2018a). High frequency identification of monetary non-neutrality: The information effect. *Quarterly Journal of Economics, 133*(3), 1283–1330.

Nakamura, E., & J. Steinsson (2018b). Identification in macroeconomics. *Journal of Economic Perspectives, 32*(3), 59–86.

Obstfeld, M., & K. Rogoff (1995). Exchange rate dynamics redux. *Journal of Political Economy, 103*(3), 624–660.

Obstfeld, R., J. Shambaugh, & A. Taylor (2005). The trilemma in history: Tradeoffs among exchange rates, monetary policies and capital mobility. *Review of Economics and Statistics, 87*, 423–438.

Oded, G., & D. Weil (2000). Population, technology, and growth: From Malthusian stagnation to the demographic transition and beyond. *American Economic Review, 90*(4), 806–828.

Okun, A. (1965). The gap between actual and potential output. In E. Phelps (ed.), *Problems of the modern economy*. New York: Norton.

Parker, J., N. Souleles, D. Johnson, & R. McClelland (2013). Consumer spending and the economics stimulus payments of 2008. *American Economic Review, 103*(6), 2530–2553.

Pissarides, C. (1985). Short-run equilibrium dynamics of unemployment, vacancies and real wages. *American Economic Review, 75*(4), 676–690.

Pissarides, C. (1990). *Equilibrium unemployment theory.* Oxford: Blackwell.

Prescott, E. (2004). Why do Americans work so much more than Europeans? *Federal Reserve Bank of Minneapolis Quarterly Review, 28*(1), 2–11.

Rebelo, S. (1991). Long-run policy analysis and long-run growth. *Journal of Political Economy, 99*(3), 500–521.

Rogerson, R. (1988). Indivisible labor, lotteries, and equilibrium. *Journal of Monetary Economics, 21*(1), 3–16.

Romer, C., & D. Romer (2004). A new measure of monetary policy shocks: Derivation and implications. *American Economic Review, 94*(4), 1055–1084.

Romer, P. (1986). Increasing returns and long-run growth. *Journal of Political Economy, 94*(5), 1002–1037.

Romer, P. (1990). Endogenous technological change. *Journal of Political Economy, 98*(5), Part 2: S71–S102.

Rotemberg, J., & M. Woodford (1992). Oligopolistic pricing and the effects of aggregate demand on economic activity. *Journal of Political Economy, 100*(6), 1153–1207.

Sargent, T. (1993). *Bounded rationality in macroeconomics.* Oxford: Oxford University Press.

Sargent, T., & N. Wallace (1981). Some unpleasant monetary arithmetic. *Federal Reserve Bank of Minneapolis Quarterly Review, 5*(3), 1–17.

Sargent, T., N. Williams, & T. Zha (2009). The conquest of South American inflation. *Journal of Political Economy, 117*(2), 211–256.

Schmitt-Grohe, S., & M. Uribe (2003). Closing small open economy models. *Journal of International Economics, 61*(1), 163–185.

Shimer, R. (2005). The cyclical behavior of equilibrium unemployment and vacancies. *American Economic Review, 95*(1), 25–49.

Smith, A. (2002). *The wealth of nations.* Oxford: Bibliomania.com.

Solow, R. (1956). A contribution to the theory of economic growth. *Quarterly Journal of Economics, 70*(1), 65–94.

Solow, R. (1957). Technical change and the aggregate production function. *Review of Economics and Statistics, 39*, 312–320.

Souleles, N. (1999). The response of household consumption to income tax refunds. *American Economic Review, 89*(4), 947–958.

Steinsson, J. (2003). Optimal monetary policy in an economy with inflation persistence. *Journal of Monetary Economics, 50*, 1425–1456.

Swan, T. (1956). Economic growth and capital accumulation. *Economic Record, 32*, 334–361.

Sweeny, J., & R.J. Sweeny (1977). Monetary theory and the great Capitol Hill baby sitting co-op crisis: Comment. *Journal of Money, Credit and Banking, 9*(1), 86–89.

Taylor, J. (1980). Aggregate dynamics and staggered contracts. *Journal of Political Economy, 88*(1), 1–24.

Taylor, J. (1993). Discretion versus policy rules in practice. *Carnegie-Rochester Conference Series on Public Policy, 39*, 195–214.

Woodford, M. (2003). *Interest and prices.* Princeton: Princeton University Press.

Woodford, M. (2011). Simple analytics of the government expenditure multiplier. *American Economic Journal: Macroeconomics, 3*(1), 1–35.

Young, A. (1995). The tyranny of numbers: Confronting the statistical realities of the East Asian growth experience. *Quarterly Journal of Economics, 110*(3), 641–680.

Index

Page numbers followed by *f* denote figures; *t* denotes tables.